WOLLSTONECRAFT

Wollstonecraft

PHILOSOPHY, PASSION, AND POLITICS

Sylvana Tomaselli

PRINCETON UNIVERSITY PRESS

PRINCETON & OXFORD

Requests for permission to reproduce material from this work
should be sent to permissions@press.princeton.edu

Published by Princeton University Press
41 William Street, Princeton, New Jersey 08540
6 Oxford Street, Woodstock, Oxfordshire OX20 1TR

press.princeton.edu

Library of Congress Control Number 2020945110
ISBN 978-0-691-16903-3
ISBN (e-book) 978-0-691-21263-0

British Library Cataloging-in-Publication Data is available

Editorial: Sarah Caro, Ben Tate, and Josh Drake
Production Editorial: Jill Harris
Jacket Design: Heather Hansen
Production: Erin Suydam
Publicity: Kate Hensley and Kate Farquhar-Thomson
Copyeditor: Karen Verde

Jacket art: Portrait of Mary Wollstonecraft, by John Opie (c. 1797),
oil on canvas, copyright © National Portrait Gallery, London

This book has been composed in Miller

Printed on acid-free paper. ∞

Printed in the United States of America

10 9 8 7 6 5 4 3 2 1

CONTENTS

ACKNOWLEDGMENTS

GRATITUDE, THOMAS HOBBES TELLS US in chapter 15 of *Leviathan*, is the fourth law of nature: "That a man which receiveth Benefit from another of meer Grace, Endeavour that he which giveth, have no reasonable cause to repent him of his good will." I hope not to be standing in breach of this, my favorite of Hobbes's nineteen laws of nature, in what follows. First, I wish to thank Madeleine Armstrong and Sam Harrison, without whose assistance this book would not have crossed the finish line in time. I am also most grateful to Eileen Hunt Botting, Stacey McDowell, and Bee Wilson for their transformative readings of the script and Bruce Baugh for his generous suggestions. My long-standing debt to Fredric Smoler for improving all I have ever sent his way must be acknowledged here. Thanks also go to Princeton University Press's readers for their most helpful comments and to its editors, Sarah Caro and Ben Tate, and to Karen Verde for her meticulous copyediting. For their learning, ways of thinking, conversations, eye-rolling, shared laughter, and all else that makes for all kinds of friendships, I am grateful to Andrew Arsan, Richard Bourke, Catherine Crawford, John Dunn, Edward Hundert, Biancamaria Fontana, Raymond Geuss, Mark Goldie, Marc Feigen, Thomas Hopkins, Susan James, Duncan Kelly, Ralph and Marie-Claire Kerr, Prakash Mishra, John Osman, John Robertson, Johannes and Adriana Schaesberg, Meg and Gordon Scoffield, Anna Sica, Joshua Simons, Gareth Stedman Jones, Nigel and Sarah Street, Chronis Tzedakis, John and Lizzie Wallwork, Paul Wood, William and Marie-Nöelle Worsley, and Anne Zwack. I would also like to thank my very brilliant students, all the kind staff members of St. John's College as well as the Fellows, and I wish to remember the late Wynne Godley, Istvan Hont, Tony and Peter Lothian, Ruby Nemser, Nicholas Phillipson, Roy Porter, Luis Racionero, and John and Jean Yolton.

WOLLSTONECRAFT

Introduction

THERE IS SOME DEGREE OF contingency at play in what becomes the topic of one's writing. Chance or choice, the question as to why it is this subject or that author, as opposed to any other subject or author, surfaces from time to time. Necessity to earn a living led Mary Wollstonecraft to write reviews, and that she could do so at all was because she knew the editor of the *Analytical Review* (1788–1798), Joseph Johnson. The publication of Edmund Burke's *Reflections on the Revolution in France* (1790) provided an opportunity, which she took up with alacrity, responding to it with *A Vindication of the Rights of Men* (1790). It prompted in turn her best-known work, *A Vindication of the Rights of Woman* (1792). The French Revolution itself gave her another reason to put pen to paper, when she sought to explain its causes in *An Historical and Moral View of the Origin and Progress of the French Revolution; and the Effect It Has Produced in Europe* (1794). The growing market in books and the interest in education had already led her to write pedagogical works, and the popularity of fiction encouraged her to try her hand at novels. Circumstances as well as events shaped the substance and genre of much of her writings. Passion and the desperate desire to reverse the unrequited love of the father of her first daughter led her to travel to Scandinavia and compose her *Letters Written during a Short Residence in Sweden, Norway, and Denmark* (1796), but its publication was driven by financial need. Like many of her contemporaries, she sought to understand the circumstances that led to the stupendous events defining her time, but more than most she weighed the ethical choices they forged on those witnessing them.

So why Wollstonecraft? To many commentators the answer is obvious: because she argued for the equality of men and women, because she was a feminist, and because of *A Vindication of the Rights of Woman*. That is not my answer. Wollstonecraft did not rest her case against the condition of women as she saw it on a claim about the natural equality between the sexes. Rather, she grounded her critique on an impassioned exposition of the flabbergasting contradictions within society's expectations of women and in women's own desires and hopes. Whether that makes her a feminist is debatable, but assessing her in this way is not the motive for this book. As for her authorship of that rightly famous work, what follows seeks to give her other writings equal weight, but if it elevates any, it is her first overtly political text, *A Vindication of the Rights of Men*. Wollstonecraft should not be celebrated only for *A Vindication of the Rights of Woman*. Hers was a philosophy of humanity. To do justice to any one of her views, especially those expressed in that now legendary work, they must be set within the context of a wider historical worldview.

My own answer to "Why Wollstonecraft?" is simple: the woman herself and her exceptional capacity to make us think about, and rethink, nature, artifice, relationships, society and its history, and the connections between the personal and the political. Progressing from what now is evidently a very limited knowledge of her, when I was asked to edit her *Vindication of the Rights of Woman* in the early 1990s, to a much deeper acquaintance has bred genuine admiration and an enduring sense of intrigue. The editors of the series, Quentin Skinner and Raymond Geuss, allowed themselves to be persuaded that her earlier work, *A Vindication of the Rights of Men* as well as *Hints*, be added to the volume as they seemed essential to understanding her most famous text. Even though I requested it, it is only relatively recently that I have come to fully appreciate the importance of reading those works together. Over time, it became clear to me that thinking of her as "the author of *A Vindication of the Rights of Woman*," as William Godwin referred to her in the title of her *Posthumous Works*, distorted our perceptions of both Wollstonecraft and her famed work. It had to be read as part of a larger corpus and she had to be thought as the author of a number of diverse works written in various genres, at different times and in various places. While the trend has been changing in recent years, and each of her works is increasingly receiving the attention they deserve, the *Vindication of the Rights of Woman* has cast a long shadow over the rest of her writing for much too long.

Wollstonecraft was an extraordinary person. This was in no small measure due to her exceptional capacity to face life's vicissitudes, to will herself to do and be what she thought the moment called for. Yes, she did twice attempt suicide. It was, one could say, out of character, or possibly not, depending on one's stance on suicide. Be that as it may, it was wrong by what we might assume to have been her own moral and religious beliefs, but it cannot easily be said to have been weak. If it be deemed weak, then these were the exceptions, albeit monumental, in a life that she forged in the face of much adversity.

The strength she possessed, or acquired, was a gift she very much wanted to share: she strove to make a case for endurance and wanted children to be made resilient. She despaired of the fact that women's education prevented them from acquiring the physical and mental strength life and human flourishing required. This is not to say that she always fully succeeded in living up to her own expectations of herself or those others might have had of her. Hers was not an easy life, and she had more than her share of sorrows from an early age, but she demonstrated courage and resourcefulness through the course of it. Her family drifted from social and economic comfort to hardship, of which she and her sister bore the brunt. Her education was uneven, though it was to widen and reach considerable depth through fortuitous encounters as well as being asked by her publisher and supporter, the Dissenter Joseph Johnson (1738–1809), to contribute extensively to the *Analytical Review*. She mostly lived from her writing, determined to pay off her debts, started a school, was a governess to Lord and Lady Kingsborough in Ireland and traveled to Portugal to assist a dear friend, Fanny, in childbirth. In Paris under the Terror, she passed as the wife of American entrepreneur and sometime novelist Gilbert Imlay (1754–1828) and undertook for his sake a perilous journey in Scandinavia with their infant daughter, Fanny (1794–1816). Her resilience to heartbreak, though repeatedly tested, faltered once prior to her northern expedition, and a second time, when it became clear that Imlay had left her, never to return. She recovered, published the *Letters*, married, but died of septicaemia at the age of thirty-eight in 1797, following the birth of her second daughter, Mary (1797–1851), the future author of *Frankenstein; or, The Modern Prometheus* (1818). Wollstonecraft had married Mary's father, William Godwin (1756–1836), in March of that year. Largely self-taught and as independent financially as any writer in her situation might be, Wollstonecraft had been an active participant in the cultural and political life of her age, battling, among others, with both Edmund Burke and the leaders of the Revolution in France.[1]

If her personality makes up part of any answer to "Why Wollstonecraft?," it is the manner in which it translated into her

1. For a detailed intellectual biography, see Todd, *Mary Wollstonecraft: A Revolutionary Life*. See also Lyndall Gordon, *Vindication: A Life of Mary Wollstonecraft* (New York: HarperCollins, 2005), and Charlotte Gordon, *Romantic Outlaws: The Extraordinary Lives of Mary Wollstonecraft and Mary Shelley* (New York: Random House, 2015). For Wollstonecraft's engagement with French writers, see Tomaselli, "*French* Philosophes," pp. 139–145.

writing that constitutes the essence of a reply. It is impressive in its variety, originality, and indeed volume, given her tumultuous existence and its difficult circumstances, not to mention her life's brevity, all of which makes her such an enthralling figure. Produced during a single decade, her literary output stretches to six or seven average-size volumes, consisting of five important texts in pedagogy and social and political thought, two novels, three translations, and many reviews and letters. Her first publication, *Thoughts on the Education of Daughters with Reflections on Female Conduct, in the More Important Duties of Life*, appeared in 1787. Just nine years later, the last work to be published in her lifetime, *Letters Written in Sweden, Norway and Denmark*, came out eighteen months before her untimely death. The unfinished novel she was writing toward the end of her life, *The Wrongs of Woman: or, Maria*, was published posthumously by Godwin in 1798.

To be sure, in a century rich in very remarkable intellectuals, Wollstonecraft could not be said to be unique. The playwright Olympe de Gouges (1748–1793), who denounced slavery and called for the rights of women and a variety of social reforms, did not have an easy life either and was to die by the guillotine.[2] Both Gouges and Wollstonecraft followed in a long line of authors on education. Mary Astell (1666–1731) and Damaris Masham (1659–1708) were just two who long preceded them in this respect in England. Neither were Gouges nor Wollstonecraft alone in tackling what might be called "the woman question" or misogyny more generally in the eighteenth century. Other women traveled the world, and several English writers reported on France during the Revolution. Wollstonecraft herself reviewed the reports of one of them: Helen Maria Williams's (1761?–1827) *Letters written in France, in the Summer, 1790, to*

2. Scott, "French Feminists and the Rights of 'Man,'" 1–21. Sandrine Bergès, "Olympe de Gouges versus Rousseau: Happiness, Primitive Societies, and the Theater," *Journal of the American Philosophical Association* 4, no. 4 (2018): 433–451.

a Friend in England; containing various Anecdotes relative to the French revolution; and the Memoirs of Mons and Madame du F. Nor, obviously, was novel-writing uncommon: Williams produced one as well as poetry, and a number of her contemporaries, most notably Elizabeth Carter (1717–1806), were distinguished translators as well. In 1790, Wollstonecraft herself published a translation or version of Maria Geertruida de Cambon's epistolary *De Kleine Grandison* from the Dutch. Living, or eking out a living, by the pen was not unusual in the eighteenth century, not even for a woman, nor was entering the political fray and pamphleteering. Moreover, Wollstonecraft's was not the only reply to Burke's *Reflections on the Revolution in France* (1790). Catherine Macaulay (1731–1791) produced one of the many, often anonymous, responses the work elicited.

So, why Wollstonecraft? Why not Williams or Carter or the great Anglo-Saxon scholar, Elizabeth Elstob (1683–1756)? The many European authors and scientists? Or the celebrated Mrs. Macaulay, renowned for her history of England at home and abroad, an impressive pedagogical and political writer and pamphleteer, who merits no less attention? Wollstonecraft admired her, was influenced by her, and there are many similarities between the two authors, not least their joint concern for the status of women. Both were also to acquire much notoriety: Macaulay in her lifetime for, among other things, her marriage to a much younger man, Wollstonecraft posthumously for having been the unmarried mother of Fanny.[3]

Notwithstanding all of the above, the answer to "why write on Wollstonecraft?" lies in her disarming frankness about what she perceived to be the human condition and her effort to be

3. For a comparison of their views, see Gunther-Canada, "Cultivating Virtue"; and "The Politics of Sense and Sensibility"; Bridget Hill, "The Links between Mary Wollstonecraft and Catharine Macaulay: New Evidence," *Women's History Review* 4, no. 2 (1995): 177–192. See also Coffee, "Catherine Macaulay," 198–210; Elizabeth Frazer, "Mary Wollstonecraft and Catharine Macaulay on Education," *Oxford Review of Education* 37 (2011): 603–617.

honest with herself in the light of changing circumstances. How many can write "that an unhappy marriage is often very advantageous to a family, and that the neglected wife is, in general, the best mother"?[4] One might be shocked or simply disagree, but it is at the very least thought-provoking. So are Wollstonecraft's reflections on raising her daughter Fanny:

> You know that as a female I am particularly attached to her—I feel more than a mother's fondness and anxiety, when I reflect on the dependent and oppressed state of her sex. I dread lest she should be forced to sacrifice her heart to her principles, or principles to her heart. With trembling hand I shall cultivate sensibility, and cherish delicacy of sentiment, lest, whilst I lend fresh blushes to the rose, I sharpen the thorns that will wound the breast I would fain regard—I dread to unfold her mind, lest it should render her unfit for the world she is to inhabit—Hapless woman! What a fate is thine![5]

Few writers are as candid as she is here about what she perceived to be the tensions between love and moral principles: should one raise one's children to thrive in the world as it is, or raise them as they ought to be, in anticipation of a world that may not be realized in their lifetime? Few were as daring as she was in *A Vindication of the Rights of Woman* in speaking of the rivalry between mothers and daughters. Few non-fiction writers

4. *A Vindication of the Rights of Woman*, in *A Vindication of the Rights of Men, A Vindication of the Rights of Woman, and Hints*, edited by Sylvana Tomaselli (Cambridge: Cambridge University Press, 1995), p. 100. See also *A Vindication of the Rights of Men*, in ibid., p. 54. All future references to both Wollstonecraft's *Vindications* and *Hints* are to this edition. Hereafter shortened to *VM*, *VW*, and *Hints*.

5. *Letters Written in Sweden, Norway, and Denmark, The Works of Mary Wollstonecraft*, edited by Janet Todd and Marilyn Butler, assistant editor, Emma Rees-Mogg, 7 vols. (London: William Pickering, 1989), Vol. 6, p. 269. (Hereafter all of Wollstonecraft's works, except for her *Vindications* and *Hints*, will be taken from that edition, shortened to *Works*.)

are as honest as she about the distorting effects of property even on parental love. Few are as clear about the interconnectedness of the personal and the public.

And how she could write! Wollstonecraft's rhetorical skills were impressive; she wrote as though she were speaking and proved more than up to the task of engaging Burke (1730–1797) or Jean-Jacques Rousseau (1712–1778).

There is also the boldness of the solutions she offered to what she saw as the problems of her day. In 1792, she called on the leadership of the French Revolution to realize that nothing short of a revolution in morals would achieve their purported aims of liberty, equality, fraternity: constitutional and political changes, no matter how momentous these might be, would not suffice to make for a society of free, equal, and fraternal beings. A total transformation of the way in which men and women conceived of themselves and each other was required. She argued for the decentralization of power and was highly critical of commercial society and its luxury economy. Yet she was surprisingly undogmatic over the course of her life. Despite her passionate disputations, she proved ready to revise her views in the light of new experiences and changed conditions that provided or needed further understanding. This can make establishing her position on a number of important subjects difficult, but thinking through these with her is never dull. While none of these biographical and intellectual features is peculiar to Wollstonecraft, combined they make her a captivating thinker.

My near final answer, then, to "Why Wollstonecraft?" is that she tackled a considerable number of important questions rendered particularly poignant by her authenticity and her eloquence. As I hope the following pages show, and as the increasing interest in her seems to indicate, Wollstonecraft continues to be someone with whom to engage on a wide range of significant topics. The personal and intellectual portrait they sketch draws on her lesser known works, such as her reviews, and highlights some of her less well-known ideas, such as those on music or humanity in its infancy, in the hope that our understanding of her best known work, *A Vindication of the Rights of Woman*, will thereby be enriched. That most important text needs to be re-situated and read within the context of the whole corpus of her work, both for its own sake and so that her thought as a whole may be better understood. It needs to be dethroned to allow for a clearer view of its author.

The scholarship on Wollstonecraft is rich and growing exponentially.[6] What follows seeks to contribute to it by highlighting the extent to which she conceived of most subjects within a historical framework and that the history of society provided the backdrop for much of her thinking. Although she did not write a stadial history of society, that is, a sequential history of humanity's stages from a state of nature to her own time, and specifically said that she would "not go back to the remote annals of antiquity to trace the history of woman,"[7] almost everything upon which she reflected was set against a shared Enlightenment understanding of the development of civilization from a primitive social condition to the present commercial age. This understanding admitted of variations between eighteenth-century authors and was not universally read as marking the progress of mankind, nor was it uniformly conceived as being in accordance with God's plan for humanity. Wollstonecraft pondered the question of the merit of this development and its relation to divine intention. However, she did not only think about the present in terms of the past or the past in terms of the present, but also thought much about futures—the future as it was likely to be, given the present, and the future as it could be.

I seek to track one of her predominant concerns, namely, finding the proper balance between the natural, the humanly created, and the divine; between what made for progress, and

6. See Tomaselli, "Mary Wollstonecraft," in *Oxford Bibliographies in Philosophy*, 2016. http://www.oxfordbibliographies.com/view/document/obo -9780195396577/obo-9780195396577-0306.xml.

7. *VW*, p. 129.

what for corruption; between enhancement and distortion, and thus the processes that underpinned each, as well as alternative futures. I also aim to stress the importance of time in her conception of individual development as well as that of humankind. Wollstonecraft did not only reflect on the nature of the progress of humanity as a whole. She was a teacher and pedagogue and thought of the mind's and the body's growth over time and at different stages of life. She thought about time, its divisions, and how it was used. She closed one of her reviews by asserting "as an irrefragable maxim, that those who cannot employ time must kill it."[8]

This book follows very loosely a format Wollstonecraft herself adopted in her first published work, *Thoughts on the Education of Daughters: With Reflections on Female Conduct, in The More Important Duties of Life* (1787), that is, bringing together her reflections on a number of subjects under eponymous headings. Her first heading was "The Nursery," followed by "Moral Discipline"; the others included "Artificial Manners," "The Observance of Sunday," "Card-Playing"; and the last was entitled "Public Places." Her thoughts are gathered here under specific headings, not only for the sake of clarity, but in order to highlight some of her lesser known views. This seemingly piecemeal approach facilitates a reconstruction of her philosophy of mind and history as well as her reflections on human nature, society, and Providence. It also allows for the tracing of continuities between the various objects of her reflections over an all too brief life.

Having spent much ink, as many other commentators have, on all that she censured, denigrated, and loathed, of which there was plenty, it is essential to consider all that she liked and loved. Wollstonecraft was a severe critic, a harsh reviewer, and unrestrained in her denunciations of individuals as well as institutions. It is all too easy to gain and give the impression that she

8. *Analytical Review*, Vol. 6 (1790), *Works*, Vol. 7, p. 224.

was an arch and bitter derider. She was not. She took pleasure in many things and was eager to share her joys. It is the aim of the opening chapter to highlight these.

Wollstonecraft thought of herself as a philosopher and a moralist: "As a philosopher, I read with indignation the plausible epithets which men use to soften their insults; and, as a moralist, I ask what is meant by such heterogeneous associations, as fair defects, amiable weaknesses, &c.?"[9] Everything she wrote, whatever the genre, she wrote as a philosopher and moralist. She had much to say on a wide variety of topics. This book cannot do justice to all of her reflections. Nor can it be written from every point of view or disciplinary approach. As I came and now still come to Wollstonecraft primarily from political philosophy, her fictional works, which have received much valuable attention, while by no means ignored, are not treated here as they would have been had I been a literary scholar.[10] I should also acknowledge from the start that I have endeavored to avoid "isms" as much as possible in this book, leaving readers to attribute any should they so wish. For my part, I find that labels often obscure more than they reveal or need to be qualified to the point of becoming meaningless. Moreover, the labels one might be tempted to apply to Wollstonecraft or her writings are likely to be anachronistic. Although she engaged with the works of others, she thought for herself and thought of herself as doing so. It is hoped that something of her personality as a whole and her understanding of the past and present, as well as her aspirations for the future, might emerge through what follows. Had she lived longer, we would likely have a more complete picture of the realistic utopia that she was gradually sketching out.

9. *VW*, p. 104.

10. Most significantly, Taylor, *Mary Wollstonecraft and the Feminist Imagination*; Mary Poovey, *The Proper Lady and the Woman Writer: Ideology as Style in the Works of Mary Wollstonecraft, Mary Shelley, and Jane Austen* (Chicago: Chicago University Press, 1984); and Johnson, *Equivocal Beings*.

CHAPTER ONE

What She Liked and Loved

OF ALL THE THINGS Mary Wollstonecraft might have wished for her sisters, friends, or indeed herself and humanity, self-command or, as she would have termed it, fortitude, would be highest. She has Maria, the protagonist of her posthumous novel, *The Wrongs of Woman: or, Maria*, recall her uncle defining "genuine fortitude" thus: it "consisted in governing our own emotions, and making allowance for the weaknesses in our friends, that we would not tolerate in ourselves."[1] Control over one's self was central to her conception of character, and it was something that she viewed as sorely missing in the world: "Most women, and men too, have no character at all," she wrote in her first published work, *Thoughts on the Education of Daughters: with Reflections on Female Conduct, in the More Important Duties of Life* (1787).[2] She stressed the essential nature of control of one's self in all her writings in one form or other. Self-command or self-governance, as Catriona MacKenzie refers to it in an important article on the subject, was the foremost virtue for her since it was the necessary

---

1. *The Wrongs of Woman: or, Maria, Works*, Vol. 1, p. 164.
2. *Thoughts on the Education of Daughters: with Reflections on Female Conduct, in the More Important Duties of Life, Works*, Vol. 4, p. 36.

condition of all the others.[3] She was not alone in seeing it as the bedrock of human personality. Adam Smith (1723–1790), with whose work on moral personality she engaged, thought likewise; he spoke of the "great school of self-command" and saw it as the basis of every other virtue;[4] so, of course, had a long line of philosophers reaching all the way back to Socrates. To be sure, all philosophers, when pressed, would agree that ultimately nothing can be achieved, no virtue exercised, without the power to will oneself to do or to forbear. Wollstonecraft made that point emphatically. She believed European society to be in particular need of being told this. Although she did see, or hoped to see, some signs of a potential moral rejuvenation in the revolution in France, she judged contemporary society to be corrupt and the bulk of her contemporaries to be degenerate in some way. While she expended much intellectual energy understanding how self-control could be taught and developed, and which social forces enhanced and which weakened it, she used most of her ink exposing what she took to be the folly of the world, its vanity, and delusions: its sheer stupidity. This is particularly true of her *A Vindications of the Rights of Men* (1790) and *A Vindication of the Rights of Woman* (1792). Wollstonecraft found little to praise in either sex. Neither women, with very rare exceptions, nor men emerge unscathed from her pages or fulfill their human potential. While she certainly did not hold what is commonly referred to as a pessimistic view of human nature, much of her writing is condemnatory and her tone, cutting. Her book reviews are mostly damning when they are not dismissive, her own books rich in disapproval of nearly everything she depicted in them, likewise her correspondence. It was, to be sure, the style of the time, of the

3. Catriona MacKenzie, "Reason and Sensibility: The Ideal of Women's Self-Governance in the Writings of Mary Wollstonecraft," *Hypatia* 8, no. 4 (1993): 35–55. *JSTOR*, www.jstor.org/stable/3810368.

4. Smith, *The Theory of Moral Sentiments*, p. 146, see also pp. 145–156. See also Leddy, "Mary Wollstonecraft and Adam Smith."

genres in which she wrote, and in many ways the product of her circumstances, but it did become her.

As a result, it would be all too easy to think of her as all denunciation and a thorough killjoy. Indeed, that is how she has been viewed, and Julie Murray has rightly challenged this.[5] It therefore may not be amiss to begin a study such as this by evoking some of the things Wollstonecraft did appreciate or even love and wish others to relish. It is also worth noting that while she thought forms of abstemiousness often necessary and the capacity to exercise them vital to the individuals themselves, their relations, and society more generally, she did not think of self-command as equating to, or necessarily entailing, self-denial. In considering what she divulged, or appeared to be, enjoying and what she thought constituted a good life, we gain both in understanding of her as a person and comprehension of her philosophical outlook. It allows us to see and, in some cases, tease out what she deemed the philosophical challenges a reflecting mind such as hers faced, for even the seemingly most simple pleasures entailed serious considerations on her part. Most, it would appear, if not all, had to be in the service of the development of a particular kind of personality, one with character. What made for character or contributed to its making emerged in part from what she wrote of the arts.

The Theater

Wollstonecraft did value many things for the sheer enjoyment they gave her and others. This was especially evident in her youth, before "misfortune had broken [her] spirits," as she described it when she was only twenty-two.[6] She prized the

5. Julie Murray, "Mary Wollstonecraft, Feminist Killjoy," in *Romantic Circles*, Praxis Series, https://romantic-circles.org/praxis/wollstonecraft/praxis.2019 .wollstonecraft.murray.htm.

6. *The Collected Letters of Mary Wollstonecraft*, edited by Janet Todd (New York: Columbia University Press, 2003), p. 28 (hereafter *Letters*).

performing arts from an early age and, in one of the earliest extant letters of 1773, expressed excitement at the prospect of seeing a play: "I am going to see the Macaroni if it be performed, and expect a great deal of pleasure."[7] The theater was for Wollstonecraft a lasting source of delight. She began the final of her *Letters Written during a Short Residence in Sweden, Norway, and Denmark* by reporting that there was "a pretty little French theatre at Altona; and the actors are much superior to those I saw at Copenhagen," and noted that the theaters at Hamburg would soon open.[8] Her correspondence toward the end of her life also attests to her continued enjoyment of the theater, a milieu in which Godwin and she had a number of friends, and her copious quotations show that she not only attended performances but read plays.

Pleased to be given a new edition of Shakespeare while in Dublin in 1787, she cited him frequently and throughout her life, drawing on a great many of his plays, including *As You Like It*, *Hamlet*, *Julius Caesar*, *Macbeth*, *A Midsummer Night's Dream*, and *The Tempest*, and providing lengthy extracts from these in *The Female Reader* (1789). On seeing "some heart's ease," she evoked *A Midsummer Night's Dream* when she wrote to Imlay that "[if] you are deep read in Shakespeare, you will recollect that this was the little western flower tinged by love's dart, which 'maidens call love in idleness.'"[9] Her novels are infused with his words, and in a 1788 review for the *Analytical Review* of *Essays on Shakespeare's Dramatic Character of Sir John Falstaff and on his Imitation of Female Characters. To which are added, some general Observations on the Study of Shakespeare* by the Glasgow Professor of Humanity, William Richardson (1743–1814), it is clear that she thought of herself as someone who, unlike many,

---

7. Ibid., p. 8. Wollstonecraft is referring to *The Macaroni, A Comedy*, by Robert Hitchcock, published anonymously in York in 1773 and performed in 1774 in Beverly, where Wollstonecraft lived at the time.

8. *Letters Written in Sweden, Norway, and Denmark, Works*, Vol. 6, p. 344.

9. Ibid., p. 247.

had a genuine understanding of Shakespeare's works.[10] She agreed with Richardson's claim that "half critics" were mistaken in thinking that Shakespeare "has exerted more ability in his imitation of male, than female characters," though she could not concur with "the cordial praise he bestow[ed] on Ophelia." Ophelia's conduct in *Hamlet*, she maintained (unknowing what lay in her own future), "was mean and unjust; if she acted like a female we pity her weakness, but should not either praise or palliate a fault that no mistaken notion of duty could justify without confounding the distinction between virtue and vice."[11]

If she condemned the action of his character, Ophelia, she did not fault the playwright. She thought that, unlike most dramaturges, he had succeeded in what she considered one of the great challenges that only great art could meet, namely, finely delineating the "almost imperceptible progress of the passions."[12] Given how little she was given to unqualified commendation, her expressed admiration for "our incomparable poet" is striking and the grounds for it of particular interest.[13] Commenting in a review in 1789 on the number of novels being published and how very few of them were "tolerable," she wrote of Shakespeare by contrast as follows:

> Shakspeare [*sic*] created monsters; but he gave such reality to his characters, that we should not hesitate a moment to deliver our imaginations, and even reason, into his hands; we follow their wild yet not fantastic foot-steps through wood and bog, nothing loath—thinking them new, though not unnatural.[14]

Here Wollstonecraft tells us that great, true art, even when fantastic, is "not unnatural." A great artist was one to whom his or

10. *Analytical Review*, Vol. 2 (1788), *Works*, Vol. 7, pp. 55–57.
11. Ibid., p. 57.
12. *Education of Daughters*, *Works*, p. 47.
13. *Analytical Review*, Vol. 12 (1792), *Works*, p. 423.
14. *Analytical Review*, Vol. 3 (1789), *Works*, p. 66.

her audience surrendered themselves fully, as in an act of love. Such artists were magicians, but their powers did not affect everyone: "nay, even Shakespear's [*sic*] magic powers are only for those who cultivate their reason."[15] Her knowledge of the theater extended well beyond him, however, and she could not resist speaking of Molière, Corneille, Dryden, and Racine in *The French Revolution* praising the first as an extraordinary author who wrote on "the grand scale of human passions, comparing the second to the third, and describing the last as 'the father of the french [*sic*] stage.'"[16]

Her first published work, *Thoughts on the Education of Daughters*, included a piece on 'The Theatre' as one of its constituent short essays.[17] She began by declaring it the site of the most rational amusements, especially to "a cultivated mind," though she warned that to one less so, it might prove a schooling in affectations. This was not a minor consequence for Wollstonecraft. Authenticity mattered to her. Exaggerated displays, false emotions, and all forms of distortions of personality were anathema to her. When writing to Imlay from Scandinavia, she even declared always having been "of the opinion that the allowing actors to die, in the presence of the audience, has an immoral tendency; but trifling when compared with the ferocity acquired by viewing the reality as a show."[18] The theater was therefore not free of moral danger, as it could easily be the scene of "a false display of the passions" and lead spectators to copy extreme ones, while being oblivious to the "more delicate touches." Wollstonecraft confessed that she herself had been affected "beyond measure" by Lear's line on seeing Cordelia: "I think that Lady is

<hr/>

15. *Analytical Review*, Vol. 6 (1790), *Works*, p. 224.

16. *The French Revolution*, *Works*, Vol. 6, p. 25.

17. For an extensive and wide-ranging discussion of Wollstonecraft's view of the theater, see Crafton, *Transgressive Theatricality, Romanticism, and Mary Wollstonecraft*.

18. *Letters Written in Sweden, Norway, and Denmark*, 19, *Works*, Vol. 6, p. 323.

my daughter," yet had been unmoved by the unfaithful, deceitful, but ultimately penitent Calista's declamations about the cave in which she would live "Until her tears had washed her guilt away."[19] Wollstonecraft, no less than anyone else, needed to be taught to be sensitive to the more subtle emotions and complex moral predicaments depicted on stage. However, her awareness of her own limitations had not stopped her questioning the value of Greek tragedies and, taking *Oedipus* as an example, asked what moral lesson could conceivably be drawn from a story of someone impelled by the gods "and, led imperiously by blind fate, though perfectly innocent, he is fearfully punished, with all this hapless race, for a crime in which his will had no part."[20] Sheer destiny was, we can infer, of no psychological interest to her. What she wanted to see staged were moral dilemmas facing characters who had genuine choices and were not shackled to a preordained fate. Whether Ophelia was in such a position is questionable, but one may assume, given what she argued, that Wollstonecraft thought Hamlet had faced such a choice.

So, while Wollstonecraft did express some concern about the potential of drama to have an emotionally distorting impact, her brief composition on the subject made clear her genuine interest in it as well as providing further evidence of her love of Shakespeare. The theater could enhance our understanding of humanity and thereby contribute to the making of our own selves. To be sure, this was by no means always the case. She could be critical of individual plays for their want of plot or character development without rejecting the art itself.[21] That her concern was far from the virulent critique of the theater articulated by Plato and

19. *Works*, vol. 4, p. 46. The references are to *King Lear* (IV.vii.68–70), and Nicholas Rowe, *The Fair Penitent* (1703), IV.i. See S. Harris, "Outside the Box: The Female Spectator, 'The Fair Penitent,' and the Kelly Riots of 1747," *Theatre Journal* 57, no. 1 (2005): 33–55.
20. *The French Revolution, Works*, Vol. 6, p. 112.
21. E.g., her review of *The Fugitive. A Comedy. As it is performed at the King's Theatre in the Haymarket. Works*, Vol. 7, pp. 454–455.

famously in the mid-eighteenth century by Jean-Jacques Rousseau might be somewhat surprising, not so much because she engaged with the thought of both these authors, but because, like the latter, she was so hostile to anything that might encourage men and women to appear other than they were or indeed to all that contributed to the making of the hall of mirrors in which much of society was entrapped.[22]

She was also aware that the theater and theater audiences were not the same the world over. They reflected deep cultural, social, and psychological differences between people. As Lisa Plummer Grafton has argued, Wollstonecraft thought the French people particularly theatrical, and claimed they imbibed the fondness for public places, and the theater in particular, as they suckled their mothers' milk.[23] Indeed, she was initially critical of their national character for being so much shaped by their theatrical amusements. She thought that the continual gratification of their senses in which the theater played a large part made the French fickle, unable to reflect on their feelings, and stifled their imagination.[24] Once in Scandinavia, she was to revise her opinion on this subject, as we will have occasion to see later, and began her *Letter XX* in her disarmingly confessional tone: "I have formerly censured the french [*sic*] for their extreme attachments to theatrical exhibitions, because I thought that they tended to render them vain and unnatural characters."[25] She now considered that money spent at the theater was far better spent than in drinking and commented on the sobriety of the French people, remarking that it was precisely this that made "their fêtes more interesting" and their common people superior to that of every other nation.

22. For an illuminating treatment of this subject in relation to Rousseau, see David Marshall, "Rousseau and the State of Theatre," *Representations* no. 13 (1986): 84–114, www.jstor.org/stable/2928495.

23. *The French Revolution, Works*, Vol. 6, p. 25. *Transgressive Theatricality, Romanticism, and Mary Wollstonecraft*, p. 50.

24. *The French Revolution, Works*, Vol. 6, p. 25.

25. *Letters Written in Sweden, Norway, and Denmark, Works*, Vol. 6, p. 327.

Moreover, she noted, responses to performances did not vary greatly between social classes in France, where audiences responded as one socially unified whole, whereas differences were far more marked in England:

> At our theatres, the boxes, pit, and galleries, relish different scenes; and some are condescendingly born by the more polished part of the audience, to allow the rest to have their portion of amusement. In France, on the contrary, a highly wrought sentiment of morality, probably rather romantic than sublime, produces a burst of applause, when one heart seems to agitate every hand.[26]

Thus plays, performances, and reactions to them were of great interest to her on several different levels. The powerful impact of art on individuals and large audiences, as we will have cause to see again in relation to music and other forms of creations, was a subject on which she deliberated.

If she rejected artificiality, she did not reject the fine arts any more than she did the theater. Both needed conditioning or training of some kind. In *A Vindication of the Rights of Woman*, Wollstonecraft argued that "[a] taste for the fine arts requires cultivation; but no more than a taste for the virtuous affections; and both suppose that enlargement of mind which opens so many sources of mental pleasure."[27] This brief statement is one of her most revealing and warrants highlighting. One had to acquire a desire for being a certain kind of person. The yearning to be a cultivated and moral being had itself to be nurtured. Both called for effort. Both called for intellectual development, which in turn produced greater fonts of enjoyment. The desire to be cultivated and virtuous had to be inculcated by thoughtful

26. *The French Revolution, Works*, Vol. 6, p. 19.
27. *VW*, p. 261; see M. Ahmed Cronin, "Mary Wollstonecraft's Conception of 'True Taste' and Its Role in Egalitarian Education and Citizenship," *European Journal of Political Theory* 18, no. 4 (2019): 508–528.

parenting, sustained by appropriate education, and not thwarted by society.[28] The theater could, given the right preparation on the part of individuals in the audience, contribute to that process, as could—and indeed should in Wollstonecraft's view—the other arts.

Painting

Of the art of painting itself Wollstonecraft wrote relatively little directly, or if she did, it has not survived the destruction of many of her letters.[29] She probably sat for her portrait for John Williamson (1751–1818) in 1791, a work commissioned by her admirer, the Liverpool lawyer, William Roscoe (1753–1831), and for John Opie (1761–1807) around 1792 and again in 1797, and was on very good terms with him and his wife.[30] They are mentioned in her letters, as are brief references to her posing amidst accounts of social engagements. She encountered illustrators and painters when she joined the circle of Joseph Johnson, her publisher. He patronized William Blake and Henry Fuseli (1741–1825), who rose to fame following the exhibition at the Royal Academy in 1782 of *The Nightmare* (1781), his erotically charged and disturbing painting.

Wollstonecraft became wildly besotted with him, but although she referred to him as an "original genius,"[31] we do not know whether her infatuation with the married artist owed

28. For a useful overview of Wollstonecraft's views on education, see Ferguson, "Theories of Education."

29. Her letters to the painter Henry Fuseli have not survived. See Janet Todd on this subject, *Letters*, pp. xvi–xvii.

30. The first Opie painting is dated c. 1790–1791 by Tate Britain, its current owner. The portrait attributed to John Williamson is in the Walker Art Gallery, Liverpool. See Eileen Hunt Botting, "The Earliest Portraiture of Wollstonecraft, 1785–1804," in *Portraits of Wollstonecraft*, edited by Eileen Hunt Botting (London: Bloomsbury, forthcoming).

31. *Letters*, p. 167.

much to his art, much less which aspect of it.[32] Writing to
Roscoe, she disclosed that she did not anticipate liking Fuseli's representation of Eve in his series of depictions of Milton's
poems. Rather than describe the early sketches, she urged Roscoe to see them for himself, adding, "[w]e have all an individual
way of feeling grandeur and sublimity."[33] Blake was to illustrate
her *Original Stories from Real Life; with Conversations Calculated to Regulate the Affections, and Form the Mind to Truth and
Goodness* (1788), but again, we do not know what she thought
of his engravings.

Her review of Joshua Reynolds's *A Discourse Delivered to the
Students of the Royal Academy, on the Distribution of the Prizes,
Dec. 10, 1788* gives almost nothing away about either Reynolds
himself or his subject, Thomas Gainsborough. Yet her relatively
lengthy citations of his *Discourse* do provide an indication that
she agreed with Reynolds in thinking that, while students might
learn from past and present masters, the latter should not be
turned into rigid models for pupils, as these would become "bad
copies of good painters, instead of excellent imitators of the great
universal truth of things."[34] She shunned imitation, whatever
the context. Independence of mind was of prime importance
to Wollstonecraft. How that could be achieved, how one could
be true to nature, yet taught or schooled, and, what is more, be
original was an unresolved difficulty to which she returned time
and again in a number of ways. Rendering nature on those terms
clearly presented a great challenge whatever the medium, but
as we saw earlier, Shakespeare had, in her estimation, achieved
something comparable in his medium.

Reviewing four of the works of the parish priest, schoolmas-
ter, and highly prolific writer and artist William Gilpin (1724–1804)
gave her cause to reflect on the nature of beauty and the beautiful

32. See Pop, *Antiquity, Theatre, and the Painting of Henry Fuseli*,
pp. 159–166.
33. *Letters*, pp. 194–195.
34. *Analytical Review*, Vol. 5 (1789), *Works*, Vol. 7, p. 160.

in nature, as well as travel literature, of which she was to become a noted practitioner when reporting on her journey through Scandinavia in 1795. The way Gilpin integrated his views of nature into his ethics and theology was, in any event, likely to appeal to Wollstonecraft.[35] She valued his *Observations on the River Wye, and several parts of South Wales, etc. relative chiefly to picturesque Beauty, made in the Summer of the Year 1770*, the second edition of which she considered for the September 1789 issue of the *Analytical Review*, "as it contains the principles of picturesque beauty, as far as it is capable of being reduced to principles, and transmitted from one man to another." Like Immanuel Kant (1724–1804), whose *Critique of Judgment* (1790) she knew and cited in her *Hints* in relation to the ideas of the sublime and the beautiful, but contra Friedrich Schiller (1759–1805), who believed in a universal aesthetic standard, she thought taste was, to a large extent, an individual matter.[36] Possibly as a result, expressing one's taste, verbalizing it, was intrinsically difficult. In contrast to matters of fact, which could be conveyed "by the most direct road" with precision and clarity from one mind to another, "pleasures arising from taste and feeling are more complex and accidental" and "almost incommunicable."[37] While Wollstonecraft thought Gilpin's drawings did help to share his perceptions of what he saw in the course of his travels as they fixed the attention on specific moments and spaces, they also limited the nature of the shared experience: "from the size of the drawings, their studied neatness, and perhaps, the imperfection

35. On Gilpin's aesthetic and theology, see Mayhew, "William Gilpin and the Latitudinarian Picturesque." On Wollstonecraft's responses to the picturesque and him, see Bahar, *Mary Wollstonecraft's Social and Aesthetic Philosophy*, pp. 152–153 and 161–162.

36. *Hints* first appeared in *Posthumous Works*, Vol. 4. The notes were intended for the projected second part of *A Vindication of the Rights of Woman*. Wollstonecraft's only mention of Schiller is in a review of Volume 1 of *The Spectator* (1790), which appraises German tragedians, *Analytical Review*, Vol. 9 (1791), *Works*, p. 361.

37. *Analytical Review*, Vol. 5 (1789), *Works*, Vol. 7, p. 161.

inseparable from art, his elegant sketches oftener gave us an idea of the beautiful than the sublime."[38] However good, the logic of composition, its inevitably restricted span, the artifice it introduced, meant that representative art could not but provide a diminished experience of nature. This said, neither Gilpin nor she thought that art should or indeed could seek to replicate nature. In fact, in a review some months later, Wollstonecraft went further, asserting that art required *"artificial effects."* Furthermore, she thought Gilpin himself was more committed to this view than he seemed to realize: "we are apt to believe, from experience, that a small landscape, when it is tinted, assumes a more diminutive and artificial appearance than plain, shadowy drawings, because the unnatural, striking glow in them, awakens the imagination, which bold strokes might have cheated, if the veil had not been removed; for unnatural must the charming tints of nature ever appear, when they are not mellowed, by melting into a large expanse of grey air."[39]

Wollstonecraft's third review of Gilpin's works, *Remarks on Forest Scenery, and other Woodland Views, (relatively chiefly to Picturesque Beauty). Illustrated by the Scenes of New Forest in Hampshire*, in August 1791, merits special attention. It reveals, first, that she thought aesthetic taste had to have some form of theoretical grounding. She believed this showed, as will be discussed further in the next chapter, "that reason and fancy are nearer akin than cold dullness is willing to allow."[40] In other words, a genuinely perceptive person would intuit that however much reason and the imagination were generally thought of as opposite/opposing terms, they were in fact profoundly connected. Second, after citing Gilpin on the comparative advantages of exhibiting "incidental beauties" of the meridian and the rising sun, she approvingly quoted the following:

38. Ibid., p. 162.
39. Ibid., p. 197.
40. Ibid., p. 387.

[i]n general, the poet had great advantages over the painter, in the process of *sublimification*, if the term may be allowed. The business of the former is only to excite ideas; that of the latter, to represent them. The advantage of excited over represented ideas is very great, inasmuch as they are in some degree the reader's own production, and are susceptible of those modifications, which make them peculiarly acceptable to the mind in which they are raised. Whereas the others being confined within a distinct and unalterable line, admit of none of the modifications, which flatter the particular taste of the spectator, but must make their way by their own intrinsic force.[41]

Gilpin was writing as an artist. Wollstonecraft was citing him from her point of view, namely as a viewer. There is reason to think from what she wrote of the other arts that she preferred what was conducive to the process of sublimification (Gilpin's coinage) rather than having an effect forced upon her mind, which is to say that she preferred art that excited ideas in the viewer rather than a mere representation of the ideas. This applied to viewing art, not producing it. When writing, in the fourth and final review of Gilpin, from the point of view of the practitioner, she did assert that "[l]andscape sketching is certainly a most pleasing amusement, and affords the idle, we mean the rich, an employment that by exercising the taste, leads to moral improvement."[42] Thus, the practice of drawing was morally edifying in her view: it gave the practitioner something to do and developed his or her aesthetic judgment in so doing.

This said, although Wollstonecraft did not consider painting in much detail, she often visualized political and human relations more generally, and wrote about them as if they were tableaux, tableaux of pastoral idylls or urban poverty, and of women in each other's company, for instance. Thus, we find another

41. Ibid.
42. Ibid., pp. 456–457.

glimpse of her thoughts on the subject in an unexpected context, namely that of her first *Vindication*. Burke's *Reflections on the Revolution in France* was partly prompted and shaped as a response to a young Frenchman of his acquaintance asking for his opinion of the unfolding events. Part of Burke's withering answer focused on the composition of the National Assembly. Attacking Burke's deprecating comments, Wollstonecraft evoked the quasi-pedagogical relationship between the young Frenchman and the older Member of Parliament, and argued that

> [i]f you had given the same advice to a young history painter of abilities, I should have admired your judgment, and re-echoed your sentiments. Study, you might have said, the noble models of antiquity, till your imagination is inflamed; and, rising above the vulgar practice of the hour, you may imitate without copying those great originals. A glowing picture, of some interesting moment, would probably have been produced by these natural means; particularly if one little circumstance is not overlooked, that the painter had noble models to revert to, calculated to excite admiration and stimulate exertion.[43]

Here we see her, as we have already noted and will see again, deliberating on the relation between imitation as obsequious copy and imitation that is nothing of the sort, but rather takes a model as inspiration in a manner that transcends them. It was a major concern of hers that all forms of servile replication be eradicated in every aspect of human existence, not just the visual arts. Wollstonecraft's reflections on the latter and the arts more generally, however, do shed some light on what she thought the relation between imitation and inventiveness ought to be.

While these topics, whether singly or in combination, were hardly Burke's monopoly, and Wollstonecraft had more than one reason to come to them, his *Philosophical Enquiry into the*

43. *VM*, pp. 41–42.

Origin of our Ideas of the Sublime and Beautiful (1757), which she ransacked in aid of her unrestrained attack on his *Reflections on the Revolution in France* (1790), brought them to the fore. Although Burke was by no means averse to change and is well-known for his pronouncement that "[a] state without the means of some change is without the means of its conservation,"[44] both of these works addressed the issue of the reproduction of society through the combined activity of the imitative capacity of mankind and the transformative effect of the ambitious among it. As we shall have occasion to see further on, much of what Wollstonecraft wrote was shaped by her engagement with him on this subject and by his conception of the sublime and the beautiful and his comments about women within it.

Music

Given that she was asked to review the subject of music as well as poetry, it would seem that the *Analytic Review*'s editor, Joseph Johnson, must have thought Wollstonecraft might not only appreciate these arts, but also be well-placed to reflect on their particular nature. Already in her first published work, *Thoughts on the Education of Daughters: with Reflections on Female Conduct, in the More Important Duties of Life* (1787), she stated that "[m]usic and painting, and many other ingenious arts, are now brought to great perfection, and afford the most rational and delicate pleasure."[45] In a work of the same period, *Original Stories from Real life; with Conversations Calculated to Regulate the Affections, and Form the Mind to Truth and Goodness* (1788), Wollstonecraft argued that "[e]very gift of Heaven

44. *Writings and Speeches of Edmund Burke*, gen. ed. Paul Langford, Vol. 8, edited by L. G. Mitchell and William B. Todd (Oxford: Clarendon Press, 1989), p. 72.

45. *Works*, Vol. 4, p. 18. See M. Ahmed Cronin, "Mary Wollstonecraft's Conception of 'True Taste' and Its Role in Egalitarian Education and Citizenship," *European Journal of Political Theory* 18, no. 4 (2019): 508–528.

is lent to us for improvement" and "[m]usic, drawing, works of usefulness and fancy, all amuse and refine the mind, sharpen the ingenuity and [form insensibly] the dawning judgement."[46] Artistic talent should not, therefore, be allowed to lie dormant, she contended, as they were divine gifts and great blessings that enhanced our capacity to be fully human; as we just read in her comments regarding landscape painting, it was conducive to "moral improvement."

Wollstonecraft was rather more vocal about music than she appears to have been about painting, though the latter subject did surface, as we shall see again, in her reflections on poetry and nature. That she was more expressive about music may be due to the fact that she responded emotionally more immediately to the one than the other, possibly because she found it less imitative and more consolatory, but perhaps also because her experience of its beauty led her more easily to that of the sublime. It was for her a source of joy and solace, a spiritual channel, a mirror to God's harmonious creation, and a unifying force.

Even though her *Thoughts on the Education of Daughters* was not an auto-biographical but a pedagogical work, she disclosed that she preferred "expression to execution," adding "[t]he simple melody of some artless airs has often soothed my mind, when it has been harassed by care; and I have been raised from the very depth of sorrow, by the sublime harmony of some of Handel's compositions."[47]

Music, and possibly that of Henry Purcell (1659–1695) and Georg Frideric Handel (1685–1759) in particular, had an important transcendent dimension for Wollstonecraft: "I have been lifted," she continued, "above this little scene of grief and care, and mused on him, from whom all bounty flows."[48] It afforded

46. Cronin, "Mary Wollstonecraft's Conception of 'True Taste,'" *Works*, Vol. 4, p. 415.
47. *Works*, Vol. 4, p. 18.
48. Ibid. Janet Todd writes that when Lady Kingsborough gave "Wollstonecraft, then governess to her children, tickets for both days of the

her a conduit to the celestial and likewise to writing about it and the arts more generally. In *Mary, A Fiction* (1788) composed in the summer of 1787, the heroine, upon hearing a sailor say that "he believed the world was going to be at an end," was led toward a new train of thought:

> Some of Handel's sublime compositions occurred to her, and she sung them to the grand accompaniment. The Lord God Omnipotent reigned, and would reign for ever and ever!— Why then did she fear the sorrows that were passing away, when she knew that He would bind up the broken-hearted, and receive those who came out of great tribulation.[49]

Similarly, in the posthumous novel, *The Wrongs of Woman: or, Maria*, begun just a little more than a year before her death, Wollstonecraft had its heroine, Maria, upon escaping her brutal husband, procure herself some books and music "to beguile the tedious solitary days," "and [sing] till, saddened by the strain of joy," "Come, ever smiling Liberty / And with thee bring thy jocund train" from Handel's *Judas Maccabaeus*.[50] Criticizing a poem that referred to the effect of Handel's music ("What moral is not rapt / To hear his tender wildy-warbled song"), she retorted that "[i]t is not Handel's *tender-wildly-warbled song*, with few exceptions, which demand our praise; but the grand combinations that force us to applaud his exquisite judgement— his harmony rather than his melody."[51] However, she did acknowledge that "the admirer of Handel's grand instrumental accompaniments" might be led to overlook "the melody of many

---

Handel commemoration—the *Messiah* had first been performed in Dublin— Wollstonecraft first admitted herself "'obliged.'" *Mary Wollstonecraft: A Revolutionary Life*, p. 105.

49. In *Works*, Vol. 1, p. 51.

50. Ibid., p. 161.

51. *Analytical Review*, Vol. 4 (1789), *Works*, Vol. 7, p. 114.

composers of genius," observing that "[t]hese feats tickle the ear and wonder is mistaken for admiration."[52]

The oratorio, *Judas Maccabaeus*, composed in 1746 with a libretto by the Reverend Thomas Morell (who borrowed from Milton and Shakespeare), must nonetheless have been a favorite of hers.[53] She included a reference to the oratorio in the fourteenth of her *Letters Written in Sweden, Norway, and Denmark* (1796) as she related the effect reports of the honest and incorruptible farmers of northern Norway had had on her: "[t]he description I received of them carried me back to the fables of the golden age: independence and virtue; affluence without vice; cultivation of mind, without depravity of heart; with 'ever smiling liberty'; the nymph of the mountain."[54] *Judas Maccabaeus* was composed to celebrate the victory of William, Duke of Cumberland, over Charles Edward Stuart the Pretender at the battle of Culloden on April 16, 1746, which, among other things, was a Catholic defeat. One of Handel's most popular works from its first performance, it tells of the Israelites rallying behind Judas following the death of his father, the leader Mattathias, and of Judas's heroic victory against the Seleucid Empire which had proscribed Judaism and forced Jews to worship Hellenistic divinities. The reason behind Handel's choice of biblical stories was therefore clear. Whether, as a fervent anti-Catholic for much of her life, although not its entirety, Wollstonecraft's liking of the musical work was partly due to this connection can only be surmised. Be this as it may, the smiling liberty of which her novel's heroine, Maria, sang was, as for the Jewish people in Handel's work, to praise God.

These were not the only instances of her conception of music as a link between the human and the divine. Commenting on Charles Burney's four-volume study, *A General History of Music,*

52. *Analytical Review*, Vol. 6 (1790), *Works*, Vol. 7, p. 211.
53. See Smither, *A History of the Oratorio*, p. 200.
54. In *Works*, Vol. 6, p. 308.

from the earliest Ages, to the present Period. To which is prefixed,
A Dissertation on the Music of the Ancients in the February 1790
issue of the *Analytical Review*, within months of writing *A Vin-*
dication of the Rights of Men, Wollstonecraft produced one of her
longest and most positive reviews, notwithstanding her divergence from the author on some points. The article makes evident
her musical knowledge and sensibility, lauds the composition
of Purcell and Handel, and reaffirms her view of the art as both
divine manifestation and prayer. After extending to Burney the
"warmest praise for his indefatigable industry" and re-entitling
the work "An Historical Dictionary of Music," she wrote:

> Every lover of this captivating art, must thank the author,
> emphatically, for his unwearied researches, whilst the unim-
> passioned philosopher may coldly connect a more grand and
> comprehensive interest with the enquiry, and drawing meta-
> physical inferences from the ingenuity displayed in the pro-
> gressive improvement of music, advance a step further into
> the *terra incognita* of the human mind. From the vocal shell
> to the bent horn; from the rustling of the breezes amongst
> reeds, or the sweep of winds across stiff aquatic plants, to the
> rude syrinx, and perforated flute; from the deep tone lyre, to
> our admirable violin, which a skilful hand and feeling heart
> can almost make articulate every gradation of passion; how
> slow, yet striking the improvement, in the aggregate! Con-
> nected thus with universal harmony, though music may be
> called the food of passion and sensation, it affords the con-
> templative mind the most exalted intellectual pleasure, and
> becomes the food of devotion; if the effusions of awful grati-
> tude, and reverential love, on discovering any fresh glimpse
> of order and wisdom in creation, is the most perfect homage
> of a being, who gropes in the dark for proofs of its great ori-
> gin and destination.[55]

55. *Analytical Review*, Vol. 6 (1790), *Works*, Vol. 7, pp. 210–211.

We saw earlier that Wollstonecraft approved of artistry that suggested ideas rather than seeking to reproduce them literally. We also noted that she believed the cultivation of aesthetic and moral sense led to other pleasures. In this February 1790 review, we see these to be the delights of piety: divine faith was deliciously pleasurable in her account.

Burney had asked, "What kind of music is most pleasing to mankind?," and replied: novelty, refinement and "ingenious contrivance" to the connoisseurs, the "familiar and common" to those who were not. Wollstonecraft thought he ought to have added that "people of taste and feeling, who are not professed performers, are most touched by strains addressed to the heart." One can only presume she was speaking for herself when she also noted that neither "novelty of harmony" nor "ingenious contrivance" was pleasing; indeed, she thought that listeners would be as disgusted by them as by "fine attitudes in an actor, which, so far from being the expression of passion, spring from study, to produce stage effect." Thus, while Wollstonecraft disapproved of mere copying and admired originality, she did not wish the latter to be forced and unnatural. She thought that on this part of his subject, Burney was speaking too much like "a mere musician, whose heart and ears were not connected, or to use the language of Rousseau, whose ears were *depraved* by harmony."[56] That music ought to make the sensible heart vibrate was a thread running through the review, something she clearly thought Burney could not fully appreciate, though she did not quite explain how music could succeed in so doing. Despite her positive response to the book under review, she distinguished herself from its author in another important respect. She read his claims about music from the perspective of an audience member, not that of a composer or performer. Her comments are illuminating, moreover, not only of her as a listener, but of her views about the history of humanity.

56. Ibid., p. 211.

While Wollstonecraft was willing to allow that the ancients might not have used "*simultaneous harmony,* that is, *music in different parts,*" she was not inclined to follow Burney in denying ancient music its powerful effects. The praise its powers had received from poets and historians could not be discarded, she argued. She thought the reactions of the learned needed to be distinguished from those of the "vulgar of most nations [who] will never perceive the delicate graces of harmony, or feel the melodious shades of passion—words are sufficient for them; refinement has not fostered those sentiments, to which tones only can give articulation."[57] This was obvious if one considered popular tunes, given their monotonousness and the repetitiveness of a "particular *motivo*" in them. Yet, speaking again as a listener, she imagined that the sudden effect of a "wild melody" on a large assembly would have been wondrous. National music should not be slighted; even "a heart of sensibility will sometimes beat with the crowd, though it understands a superior language."[58] The ignorant could be moved and united to good effect. By contrast, she thought "the immoderate indulgence of genuine feelings, or the sickly appetite of fastidious refinement, the melody of passion, the graces of harmony, pall on the sense."[59] Like a tight-rope artist, Wollstonecraft walked the thin line between wishing to acknowledge taste and discernment and railing against denaturation through over-refinement. As with painting, the question revolved around the extent to which learning enhanced perception and feeling or corrupted them in the formation of taste.

Thinking of this in relation to music, Wollstonecraft was eager to resist a division between heart and mind, passion and understanding, sound and language. Some music required no explanation. Listening to it and comprehending it were one.

57. Ibid., p. 213.
58. Ibid.
59. Ibid.

Its absorption was instantaneous. "We perfectly agree with Dr
B[urney]," she declared,

> [t]hat there is some kind even of instrumental music, so
> "divinely composed, and so expressively performed, that it
> wants no words to explain its meaning: it is itself the lan-
> guage of the heart and of passion, and speaks more to
> both in a few notes, than any other language composed of
> clashing consonants, and insipid vowels, can do in as many
> thousand."[60]

However, she firmly disagreed with him in opposing music to
poetry. In this, we see her thinking of the interconnectedness of
feeling and understanding in the first months of 1790 as she had
begun to in her earliest work and would do for the remainder of
her short life. "We cannot subscribe," she continued, with what
Burney took as the inference that "'upon the whole, it seems
as if poetry were more immediately the language of the head,
and music that of the heart; or in other words, as if poetry were
the poorest vehicle of instruction, and modulated sound that of
joy, sorrow and innocent pleasure.'"[61] Neither music nor poetry
were, in her view, or, at least should be, didactic. They did not, or
ought not, seek to teach. Given how prone she was never to miss
an opportunity to moralize, these pronouncements on music and
especially poetry are striking. She believed they sought or ought
to seek to move. It may be that she thought that is how they edi-
fied. But in moving listeners or readers, they did not skirt understanding. They involved it seamlessly. Although, as we shall see
shortly, Wollstonecraft could often speak of the different mental
faculties as if they were neatly divided and indeed conflicting,
that is not how she thought they ought to be conceived or how
one should think of the human psyche in its entirety.

60. Ibid., p. 214.
61. Ibid.

Poetry

Unsurprisingly, if judged only by what we saw of her admiration of Shakespeare, poetry, the music of words, was much loved by Wollstonecraft.[62] She cited poems in her correspondence as well as in her published writings, such as those of John Milton (1608–1674), John Dryden (1631–1700), James Thomson (1700–1748), and William Cowper (1731–1800). Read by Samuel Taylor Coleridge (1772–1834), who drew on *A Vindication of the Rights of Woman* in his account of the status of women within Germanic tribes in *The Watchman*,[63] she became the subject of poetry herself. Shortly after her death, Robert Southey, counterbalancing the many satires of which she had been the target, wrote a sonnet in her praise:

> Who among Women left no equal mind
> When from this world she pass'd; and I could weep,
> To think that She is to the grave gone down![64]

Her influence on the first generation of Romantics—Coleridge, William Wordsworth, Southey, William Hazlitt—extended beyond the radical politics that she and William Godwin shared in common in them in the 1790s. The young poets were frequent visitors to Wollstonecraft's and Godwin's intellectual *salons*, where Wollstonecraft's conversation dazzled them. Hazlitt has left a vivid recollection of a conversation with Coleridge on this subject in 1798:

> [Coleridge] asked me if I had ever seen Mary Wollstonecraft, and I said, I had once for a few moments, and that

---

62. See Wolfson, "Mary Wollstonecraft and the Poets," pp. 160–188.

63. N. 3, March 17 (1796) in *The Collected Work of Samuel Taylor Coleridge*, p. 91. I am grateful to Lee Borocz-Johnson for drawing my attention to this and to Bruce Baugh for his comments on her influence on the Romantics

64. See Susan J. Wolfson, *Romantic Interactions: Social Being and the Turns of Literary Action* (Baltimore, MD: Johns Hopkins University Press, 2010), pp. 93–109.

she seemed to turn off Godwin's objections to something she advanced with quite a playful, easy air. He replied that "this was only one instance of the ascendancy which people of imagination exercised over those of mere intellect."[65]

Given Coleridge's high estimation of the imagination, this was no small praise. But it was Wollstonecraft's *Letters Written in Sweden, Norway, and Denmark* that most influenced the Romantics.[66] All of them frequently mention this work in their correspondence; critics have argued that the imagery of Coleridge's "Kubla Khan" is directly influenced by Wollstonecraft's description of "the impetuous dashing of the rebounding torrents from the dark cavities" in Wollstonecraft's travelogue.[67] Wollstonecraft's *Letters Written in Sweden, Norway, and Denmark* also inspired Coleridge to plan (but not to execute) a pedestrian tour of Denmark, Sweden, and Norway.[68] She became the Romantics' ideal of a person—indeed, a woman—in whom Reason and Imagination, politics and poetry, were perfectly combined.

As with music, poems led Wollstonecraft to reflect on the activity of the mind in reading or hearing it. "Poetry," she wrote in *A Vindication of the Rights of Men*, "naturally addresses the fancy, and the language of passion is with great felicity borrowed from the heightened picture which the imagination draws of sensible objects concentred [*sic*] by impassion reflection."

65. William Hazlitt, "My First Acquaintance with Poets" (1823), in Hazlitt, *Selected Writings*, edited by Ronald Blythe (Harmondsworth: Penguin Books, 1982), p. 59.

66. See Richard Holmes, "Introduction," in Wollstonecraft, *Letters Written during a Short Residence in Sweden, Norway, and Denmark*, and William Godwin, *Memoirs of the Author of "The Rights of Woman,"* edited by Richard Holmes (Harmondsworth: Penguin Books, 1987), pp. 36, 39–42.

67. Jonathan Livinston Lowes, *The Road to Xanadu: A Study in the Ways of the Imagination* (Boston: Houghton & Mifflin, 1955 [1927]), pp. 148, 161–62, 545 n.127; Holmes, "'Introduction' to Wollstonecraft, *Letters Written during a Short Residence in Sweden, Norway, and Denmark*," pp. 39–41.

68. Richard Holmes, *Coleridge: Early Visions* (London: Hodder & Stoughton, 1989), p. 236.

Quoting from *A Midsummer Night's Dream,* she added, "during this 'fine phrenzy,' reason has no right to rein-in the imagination, unless to prevent the introduction of supernumerary images; if the passion is real, the head will not be ransacked for stale tropes and cold rodomontade."[69] Wollstonecraft did not only enjoy poetry, but as with everything else, she reflected on its nature and its history, and as with music, her views on the subject open a door on to her other beliefs. She thought poetry at its most vivid in the early history of humankind, "the infancy of civilization," as she termed it, when the imagination ruled supreme before it began to be unseated by reason "which clips the wing of fancy—the youth becomes a man."[70] In *Hints,* the notes we have of what was to be a sequel or second volume to *A Vindication of the Rights of Woman,* in which she meant to consider the question of women's legal status and rights more particularly, we find her reiterating this view of humanity: "I am more and more convinced, that poetry is the first effervescence of the imagination, and the forerunner of civilization."[71] Her juxtaposition of the imagination and reason went further. Speaking of a period when the Arabs had "no trace of literature or science," she noted that they "composed beautiful verses on the subjects of love and war," adding that the "flights of the imagination, and the laboured deductions of reason, appear almost incompatible," and again that "[p]oetry certainly flourished most in the first rude state of society. The passions speak most eloquently, when they are not shackled by reason."[72] We saw earlier that Wollstonecraft believed discernment could make one realize that the imagination and reason were not as opposed as one might think. We should also be wary of thinking that she thought dichotomously of feelings and reason from such passages, but there is

69. *VM*, p. 28.
70. Ibid.
71. *Hints*, p. 300.
72. Ibid.

no doubt that she also thought that a certain kind of reasoning could have a baneful effect on creativity.

The origins and power of poetry was a subject that continued to preoccupy Wollstonecraft, as she was to devote a very condensed work to it toward the end of her life. In April 1797, just five months before she died, "On Poetry, and Our Relish for the Beauties of Nature" appeared in the *Monthly Magazine*.[73] While only a few pages long, it is not an easy text, as Wollstonecraft seems to be carried away by the force of her own prose, weaving together several of her most important concerns. As a result, it encapsulates much of her view of the world. Beginning with a theme we touched on already in relation to the theater and painting—the divide between true feeling and false sensibility— it contrasts nature and artifice, the beginnings of civilization and its current stage, sensual love and friendship, happiness and contentment. In the present state of society, Wollstonecraft began, "[a] taste for rural scenes," though frequently seemingly displayed, was often not genuine. It was mediated by poetry and romances rather than by a direct or "real perception of the beauties of nature."[74] In such circumstances, poetry distanced its readers from nature, creating a sham encounter with it.

Thinking historically about this as she did about all else, Wollstonecraft went on to say that she had often wondered why poetry written in the infancy of society was most natural. Which early poets she had in mind was not made explicit, but it would seem she had Ancient Greek, probably Homeric, poetry in her thoughts, though, given her biblical knowledge and her liking of *Judas Maccabaeus*, she might also have been thinking of the poetry of the Ancient Hebrews.

She did own that "natural" had an indeterminate meaning and explained that in relation to poetry at least, it should

73. For a discussion of this work, see Devine, "'A Kind of Witchcraft,'" pp. 235–245; Hodson, *Language and Revolution*.

74. *Works*, Vol. 7, p. 7.

be read as "the transcript of immediate sensations, in all their native wildness and simplicity, when fancy, awakened by the sight of interesting objects, was most actively at work."[75] In such moments, she thought, similes and images spontaneously came to mind, without the understanding or memory laboriously searching for words and effects. Judging by her tone, that was the poetry she thought most affecting. "The poet, the man of strong feelings," she wrote,

> Gives us only an image of his mind, when he was actually alone, conversing with himself, and marking the impression which nature had made on his own heart.—If, at this sacred, moment, the idea of some departed friend, some tender recollection when the soul was most alive to tenderness, intruded unawares into his thoughts, the sorrow which it produced is artlessly, yet poetically expressed—and who can avoid sympathizing?[76]

Following this passage, Wollstonecraft writes of poetry and its effects, as she had of music, within the framework of contemplation of the divine creation. Indeed, she thought of poetry, in what one might call its purity, when a most direct reflection of sensory impressions of nature or feelings, as devotional:

> Love to man leads to devotion—grand and sublime images strike the imagination—God is seen in every floating cloud, and comes from the misty mountain to receive the noblest homage of an intelligent creature—praise. How solemn is the moment, when all affections and remembrances fade before the sublime admiration which the wisdom and goodness of God inspires, when he is worshipped in a *temple not made with hands*, and the world seems to contain only the mind that formed, and the mind that contemplates it! These are not the weak responses of ceremonial devotion; nor, to

75. Ibid.
76. Ibid., p. 8.

express them, would the poet need another poet's aid: his heart burns within him, and he speaks the language of truth and nature with resistless energy.[77]

Such spiritual elation was known in ancient times as its peoples were closer to nature. They saw it for themselves and responded to it. "In a more advanced state of civilization," she claimed, "a poet is rather the creature of art, than of nature."[78] Literary exposure interceded between nature and modern poets. This could be seen in classically educated boys, who could write according to prescribed forms, but expressed very little, if anything. They could not be un-read, and in meeting the rules of various poetic styles, in their desire to be elegant, and in their attention to their choice of words, they deprived themselves of "sublime, impassioned thoughts."[79] Knowledge and understanding interfered far too much, dampening flights of fancy. Moderns were caught in a hall of mirrors, imitation imitating imitation ad infinitum—a view that has now become associated with postmodernism.

Taking Burke up on the question of whether the "spirit of romance and chivalry" was on the wane in *A Vindication of the Rights of Men*, Wollstonecraft gave "romantic" "one definition— false, or rather artificial, feelings," and went on to say that sentiments were being imitated because they were deemed fashionable, "not because they were forcibly felt." Turning to poetry more specifically, she claimed that "[i]n modern poetry, the understanding and memory often fabricate the pretended effusions of the heart, and romance destroys all simplicity; which, in works of taste, is but a synonymous word for truth."[80] She thought this "romantic spirit [had] extended to our prose, and scattered artificial flowers over the most barren heath; a mixture of verse and prose producing the strangest incongruities." She

77. Ibid. The reference is to *Revelation*, pp. 21, 22.
78. Ibid. p. 9.
79. Ibid.
80. *VM*, p. 28.

believed it had contaminated Burke's style or his character, making one doubt his sincerity.[81]

This is not to say that she thought that "the first observers
of nature, the true poets" were devoid of understanding. On
the contrary, they "exercised their understanding much more
than their imitators": [b]ut they exercised it to discriminate
things, whilst their followers were busy to borrow sentiments
and arrange words."[82] Yet, she could waver on the relation of the
understanding to the imagination, as when she took issue with
Kant in her *Hints*:

> Mr. Kant has observed, that the understanding is sublime,
> the imagination beautiful—yet it is evident, that poets, and
> men who undoubtedly possess the liveliest imagination, are
> most touched by the sublime, while men who have cold,
> enquiring minds, have not this exquisite feeling in any great
> degree, and indeed seem to lose it as they cultivate their
> reason.[83]

What she conceived as the just exercise of understanding had
received some elucidation five years earlier in *A Vindication of
the Rights of Woman* (1792). Depicting a scene in which a poem
that left her breathless, whose "melody [had] almost suspended
respiration," was met by "a languid yawn" from a lady more eager
to discuss the provenance of a gown, she explained that "[t]rue
taste is ever the work of the understanding employed in observing nature's effects." Men of true genius, she observed,

> have appeared to have the highest relish for the simple
> beauties of nature; and they must have forcibly felt, what
> they have so well described, the charm which natural affec-
> tions, and unsophisticated feelings spread round the human
> character. It is this power of looking into the heart, and

81. *VM*, p. 29.
82. Ibid.
83. *Hints*, pp. 301–302.

responsively vibrating with each emotion, that enables the
poet to personify each passion, and the painter to sketch
with a pencil of fire.[84]

With the progress of civilization and concomitantly, that of luxury, neither the beauties of nature nor those of poems conveying
them were forcefully felt. The countryside was found to be too
dull, its tranquility incapable of touching those enervated by the
heightened liveness of artificial pleasures.

This was not true of Wollstonecraft herself; she delighted in
it. That much is clear. What is somewhat less so is which poets
she liked. Her compilation, *The Female Reader: or Miscellaneous
Pieces in Prose and Verse; Selected from the Best Writers, and
Disposed under Proper Heads: for the Improvement of Young
Women. By Mr Creswick* (1789), contained a good number of
poems, including some by Charlotte Smith (1749–1806), Anna
Laetitia Barbauld (1743–1825), William Cooper, James Thomson, and Edward Young (1683–1765). In her other works, references were often biblical. Shakespeare's plays, we saw, she
cited very readily. The same is to a lesser extent true of John
Milton, whose *Paradise Lost* she quoted repeatedly, despite the
occasional divergence, shall we say, in their respective views
of women. In November 1796, she did ask Godwin to lend her
Mary Robinson's *Poems by Mrs. Robinson* (1775).[85] In a review
of 1788, she spoke very favorably of Dryden's fable "The Flower
and the Leaf; or, the Lady in the Arbour" (1700), and of Milton in her posthumous novel, *The Wrongs of Woman: or, Maria*
(1798).[86] But she also compared Corneille to him in *An Historical and Moral View of the Origin and Progress of the French
Revolution; and the Effect It Has Produced in Europe* (1794),
describing them both as "often tottering on the brink of absurdity and nonsense," though she was quick to avoid being seen

84. *VW*, p. 261.
85. *Letters*, p. 375.
86. *Works*, Vol. 7, p. 45; Vol. 1, pp. 93 and 94.

as dismissive, explaining that the former (and possibly also the latter) "still delights his readers by sketching faint outline of gigantic passion; and, whilst the charmed imagination is lured to follow him over enchanted ground, the heart is sometimes unexpectedly touched by a sublime or pathetic sentiment, true to nature."[87] Whether any of these authors could be described as writing unfiltered by form or influence, as she had claimed the best poetry to be, is quite another matter.

There is no doubt, however, that writing about poetry gave her occasion to think deeply about the relationship between direct sensory perception of the natural world and the ideas formed in the listener or reader through the medium of the poets' words. This emerges in several of her reviews of poetry, as in that of *Poems. Consisting of Odes, Songs, Pastorale, Satires, etc. and a descriptive Poem, in Four Books, called Prospects*, by the Rev. Geo. Sackville Cotter (1788). She called these poems "neither sublime nor beautiful" but "pretty," by which she meant, drawing on Samuel Johnson's (1709–1784) definition of the word, "beauty without dignity; neat elegance without elevation."[88] Descriptive poems could be pleasing, but they generally lacked interest and were likely to be the refuge of clichés ("the morning came to disperse the dews" and "the lark ascended with the rising mist"). Evoking rustic sounds could affect the reader to a degree, but the latter needed to be made to hear the music of nature and see it. What was required was generating an emotion to unify the reader to the poet, to make them one. "We cannot accompany the poet quickly from one [the impression of morning] to the other [the impression of evening]," she explained.

> We must follow the foot-steps of a fellow creature, a social passion must connect the whole, to give warmth and continuity to our most refined instincts, or we flag, particularly in cultivated scenes, more wild ones remind us of the *present*

87. *Works*, Vol. 6, p. 25.
88. *Works*, Vol. 7, pp. 42–43.

God; the soul asserts its dignity and claims kindred with the Being who inhabits the gloomy waste. A pleasing sympathy draws us to woods and fields, from the vegetable to the animal world; the moistened eye surveys the attractive prospect, and expansive tender love fills the heart; but, when nature seems to rest from her labours, and the features of chaos appear, we tread with firmer step, and feel immortal.[89]

Writing of cultivated or untouched landscapes, beautiful and sublime poetry drew its listeners and readers where "pretty" poems could not, that is, to thoughts of the divine and immortality. The word must bring nature, man, and God into harmony.

What is also certain is that Wollstonecraft wanted everyone to try to form "an opinion of an author themselves" rather than just praise only those "whose merit is indisputable," as she put it in *Thoughts on the Education of Daughters: with Reflections on Female Conduct, in The More Important Duties of Life* (1787):

I am sick of hearing of the sublimity of Milton, the elegance and harmony of Pope, and the original, untaught genius of Shakespear [*sic*]. These cursory remarks are made by some who know nothing of nature, and could not enter into the spirit of those authors, or understand them.[90]

Such was most definitely not Wollstonecraft's view of herself. She knew nature and understood these authors. Ultimately, as she expressed it already in the summer of 1790 in a review of an English translation of a sequel to Rousseau's *Julie, ou la Nouvelle Héloïse*, "neither poetry nor painting, music or eloquence, have much power over the passions, to move them to virtuous or vicious exertions, if they are not natural and excellent."[91]

89. Ibid., p. 44.
90. *Works*, Vol. 4, p. 21.
91. *Analytical Review, Works*, Vol. 7, p. 283.

Nature

Wollstonecraft did make plain her liking of the countryside.[92] Whilst residing at Bath in 1780, she wrote to Jane Arden, her close friend from when the Wollstonecraft family lived in Beverley in Yorkshire, that were she to have a choice in the matter, she would not live in a large town, explaining: "as I am fond of the country."[93] She enjoyed physical exercise and was particularly fond of walking and riding among fields as well as swimming. In Yorkshire, she exclaimed affectionately of a nearby commons: "I long for a walk in my darling Westwood."[94] In a letter from Henley in mid-September 1787, she told her publisher Joseph Johnson that

[s]ince I saw you, I have, literally speaking, enjoyed solitude. My sister could not accompany me in my rambles; I therefore wandered alone, by the side of the Thames, and in the neighbouring beautiful fields and pleasure grounds: the prospects were of such a placid kind, I *caught* tranquillity while I surveyed them—my mind was *still*, though active. Were I to give you an account how I have spent my time, you would smile.—I found an old French bible here, and amused myself with comparing it with our English translation; then I would listen to the falling leaves, or observe the various tints the autumn gave them—At other times, the singing of a robin, or the noise of a water-mill, engaged my attention—partial attention—, for I was, at the same time perhaps discussing some knotty point, or straying from this tiny world to new systems. After these excursions, I returned to the family meals, told the children stories (they think me

92. She is increasingly read for her stance on the environment; see Seeber, "Mary Wollstonecraft: 'Systemiz[ing] Oppression,'" pp. 173–188.

93. *Letters*, p. 27.

94. Ibid., p. 14; Janet Todd notes that "[w]hen Wollstonecraft later remembered the good time at Beverley she mentioned the walks with Jane Arden on Westwood Commons," p. 14, n.36.

vastly agreeable), and my sister was amused.—Well, will you allow me to call this way of passing my days pleasant?[95]

The sight of nature transported her. She wanted to live in the forest outside Windsor every time she rode through it.[96] This was true not only in her youth. Natural beauty had a profound effect on her throughout her life, invigorating her and restoring her to physical and emotional health. Writing to Imlay from Tønsberg, Norway, at the end of July 1795, she declared: "I never was so much in the air.—I walk, I ride on horseback—row, bathe, and even sleep in the fields; my health is consequently improved."[97] Adding, a few days later,

> Employment and exercise have been of great service to me; and I have entirely recovered the strength and activity I lost during the time of my nursing. I have seldom been in better health; and my mind, though trembling to the touch of anguish, is calmer—yet still the same.—I have, it is true, enjoyed some tranquillity, and more happiness here, than for a long—long time past.—(I say happiness, for I can give no other appellation to the exquisite delight this wild country and fine summer have afforded me.)[98]

She also declared her love of the country to Godwin, longed to be in it with him, and imagined herself smelling "the fragrant gale" and feeling both the sun and moonshine on her in one of his travels.[99] As with music and poetry, the thought of God was never far behind in her reflections on nature. "As I love the country and think with a poor mad woman, I knew," she wrote to Godwin in May 1797, less than four months before she died, "that there is God, or something, very consolatory in the air."[100]

95. Ibid., pp. 133–134.
96. Ibid., p. 33.
97. Ibid., p. 315.
98. Ibid., p. 316.
99. Ibid., p. 417.
100. Ibid., p. 415.

Indeed, she marveled at the Creation in individual instances and its entirety, and though Wollstonecraft's faith often manifested itself in relation to somber thoughts of death, she did take pleasure in seeing the world explained in such a way as to reveal God's omniscience. Thus, reviewing the Rev. Samuel Stanhope Smith's *An Essay on the Causes of the Variety of Complexion and Figure in the Human Species. To which are added, Strictures on Lord Kaims's* [sic] *Discourse on the original Diversity of Mankind* shortly after its publication in 1788, she concluded: "We cannot dismiss this article without expressing the pleasure the perusal has afforded us; [. . .] whatever tends to make *visible* the wisdom of the Supreme Being in the world we inhabit, is of the utmost importance to our happiness."[101]

This expression of delight might explain why Wollstonecraft was asked to review a number of works of natural history, including *Buffon's Natural History, abridged* and William Smellie's *The Philosophy of Natural History.* Although we do not know whether she asked Johnson to have them sent her way, she did appear to take a genuine interest in them. Such comments also explain why, in the June 1791 issue of the *Analytical Review*, she said that she had "long been persuaded that the first study of children should be natural history."[102] To be in nature, particularly walking through it, and to see oneself at one with it through its study was clearly essential to well-being in her view. The centrality of this belief to her view of pedagogical and moral and political philosophy cannot be overstated.

Wollstonecraft's love of nature did not entirely blind her, however, to the charms of some towns, though her liking of them tended to be connected to nature in some way. She thought Bath very attractive, and if she were to have to settle in a town would

101. *Analytical Review*, Vol. 2 (1788), in *Works*, Vol. 7, p. 55. This refers to Henry Home, Lord Kames's (1696–1782) *Diversity of Men and of Languages*, sketch 1 in *Progress of Men*, Book I, *Sketches of the History of Man* (1774).

102. *Works*, Vol. 7, p. 382.

have chosen it, if only for its situation.[103] She liked Southampton, where she sea-bathed.[104] She found its inhabitants particularly friendly, and her appreciation of places was also tied to the character of the people in them. She longed to visit Ireland and

> in particular the dear county of Clare.—The women are all handsome, and the men all agreeable; I honor their hospitality and doat on their freedom and ease, in short they are the people after my own heart.—I like their warmth of Temper, and if I was my own mistress I would spend my life with them.[105]

She changed her mind once on the island, but that had more to do with her social life while residing in Dublin and working as governess to the Kingsboroughs' children than it had with Ireland or the Irish per se.[106]

Thus, while most of her letters are those of a troubled and unhappy friend, sister, and lover, what she called her "melancholy" and the painful reality of her circumstances should not obscure the fact that, had things been otherwise, she had the capacity to rejoice in a great variety of experiences.[107] Similarly, her very extensive critiques of her contemporaries at home, in Portugal, Ireland, France, and Scandinavia, should not be taken to mean that she was essentially censorious, though she could, naturally enough, be envious, of the happiness of others. Writing to Jane Arden from Windsor in the spring of 1781, she confessed:

> This is the gayest of all gay places;—nothing but dress and amusements are going forward;—I am only spectator—I

---

103. *Letters*, p. 27.
104. Ibid. See Janet Todd's comment, p. 26, n.63.
105. Ibid., p. 37.
106. Ibid., p. 110.
107. Ibid., p. 23. Wollstonecraft was relatively open about the financial and social adversity brought about by her father, whom she described as having a "violent temper and extravagant turn of mind." What is more, she made no secret that his neglect and physical violence had broken her.

have lost all my relish for them:—early in life, before misfortune had broken my spirits, I had not the power of par-
taking of them, and now I am both from habit and inclination averse to them.—My wishes and expectations are very
moderate.—I don't know which is the worst—to think too
little or too much.—'tis a difficult matter to draw the line,
and keep clear of melancholy and thoughtlessness; I really
think it is best sometimes to be deceived—and to expect
what we are never likely to meet with[.][108]

Although her tribulations afforded her few opportunities to
express joy, she made the most of the occasions she had to experience happiness whether in nature or evoked by music and
poetry or through close relationships. Her love of nature did
not preclude her appreciation of the arts, nor did they need to
be imitative of nature to warrant her approval. On the contrary,
we saw that she believed that while art should not be made to
act or appear as a substitute for nature, at its best art enhanced
appreciation and awareness of the natural environment, and in
so doing brought humans closer to the divine.

Art had to elevate. Wollstonecraft made this point several
times in relation to its various forms, including when speaking of architecture. She thought Grecian buildings graceful;
seeing them filled the mind with pleasing emotions, because,
in her view, elegance, beauty, and utility never failed to satisfy
a cultivated mind, "things appear just what they ought to be."
This led to "a calm satisfaction," but while "this kind of pleasure
may be lasting," she wrote, "it is never great."[109] Great pleasure
could only be had if the beholder was somehow transported.
"[R]easonable content" was pleasing, but as it left the imagination unexercised, it could not engender sublime feelings. Art,
whether architectural, statuary, musical, or in any other form
had to affect beyond contentment. It had to elate. For this to

108. Ibid., pp. 28–29.
109. *Hints*, p. 302.

happen, the viewer or listener had to be prepared, that is, be educated so as to be receptive to the artistry and yet, were it to be either slavishly imitative or overly refined, the effect would not be achieved. Similarly, an overly sophisticated spectator or listener would not be open to being taken wherever the art form might lead.

Reading

Wollstonecraft read, translated, and wrote, but wrote only of the pleasures of reading, though Susan J. Wolfson has written incisively about the way Wollstonecraft read texts and society as a text.[110] One of the Letters from *Young Grandison. A Series of Letters from Young Person to their Friends, translated from the Dutch of Madame de Cambon. with alterations and improvements* ends with the following advice: "If you would learn to be qualified for general conversation, learn to think when you read, and through the assistance of rational books, many hours of retirement may pass pleasantly away, without your wishing for the noise of society—Books are never failing friends."[111] Her *Thoughts on the Education of Daughters* included a piece, "Reading," that presented reading "as the most rational employment, if people seek for food for the understanding, and do not read merely to remember words; or with a view to quote celebrated authors, and retail sentiments they do not understand or feel."[112] As with the fine arts, she thought a "relish for reading" should be cultivated in early life; however, as with the arts, she thought that certain kinds of works were appropriate only when individuals had acquired a sufficient degree of judgment. As we saw in relation to the theater, she was concerned with the potentially distorting psychological effect of some texts:

---

110. Wolfson, "Mary Wollstonecraft and the Poets," pp. 160–188.

111. *Works*, Vol. 2, p. 290.

112. *Works*, Vol. 4, p. 20.

Those productions which give a wrong account of the human passions, and the various accidents of life, ought not to be read before the judgement is formed, or at least exercised. Such accounts are one great cause of the affectation of young women. Sensibility is described and praised, and the effects of it represented in a way so different from nature, that those who imitate it must make themselves ridiculous. A false taste is acquired, and sensible books appear dull and insipid after those superficial performances, which obtain their full end if they can keep the mind in a continual ferment. Gallantry is made the only interesting subject with the novelist; reading, therefore, will often co-operate to make his fair admirers insignificant.[113]

By this, Wollstonecraft did not mean that she only recommended "books of an abstract or grave cast." Instruction and amusement could be combined, and she recommended a periodical, *The Adventurer*, to which Samuel Johnson contributed, as a successful example of this.[114] Once the mind was formed, "everything will then instruct," she thought.

Generally speaking, and despite writing two of them herself, she did not think much of novels, though she was not entirely against them.[115] She did on occasion ask for some to be brought to her, and said of at least one of them, *Caroline de Lichfield. Par made de **** [Baroness de Montolieu], that it was "one of the prettiest things I have ever read." Moreover, Wollstonecraft did wish to marry two men who happened to be novelists, among others things.[116] Imlay, who rejected her, tried his hand at one, *The Emigrants* (1793), and Godwin, whom she did marry, wrote several multi-volume works, including *Things as They Are; or*

113. Ibid.
114. Ibid.
115. For a seminal assessment of her own novels, see Claudia L. Johnson, *Mary Wollstonecraft's Novels*, in *The Cambridge Companion to Mary Wollstonecraft*, pp. 189–208.
116. *Letters*, p. 98.

The Adventures of Caleb Williams (1794). It is not unlikely, as Janet Todd and others have argued, that Wollstonecraft might have contributed at least some of the polemical passages on the condition of women to Imlay's work.[117] We do not know what she thought of it in the main, but do know that she noted the disparity between what Imlay had written of the protection men owed to women and his own treatment of her as he abandoned her and their daughter, Fanny: "Reading what you have written relative to the desertion of women, I have often wondered how theory and practice could be so different, till I recollected, that the sentiments of passion, and the resolves of reason, are very distinct."[118] As for Godwin, she did ask him for the second volume of *Caleb Williams*, and it shares some features with her posthumous novel, *The Wrongs of Woman: or, Maria*.

In the preface of that novel, she wrote, in a language we saw her use to describe Shakespeare's achievement, that her aim was the "delineation of finer sensations," which in her opinion constituted the "merit of our best novels."[119] She had the heroine of that novel, Mary, read Rousseau's *Julie, ou la Nouvelle Héloïse* (1761), fantasize about its hero, St. Preux, and transcribe some of its passages.[120] Wollstonecraft herself liked German novels, as they told of "a simplicity of manners and style," and thus served as an antidote to the "deluge of sentiments and gallantry" in French and English ones.[121] She said the same again in a review in 1796 of *Albert de Nordenshild: or the Modern Alcibiades. A Novel translated from the German* (1794), remarking that "[a]n interesting warmth of imagination, and truth of passion, appear in this translation, which seems to characterize german [*sic*]

---

117. Ibid., pp. 222–223, n.520; see Tysdahl, *William Godwin as Novelist*; Andrews, "Women and Emigrants: Mary Wollstonecraft and Gilbert Imlay," in *The Rediscovery of America*, 170–186; Verhoeven, *Gilbert Imlay: Citizen of the World*.

118. *Letters*, p. 283 and n.641.

119. *Wrongs of Woman, Works*, Vol. 1, p. 84.

120. Ibid., p. 96.

121. *Analytical Review*, Vol. 7 (1790), *Works*, Vol. 7, p. 281.

works of fancy, at the very period when the romantic rants of false refinement in the majority of novels of France and England, only excite a restless curiosity, which fatigues the head, without touching the heart." (She did, however, think the novel was not as successful as it might have been because it included too many ill-conceived incidents and too many characters.) Thus, while she abhorred excess and affectation in novels, she did admire those that portrayed genuine affection and feelings. She valued simplicity in the story line and depth of character analysis. She also sought consistency and deplored the want of it, as for instance in M. G. Lewis's sensationally popular Gothic novel, *The Monk: a Romance* (1796), when "the language and manners of the personages are not sufficiently gothic in their colouring, to agree with the superstitious scenery, borrowed from those times."[122] By and large, she thought novels the "spawn of idleness" and that it would be easy to think them "one of the lowest order of literary productions" were it not for the "small number of good ones which appear."[123] As with all else, she believed that different kinds of novels were appropriate at different stages of life. Illustrating that there was a time in life for the prevalence of the imagination and a time for that of understanding, she wrote: "[f]or example, I am inclined to have a better opinion of the heart of an *old* man, who speaks of Sterne as his favourite author, than of his understanding."[124]

Love and Friendship

The arts and in particular music and poetry could genuinely move Wollstonecraft, and she extolled them to the extent that they did so. She wrote about music and poetry in a manner usually associated with the sensations attendant to being in love.

122. *Analytical Review*, Vol. 24 (1796), *Works*, p. 474.
123. Ibid., p. 472.
124. *VM*, p. 58. She is referring to Laurence Sterne (1713–1768), author of *The Life and Opinions of Tristram Shandy* (1759).

Wollstonecraft wrote of love as well as of being in love and lived her life as a series of passions, from those of youthful friendship to those of a lover, a mother, and wife. She loved individuals but had very strong feelings as well for or about nations and categories of persons.

Like many passionate people, the intensity of her love matched that of her abhorrence when her sentiments happened to change. While she did not wish to reside in England in 1795 for political as well as emotional reasons, even expressing "horror" at the thought of it, she had declared her love of England in earlier years. Writing to Jane Arden at the age of twenty-three, she prescribed for herself the aspiration of "a true born Englishwoman" to "endeavour to do better."[125] While in Ireland some five years later, she confessed to her sister, Everina: "I never before felt what it was to love my country; but now I have a value for it built on rational grounds, and my feelings concur to fix it, I never see an English face without feeling tenderness."[126] Despite her wavering sentiments and strong criticisms, England fared overall better than other countries in *The French Revolution* (1794); this was especially so in relation to liberty, to which, as we will see later, she thought her country had long provided its first home.[127]

Similarly, while she expressed admiration for very few women besides Catherine Macaulay, and could be very hard on her own sex, she was capable of the strongest bonds with particular individuals, and developed passionate feelings for Fanny Blood, "the main love of her youth," as Janet Todd rightly named her, and for Gilbert Imlay, the second man, after her father, to truly break her heart.[128] Writing to Jane Arden early in 1780, Wollstonecraft wrote:

125. *Letters*, p. 38.
126. Ibid., p. 110.
127. *Works*, Vol. 6, p. 190, for one example.
128. *Letters*, Janet Todd, "Introduction," p. xvi.

I enjoyed the society of a friend, whom I love better than all
the world beside, a friend to whom I am bound by every tie
of gratitude and inclination: To live with this friend is the
height of my ambition, and indeed it is the most rational
wish I could make, as her conversation is not more agreeable
than improving.

Adding,

I could dwell for ever more on her praises, and you wo.
[*sic*] not wonder at it, if you knew the many favors she has
conferred on me, and the many valuable qualifications she
possesses:—She has a masculine understanding, and sound
judgment, yet she has every feminine virtue [.][129]

Todd notes that after her death, Godwin was to write of Wollstonecraft's first meeting with Fanny in the language he borrowed from Goethe's *Sorrows of Young Werther* (1774), when
the poet described the first encounter between the love-struck
Werther and his adored Charlotte.[130] Wollstonecraft was to follow Fanny to Portugal to assist in the delivery of her child. Fanny's death upon childbirth affected her very deeply. Wollstonecraft named her own daughter, by Imlay, Fanny, and one of the
last letters we have from Wollstonecraft shows that her friend
remained with her to the last: "I was thinking of a favourite song
of my poor friend, Fanny's—In a vacant rainy day you shall be
wholly mine."[131]

Wollstonecraft delighted in her daughter Fanny, whom she
confessed to loving more than she had thought she would.[132]
She wrote of the birth, which had been relatively easy, to her
friend Ruth Barlow, adding: "I feel great pleasure at being a

129. Ibid., p. 25.
130. Ibid., p. 24, n.57.
131. Ibid., p. 426.
132. Ibid., p. 272.

mother."[133] The same letter ended with: "My little Girl begins to suck so *manfully* that her father reckons saucily on her writing the second part of the R-ts of Woman."[134] Wollstonecraft was proud to attribute Fanny's good health and sagaciousness to her breast-feeding; she enjoyed the physicality of motherhood, and spoke of her insatiable desire for kissing the baby and of playing and laughing with her.[135] The child moved her. As was her way, she studied her own feelings and told Imlay that, while her affection for "our little girl was at first very reasonable—more the effect of reason, a sense of duty, than feeling—now, she has got into my heart and imagination, and when I walk out without her, her little figure is ever dancing before me."[136] Writing to the same from Paris a few months later, in October 1794, she wrote jubilantly of Fanny's intelligence and gaiety and went on to reveal that

> I once told you that the sensations before she was born, and when she is suckling, were pleasant; but they do not deserve to be compared to the emotions I feel, when she stops to smile upon me, or laughs outright on meeting me unexpectedly in the street or after a short absence.[137]

To be sure, much of Wollstonecraft's writing about little Fanny was, of course, bound with her passionate desire for Imlay— his presence, if not his love, a vain hope, as would all too soon become clear. While there is no doubt of her utter, indeed terrible, devotion to him and physical need of him, it is difficult to find any testimony of the happiness he gave her other than through their child. The pain he caused her can be gauged by the fact that, for all her motherly love for Fanny, his leaving them drove her to two attempts on her own life. Fanny was herself to

133. Ibid., p. 253.
134. Ibid., p. 254.
135. Ibid., p. 265.
136. Ibid., p. 258.
137. Ibid., p. 269.

commit suicide in 1816, at the age of twenty-two; why she took her life remains a matter of some contention, but what is clear is that her existence in her stepfather, Godwin, and his second wife's household was never happy.[138]

Of William Godwin, Wollstonecraft grew genuinely fond. They married in March 1797 while they were expecting Mary, who was born on August 30 that year. In the short period they were together, he did make Wollstonecraft happy. She wrote in the same terms to Godwin of her sentiments for him when pregnant with Mary, as she had admitted of her feelings for her eldest daughter, Fanny,

> I begin to love this little creature, and to anticipate his [*sic*] birth as a fresh twist to a knot, which I do not wish to untie— Men are spoilt by frankness, I believe, yet I must tell you that I love you better than I supposed I did, when I promised to love you for ever—and I will add what will gratify your benevolence, if not your heart, that on the whole I may be termed happy. You are a tender, affectionate creature; and I feel it thrilling through my frame giving, and promising pleasure.[139]

Though they had their differences of opinion and he could make her jealous, she was proud of being "Mrs. Godwin," even before she could be called such. Recalling his notorious denunciation of marriage in an *Enquiry Concerning Political Justice and Its Influence on Morals and Happiness* (1793), she wrote in November 1796: "I send you your household linen—I am not sure that I did not feel a sensation of pleasure at thus acting the part of a wife, though you have so little respect for the character." And, as if that were not saying enough, she continued: "There is such a magic in affection that I have been more gratified by your clasping your hands round my arm, in company, than I could have

---

138. See Todd, *Death and the Maidens*.
139. *Letters*, p. 417.

been by all the admiration in the world, tho' I am a woman—and to mount a step higher in the scale of vanity, an author."[140]

While it would be easy to think otherwise, as she was herself aware, from what she said of physical appearance and sexuality in *A Vindication of the Rights of Woman* and elsewhere, Wollstonecraft was by no means indifferent to physical beauty or love, and as with everything else, she reflected on their nature. She commented on men's and women's looks as well as her own, and challenged contemporary notions of physical beauty, especially in women. As we observed with other subjects, she thought of physical beauty historically, believing "that the human form must have been far more beautiful than it is at present, because extreme indolence, barbarous ligatures, and many causes, which forcibly act on it, in our luxurious state of society, did not retard its expansion, or render it deformed."[141] She admired Greek representations of the body, not in spite of their being idealizations, but because they were. However much she loved nature, and shunned artificiality, in sculpture as in other arts, the imagination had to play its part for statuary to be great, according to her. It is worth considering in full a passage toward the end of her *Vindication of the Rights of Woman* as it shows some of the complexity of her thoughts on the just relationship between nature and its representation:

> I do not forget the popular opinion that the Grecian statues were not modelled after nature. I mean, not according to the proportions of a particular man; but that beautiful limbs and features were selected from various bodies to form an harmonious whole. This might, in some degree, be true. The fine ideal picture of an exalted imagination might be superior to the materials which the statuary found in nature, and thus it might with propriety be termed the model of mankind than

140. Ibid., p. 374.
141. *VW*, p. 267.

of a man. It was not, however, the mechanical selection of limbs and features; but the ebullition of an heated fancy that burst forth, and the fine senses and enlarged understanding of the artist selected the solid matter, which he drew into this glowing focus.

I observed that it was not mechanical, because a whole was produced—a model of that grand simplicity, of those concurring energies, which arrest our attention and command our reverence. For only insipid lifeless beauty is produced by a servile copy of even beautiful nature.[142]

As we have seen already in relation to the other arts and we will have cause to note in relation to her observations on women and men, the imagination and understanding had to be combined with the endeavor to remain true to nature and yet surpass it for a depiction of the human form to merit the appellation of art. Facsimiles of nature could at best be blandly beautiful. The contribution of the imagination was essential in making it more than this. It alone could take the mind beyond nature, according to Wollstonecraft.

While scholars such as Mary Poovey, Cora Kaplan, and Barbara Taylor have debated her attitude toward sex and sexuality, Wollstonecraft, it would seem, was no more immune to physical desire than she was to physical beauty, whether in living bodies or rendered in various forms.[143] As early as her first publication, she warned against platonic attachments, thinking nothing could destroy peace of mind more than they did. She hastened to add that she did not think friendship between the sexes impossible, but where there was physical attraction the matter

142. Ibid.

143. See Taylor, "The Religious Foundations of Mary Wollstonecraft's Feminism"; Jones, "Mary Wollstonecraft and the Literature of Advice and Instruction," pp. 112–116 and 119–120; Taylor, *Mary Wollstonecraft and the Feminist Imagination*.

was altogether different. Pretense would not do. She thought it ridiculous to try to raise oneself above the human condition: "we cannot extirpate our passions, nor is it necessary that we should, though it may be wise sometimes not to stray too near a precipice, lest we fall over before we are aware."[144]

Graf von Schlabrendorf, who only realized he had fallen in love with her once she had left Paris where they had met, said that "Mary was the most noble, virtuous, sensuous female creature, that I ever met."[145] Her letters leave no doubt as to the extent of her passion for Imlay, but even those to Godwin, for whom she did not feel the same burning physical desire at least initially, are not altogether coy about their lovemaking. Living separately, they exchanged notes every day and sometimes more than once a day. In a letter composed on a Sunday morning in November 1796, just over nine months before Mary Godwin's birth, Wollstonecraft writes,

> If the felicity of last night has had the same effect on your
> health as on my countenance, you have no cause to lament
> your failure of resolution: for I have seldom seen so much
> live fire running about my features as this morning when
> recollections—very dear; called forth the blush of pleasure,
> as I adjusted my hair.[146]

She was unabashed also in her published works, insisting in a manner reminiscent of her views of art, that she did not decry sexual desire, but only raw lust unmixed with what she would call feelings of the heart. This was most explicit in her letters to Imlay as she sought to convince him to love her (again). She claimed that he had given in to "inferior feelings" and told him: "you have sought in vulgar excess, for that gratification which

144. *Works*, Vol. 4, p. 30.
145. *Letters*, p. 230 n.539.
146. Ibid., p. 375.

only the heart can bestow." Want of imagination was the problem with him as with "the common run of men." He and they had to have variety "to banish *ennui*" because their imagination did not lend "its magic want to convert appetite into love." He and they were never to know "the exquisite pleasure, which arises from unison of affection and desire, when the whole soul and sense are abandoned to a lively imagination, that renders every emotion delicate and rapturous."[147] She acknowledged that such pleasures required the exercise of some self-denial. Uncontrolled or rather indiscriminate satiation of desire rendered some emotions unattainable. What is more, the pursuit of mere lust had consequences for women as well as men. Thus Wollstonecraft argued that to satisfy the wantonness of some men, "women are made systematically voluptuous, and though they may not carry their libertinism to the same height, yet this heartless intercourse with the sex, which they allow themselves, depraves both sexes, because the taste of men is vitiated; and women, of all classes, naturally square their behaviour to gratify the taste by which they obtain pleasure and power."[148] Heart and mind had to be conjoined in physicality so that, in this instance as in art, something was added to mere nature for the good of both men and women. As with everything else, she thought pleasure in sex had somehow to elevate out of mere physicality, and lead to a kind of "sublimification," to borrow Gilpin's coinage. What is particularly interesting is how, writing to Imlay in June 1795, she brought nature, the imagination, and sexuality into an intriguing and wondrous mix. The emotions to be had when sex and love combined, she claimed: "appear to me to be the distinctive characteristic of genius, the foundation of taste, and of that exquisite relish for the beauties of nature, of which the common herd of eaters and drinkers and *child-begeters*, certainly have not idea."

147. Ibid., p. 297.
148. *VW*, pp. 227–228.

The strongest minds, in her view, and the most original, were those whose "imagination acts as stimulus to their senses."[149]

Concluding Reflections

Unsurprisingly given the disparaging comments about eaters and drinkers just quoted, Wollstonecraft wrote next to nothing about food or drink and what little she did leads one to suspect that she preferred meals to be plain and she disapproved of drinking.[150] She did not like cooking. She noted that Rousseau thought man was not a carnivorous animal, adding that "the long and helpless state of infancy seems to point [man] as particularly impelled to pair, the first step towards herding."[151] She thought "[i]ntoxication the pleasure of savages, and of all those whose employments rather exhaust their animal spirits, than exercise their faculties." She thought it the vice in both England and the northern state of Europe, and the greatest impediment to what she called "the general improvement."[152] From these or comparable comments, it would be easy to infer not only that she rejected many things, but that what she took pleasure in or appreciated in some manner had to be simple, plain, and as close to nature as possible. The preceding does not aspire to be an exhaustive list of her loves and likings, or indeed her displeasures, to which we will have cause to return. Nothing was said, for instance, of her love of learning foreign languages. It does however show that she held rather more complex views about the relation between the natural and the humanly

---

149. *Letters*, p. 297. For more on this and cognate subjects, see Taylor, *Mary Wollstonecraft and the Feminist Imagination*.

150. *Works*, Vol. 6, pp. 226–227. In *VW* (p.152), she wrote: "Bread, the common food of life, seldom thought of as a blessing, supports the constitution and preserves health; still feasts delight the heart of man, though disease and even death lurk in the cup or dainty that elevates the spirits or tickles the palate."

151. *VW*, p. 82.

152. *Letters Written in Sweden, Norway, and Denmark*, *Works*, Vol. 6, p. 327.

created than might be assumed and that she was preoccupied by their rightful interconnection throughout her intellectual life. It also reveals some of her views about the operations of the mind and, as Barbara Taylor, Martina Reuter, and Isabelle Bour have emphasized, the importance she granted to the imagination in these. Aesthetic judgment was an individual matter, in Wollstonecraft's view. Taste was a function of the particular workings of the mind.[153] Though formed through experience and education, it could not be dictated, any more than any passion could. It is also evident from her comments quoted in this chapter that she did not think all such judgments to be equal. It is not even clear that she thought that education and the right kind of habituation could render all taste equal though varied. This said, creativity and originality were to be encouraged in everyone, regardless of talent or genius. These are subjects that the remainder of this book will consider further.

Wollstonecraft's writings can produce contrary perceptions of her positions. She might have achieved a greater degree of consistency had it not been for the speed at which she had to meet her publisher's deadlines. This, combined with the nature and subjects of the ripostes and critical reviews she wrote, led her to adopt an adversarial tone, and caused her to be eager to contest the views of others rather than to calmly analyze and clarify her own. Her letters were also dashed off in the heat of the moment and thus might give different impressions of her sense of herself and of her opinions. Yet, it is hoped that the forgoing does offer a taste of what might be viewed as her overall enterprise or what such an enterprise might have been had her circumstances been, if not entirely changed, somewhat easier materially and emotionally, and above all had her life not been cut short. The brevity of that life must never be forgotten. Nor must her very

---

153. Martina Reuter's "Reason, Imagination, Passion," and Isabelle Bour's "Epistemology," in *The Wollstonecraftian Mind*, edited by Sandrine Bergès, Eileen Hunt Botting, and Alan Coffee (London: Routledge, 2019).

conscious emphasis on the importance of the relevance of temporality to all things human. Behind her many pronouncements on the arts and other aspects of social and political reality, one can begin to sketch the kind of personality she thought ideal, discern her desire to establish what the balance between nature and civilization might ideally be, and see her continual reflection on humanity's history and, as Barbara Taylor has underscored, a prolonged consideration over time of its ties, to its Creator.[154]

154. Taylor, "The Religious Foundations of Mary Wollstonecraft's Feminism," *The Cambridge Companion of Mary Wollstonecraft*, pp. 99–118; Taylor, *Mary Wollstonecraft and the Feminist Imagination*, pp. 95–142.

CHAPTER TWO

Who Are We? What Are We Made Of?

The Unity of Humanity

Wollstonecraft's belief in the unity of humanity is the stepping-stone to understanding her social and political views. She thought that whatever the observable differences between human beings across time or diverse parts of the world, all shared the same God-given nature. Thus, writing of the character of the French nation in mid-February 1793, she explained that, regardless of her criticisms, her reader needed to "[r]emember that it is not the morals of a particular people that I would decry; for are we not all of the same stock?" She wrote of the French as of humanity at a particular stage in its history, in the history of civilization as whole, and in examining them, she meant "to throw some light on the history of man."[1] Any variations between humans could, and had to, be explained by historical as well as natural causes.

This was made clear in her aforementioned very favorable review in December 1788 of *An Essay on the Causes of the*

---

1. *Works*, Vol. 6, p. 444.

Variety of Complexion and Figure in the Human Species. To which are added, Strictures on Lord Kames's Discourse on the original Diversity of Mankind, by the Rev. Samuel Stanhope Smith, D.D., Vice President and Professor of Moral Philosophy in the College of New Jersey, now Princeton.[2] Its author, an ordained Presbyterian minister, became his alma mater's seventh president and devoted his life to demonstrating the compatibility of science and Christianity. His was a most important work, in Wollstonecraft's opinion, because being based on observation as well as reason, it countered any dubious conjectures that might be deemed to cast a shadow on the harmoniousness of God's creation.[3]

As explained in a note in the *Analytical Review*, the substance of Rev. Stanhope Smith's essay had already been delivered before the Philosophical Society in Philadelphia on February 28, 1787. It had been printed both there and in Edinburgh in 1788, and challenged the views put forward in Lord Kames's "Diversity of Men and of Languages," the first sketch in *Progress of Men*, Book 1 of *Sketches of the History of Man* (1774). Kames knew he would encounter much opposition in claiming that it could be "ascertained beyond any rational doubt, that there are different races or kinds of men, and that these races or kinds are naturally fitted for different climates: whence we have reason to conclude, that originally each kind was placed in its proper climate, whatever change may have happened in later times by war or commerce."[4] He had sought to square this position with the biblical account of the creation of mankind, by turning to Scriptures's account of the erection of the Tower of Babel

2. See S. Juengel, "Countenancing History: Mary Wollstonecraft, Samuel Stanhope Smith, and Enlightenment Racial Science," *English Literary History* 68, no. 4 (2001): 897–927. *Project MUSE*, DOI:10.1353/elh.2001.0033; and Hudnut, "Samuel Stanhope Smith: Enlightened Conservative," pp. 540–552. On the continued relevance of MW, see Maoulidi, "Mary Wollstonecraft: Challenges of Race and Class in Feminist Discourse."

3. *Works*, Vol. 7, p. 55.

4. Henry Home, Lord Kames, *Sketches of the History of Man.*

and the subsequent fragmentation and dispersal of humanity. Although he had endeavored to account for the variation in the appearance and custom of human beings by appealing to climate, Kames contended that "were all men of one species, there never could have existed, without a miracle, different kinds, such as exist at present."[5] That the diversity between men could be explained by natural causes was precisely what Stanhope Smith sought to demonstrate. To say that God had created one single species that was highly adaptable to variation in geographical conditions, he believed, "surely places his benevolence in a more advantageous light" than to claim "the beneficent deity hath created the inhabitants of the earth of different colours."[6] Thus, whether humankind descended from a single pair (Adam and Eve) was a subject with significant theological and moral implications, and became an increasingly virulent debate in the eighteenth and nineteenth centuries.[7]

Wollstonecraft's review, while rich in quotations, opens with the expression of her own views on the matter, which was rather unusual compared to most of her other contributions to the *Analytical Review*. Human nature had always been an important and interesting subject, she began. Those who felt strong emotions were naturally curious about whether others felt as they did. To be sure, there were "innumerable modifications" between people, "yet there is a degree of uniformity in their variety which silently affirms that they proceed from the same source." "The untutored savage and the cultivated sage," she continued,

> are found to be men of like passions with ourselves: different external circumstances, such as the situation of the country, forms of government, religious opinions, etc. have been traced by the ablest politicians as the main causes of

5. Ibid.

6. *Works*, Vol. 7, p. 50.

7. On this controversy, see, for instance, Sebastiani, *The Scottish Enlightenment*.

national characters, the predominate feature was striking, it
pointed out the parent, and proved that it was not of equivocal generation.—But observing the heart, we may be said to
work under ground—though treating this subject we seldom
express any doubt;—the jealousy or ambition that actuates
our antipodes is not supposed to differ from the passions
which agitate us,—nor can the fortitude of an Indian, who
dies singing his death song, be distinguished from the pride
or virtue which made many heroes endure grievous calami-
ties and smile on the grim king of terrors.[8]

She followed this with a rhetorical question: given the similarity
between minds the world over, could the physical differences be
thought to prove that the earth was peopled by different species of men? Stanhope Smith, she contended, gave every reason to think that these differences were due to climate or other
such causes, and to reject therefore "vague conjectures, which
shake our confidence in the validity of the Mosaical account, and
consequently lead to a distrust of revelation."[9] True to herself,
she did not leave unmentioned what she saw as contradictions
in Stanhope Smith's work, but was happy to quote his "rational conclusion," namely, that "[a] just philosophy will always be
found to be coincident with true theology."[10] What she went on
to cite approvingly was significant, as Stanhope Smith claimed
that only those who were ignorant of nature or intent against
religion would deny the unity of the species, and that to do so
would render the science of morals meaningless, annihilate the
law of nature and nations, and make any rule of principle in
human affairs impossible. It would mean that whatever conven-
tion were developed from a study of our human nature would
not be applicable elsewhere in the world. All science and piety
would come to an end and skepticism and uncertainty would

8. *Works*, Vol. 7, p. 50.
9. Ibid., pp. 50–51.
10. Ibid., p. 54.

reign unchallenged. "The doctrine of one race," the quote went on, "removes this uncertainty, renders human nature susceptible of system, illustrates the powers of physical causes, and opens a rich and extensive field for moral science."[11] This doctrine was as foundational for Wollstonecraft as it was for the author under review. That God had created one human race and that all men had to be treated with dignity for the sake of all were to be running themes in her works, and while her first published text was on the education of daughters, in her first novel about a woman, and her reader, *The Female Reader*, she came to the subject of inequity and inequality between the sexes from that between men, and indeed races.

Slavery

Given her extensive use of the register of enslavement in speaking of the condition of women in *A Vindication of the Rights of Woman*, referring to them as "convenient slaves," "coquettish slaves," or "abject slaves," and writing of "their slavish dependence," to cite but some examples, it is noteworthy, but perhaps unsurprising, that Wollstonecraft had cause to reflect on the subjects of race and slavery before she penned her most famous work.[12] When in March 1789, she reviewed Rodolphe-Louis D'Erlach's *Code du Bonheur. A Code of Happiness: containing Maxims and Rules relative to the Duties of man towards Himself, his Fellow-Creatures, and God* (1788), she said little more than that his letters on the slave trade were "long, but interesting."[13] She was somewhat more forthcoming, however,

11. Ibid.

12. *VW*, pp. 69, 94, 76, 155. Wollstonecraft's critique of slavery and the slave trade in particular is widely acknowledged, not least thanks to the seminal work of Moira Ferguson; see Ferguson, "Mary Wollstonecraft and the Problematic of Slavery," and *Colonialism and Gender*; Howard, "Wollstonecraft's Thoughts on Slavery and Corruption." See also Brace, "Wollstonecraft and the Properties of (Anti-) Slavery."

13. *Works*, Vol. 7, p. 90.

the following month, in the May 1789 issue of the *Analytical Review*, when she reviewed *The Interesting Narrative of the Life of Olaudah Equiano, or Gustavus Vassa, the African*, which her publisher, Joseph Johnson, had just printed. She opened by declaring that "it has been a favourite philosophic whim to degrade the numerous nations, on whom the sun-beams more directly dart, below the common level of humanity, and hastily to conclude that nature, by making them inferior to the rest of the human race, designed to stamp them with a mark of slavery."[14] In that piece, she did not consider it her task to provide an account of the reasons between differences in color, nor "to draw a parallal [*sic*] between the abilities of a negro and [a] European mechanic." But she did think that while the two-volume narrative did not exhibit "extraordinary intellectual powers, sufficient to wipe off the stigma, yet the activity and ingenuity, which conspicuously appear in the character of Gustavus, place him on a par with the general mass of men, who fill the subordinate stations in a more civilized society than that which he was thrown into at his birth."[15] While this sentence might offend modern sensibilities, it would be a mistake to take this as an indication of "unconscious racism—common in abolitionist circles."[16] Though Wollstonecraft thought well of parts of the work, especially those in the first volume relating to "his being kidnapped with his sister, his journey to the sea coast, and terror when carried on shipboard [the accounts] relative to the treatment of male and female slaves on the voyage, and in the West Indies, which make the blood turn it course," she was her usual critical self when assessing its style and the rest of its content. She was therefore unlikely to claim it showed the author to be highly educated or to possess a great mind. What is more, the

14. Ibid., p. 100.
15. Ibid.
16. Taylor, *Mary Wollstonecraft and the Feminist Imagination*, p. 240.

terms of the debate about the comparative abilities of the different races were not hers. She flatly rejected the division of the human race on the basis of color. Notwithstanding differences between individuals discussed in the previous chapter, what divided mankind, as she was to make clear a few months later in *A Vindication of the Rights of Men*, was privilege, wealth, legal and political rights, and education.

It is in its opening pages that we find one of the clearest expressions of Wollstonecraft's condemnation of slavery. Burke's critique of the revolutionary events that had taken place in France constantly appealed to precedent in support of the maintenance of the status quo, in her view, and such a spirit "settles slavery on an everlasting foundation," to which she added:

> Allowing his servile reverence for antiquity, and prudent attention to self-interest, to have the force which he insists on, the slave trade ought never to be abolished; and, because of our ignorant forefathers, not understanding the native dignity of man, sanctioned a traffic that outrages every suggestion or reason and religion, we are to submit to the inhuman custom, and term an atrocious insult to humanity the love of our country, and a proper submission to the laws by which our property is secured.[17]

Wollstonecraft went beyond merely borrowing the rhetoric of the anti-slavery campaign. She had read and written on the subject of race, asserted the unity of mankind, and decried slavery before she began defending the aims of the revolution in France or vindicating the rights of woman. What is more, she was not to pass over in silence women's participation in the horrors of slavery: "Where is the dignity, the infallibility of sensibility, in the fair ladies, if the voice of rumour is to be credited, the captive negroes curse in all the agony of bodily pain, for

17. *VM*, p. 13.

the unheard of tortures they invent? It is probable that some of them, after the sight of a flagellation, compose their ruffled spirits and exercise their tender feelings by the perusal of the last imported novel."[18]

She was, to be sure, not alone in denouncing slavery. Across the Channel, Olympe de Gouges shared the same sentiment. Several of Wollstonecraft's acquaintances and friends were active in the anti-slavery movement. Becoming the chairman in 1823 of the Liverpool Anti-Slavery Society, William Roscoe, who commissioned the first portrait of her, headed an eponymous circle of like-minded people in Liverpool, and had written a number of pamphlets pleading the case by the time he met Wollstonecraft.[19] Much of Imlay's *A Topographical Description of the Western Territory of North America* (1792) decried slavery, and argued for gradual emancipation and against segregation. Thomas Jefferson was singled out in the text as having a "mind is so warped by education and the habit of thinking, that he has attempted to make it appear that the African is a being between the human species and the oran-outang."[20] It is possible that the expression of such sentiments contributed to endearing him to Wollstonecraft. It certainly helped him gain an entry into the intellectual circles she frequented. Vile though one might have thought him for abandoning her and their baby, Fanny, extensive research by Imlay's biographer, Wil Verhoeven, has revealed him to be more despicable still. A shameless hypocrite, Imlay had been very much involved in the slave trade himself, co-owning the slave carrier *Industry*: "[t]he truth is that before he left America for Europe and became involved with her, Imlay had been one of those barterers in human blood that Wollstonecraft so thoroughly despised."[21]

18. Ibid., p. 46.
19. Sutton, "Roscoe circle."
20. Verhoeven, "Gilbert Imlay and the Triangular Trade," p. 832.
21. Ibid., p. 833.

Human Nature

As so much hung on subscribing to the view that humans belonged to one species and shared one human nature, what did Wollstonecraft think of it? She was brought to reflect on human nature from the very beginning of her intellectual career, through her involvement in and works on education. From her *Original Stories*, first published in 1788, republished in 1791 and 1796, and written shortly after her arrival in London in August 1787, we know that human beings, in contrast to animals,[22] had the God-given power to "ennoble" human nature by the cultivation of the mind and enlargement of the heart. Man, by which we can presume she meant mankind, being capable of disinterested love, could "imitate Him."[23] She thought it contrary to all experience to insinuate "that it is the nature of man to degenerate rather than improve."[24] Reviewing *New Travels into the interior Parts of Africa, by the Way of the Cape of Great Hope, in the Years 1783, 83 [sic], and 85,* she applauded accounts that showed baseless prejudices for what they were:

> The hottentots have been considered as the most disgusting and brutal of the "various tribes of the many peopled earth"; a real lover of mankind must then be highly gratified by the lively and artless pictures that occur in this narrative of the domestic virtues, and moral sensibility, of the untutored wanderers in those vast rocky deserts. [. . .] The dirty customs attributed to them are evidently false, as well as the charge of tyrannizing over the weaker sex.[25]

22. *VM*, p. 31. See Botting's "Mary Wollstonecraft, Children's Human Rights, and Animal Ethics,"; Spencer, "'The link which unites man with brutes'"; and Seeber, "Mary Wollstonecraft: 'Systemiz[ing] Oppression.'"

23. *Works*, Vol. 4, p. 370.

24. *Analytical Review*, Vol. 25 (1797), *Works*, Vol. 7, p. 479.

25. Ibid., p. 480.

Similarly, in a review of William Thomson's *Manmouth; or Human Nature displayed on a grand scale: in a Tour with the Tinkers into the inland Parts of Africa*, Wollstonecraft commended him for not following Jonathan Swift in inducing "that painful sensation of disgust, and even distrust of Providence, which Gulliver's Travels never fail to excite in a mind possessed of any sensibility." Such works as Swift's led one to detest the vicious, rather than feel compassionate toward them, and question "why they were created to contradict what appears in shining characters throughout the universe, that God is wise and good."[26] "In sketches of life," she added,

> a degree of dignity, which distinguishes man, should not be blotted out; nor the prevailing interest undermined by a satirical tone, which makes the reader forget an acknowledged truth, that in the most vicious, vestiges may be faintly discerned of a majestic ruin, and in the most virtuous, frailties which loudly proclaim, that like passions unite the two extremities of the social chain, and circulate through the whole body.[27]

Whether depicting individuals or the species, in quasi-factual or fictional works, Wollstonecraft thought human beings should not be presented as degraded beyond recognition. They should, instead, be presented in such a manner as to retain "a degree of dignity."[28] Human beings were not inherently evil, in her view, and just as she had argued for our creative potential, so she thought the realization of our moral potential should be encouraged. "It may be confidently asserted," she wrote, "that no man chooses evil, because it is evil; he only mistakes it for happiness, the good he seeks." Striving to rectify mistakes was "the noble ambition of an enlightened understanding, the impulse of

---

26. Ibid., Vol. 4 (1789), p. 104.
27. Ibid., p. 105.
28. Ibid.

feelings that Philosophy invigorates," adding that "[t]o endeavour to make unhappy men resigned to their fate, is the tender endeavour of short-sighted benevolence, of transient yearnings of humanity; but to labour to increase human happiness by extirpating error, is a masculine godlike affection."[29]

Her confidence in human perfectibility was apparent throughout her works. Writing about the French in *An Historical and Moral View of the Origin and Progress of the French Revolution; and the Effect It Has Produced in Europe* (1794), Wollstonecraft expressed the view that no matter how adulterated human beings had become in the most luxurious and unequal society under an absolute government and "domineering priesthood," they could not be so debased as not to have retained "a gleam of the generous fire, an ethereal spark of the soul; and it is these glowing emotions, in the inmost recesses of the heart, which have continued to feel feelings, that on sudden occasions manifest themselves with all their pristine purity and vigour."[30] Despite the ferocity manifested during the French Revolution, she felt "confident of being able to prove, that people are essentially good, and that knowledge is rapidly advancing to that degree of perfectibility, when the proud distinctions of sophisticating fools will be eclipsed by the mild rays of philosophy, and man be considered as man—acting with the dignity of an intelligent being."[31] The notorious shadow the Revolution cast on itself could not be taken to reveal human nature. One had to wait for the anarchy to subside, Wollstonecraft claimed, before its true qualities could emerge. This is not to suggest that she was confident that the Revolution would herald a new dawn for the French people or, indeed, humanity as a whole. Chapter 4 will consider her views on that subject. Despite her concerns about the future direction of the French and civilization more

29. *VM*, p. 56.
30. *Works*, Vol. 6, pp. 231–232.
31. Ibid., p. 46.

generally, it was Wollstonecraft's fundamental belief that while mankind created the conditions under which evil occurred, it was not essentially or irretrievably so.

When writing about the theater in her first publication, she had maintained that its ability to edify was reduced to nought when the main characters were given either exalted qualities far above the common attributes of humanity or a depraved nature far below them. Crass divisions between good and evil were not only needless, but dangerous for individuals and society. The main purpose of dramatic performances, she claimed, should be "to teach us to discriminate characters," adding "I cannot help thinking, that every human creature has some spark of goodness, which their long-suffering and benevolent Father gives them an opportunity of improving, though they may perversely smother it before they cease to breathe."[32] Just preceding "The Theatre" in the same work, she had devoted a piece to "Benevolence," deeming it the "first, and most amiable virtue" and most evident in the young.[33] Selfishness only grew through imitation, from the perception and experience of the selfishness of others and the ways of the world. As we saw in relation to the arts, so with regard to moral character, imitation was nefarious. Seeing the ways of the world was more likely than not to lead to its imitation rather than disavowal. She reiterated the point in 1793, writing that "[t]he desire [. . .] of being useful to others, is continually damped by experience; and, if the exertions of humanity were not in some measure their own reward, who would endure misery, or struggle with care, to make some people ungrateful, and others idle?"[34]

Universal benevolence was the first duty, "and we should be careful not to let any passion so engross our thoughts, as to prevent our practising it."[35] Natural benevolence had to be

32. , Vol. 4, p. 46.
33. Ibid., p. 43.
34. *Letter on the Character of the French Nation, Works*, Vol. 6, p. 445.
35. *Education of Daughters, Works*, Vol. 4, p. 30.

protected and nurtured. Until such time as the world metamorphosed into a fair and equitable environment in which selfishness ceased to be a model and ingratitude no longer prevailed, it was vital that parents and educators help sustain and develop the innate benevolence of children. The means she proposed in her early pedagogical texts was to encourage young people to practice charity, by giving them an allowance or pocket money with which to do so.

"Faith, hope and charity," Wollstonecraft believed, "ought to attend us in our passage through this world." Of the three virtues, only charity could remain in our souls eternally. "We ought not to suffer," she contended, "the heavenly spark to be quenched by selfishness; if we do, how can we expect to revive, when the soul is disentangled from the body, and should be prepared for the realms of love?" While she would write to Imlay from her travels in northern Europe that he knew how she had always been "an enemy to what is termed charity," this was within the particular context of an unjust and hypocritical society in which charity was intended to cover inequities or be valued as a way of inducing servility among those in receipt of it.[36] To be sure, *A Vindication of the Rights of Men* decried the age in which [c]ivility was then called condescension, and ostentatious almsgiving humanity."[37] Charity, she argued in that text, "is not a condescending distribution of alms, but an intercourse of good offices and mutual benefits, founded on respect for justice and humanity." This again has to be seen in the context in which it is written, one in which it is the ostentatiousness as well as the need for alms that are deplored, not the act of charity itself. In the same work she also pointed to the desire to perpetuate property within families as narrowing benevolence to the confines

---

36. *The French Revolution, Works*, Vol. 6, p. 46 and *Letters Written during a Short Residence in Sweden, Norway, and Denmark, Works*, p. 337.
37. *VM*, p. 11.

of a very narrow circle.[38] A few pages later, she stated that the desire of three out of four people to appear to be richer than they are destroys "benevolence, friendship, generosity, and all those endearing charities which bind human hearts together." "[T]he iron hand of property" thereby also stopped "all the pursuits which raise the mind to higher contemplations."[39]

If the more tangible part of benevolence—charity—was necessitated by iniquitous poverty, it was for that very reason to be exercised and fostered. Its benefit also extended far beyond the immediate impact on its recipients. Writing on education in her first publication, she had declared that every act of benevolence improved its performer and described it as an active duty that fitted us for "the society of more exalted beings." Philanthropy, she continued, was said to be proof of human capability of loving God:

> Indeed this divine love, or charity, appears to me the principal trait that remains of the illustrious image of the Deity, which was originally stampt on the soul, and which is to be renewed. Exalted views will raise the mind above trifling cares, and the many little weaknesses, which make us a torment to ourselves and others. Our temper will gradually improve, and vanity, which "the creature is made subject to," has not an entire dominion.[40]

Wollstonecraft was to reiterate such sentiments toward the end of *A Vindication of the Rights of Woman*, when writing about the place of religion in national education. "What would life be," she asked, "without that peace which the love of God, when built on humanity, alone can impart?" Continuing, she declared: "Every earthly affection turns back, at intervals, to prey upon

38. Ibid., p. 21. See Eileen Hunt Botting, *Family Feuds: Wollstonecraft, Burke and Rousseau on the Transformation of the Family* (Albany: State University of New York Press, 2006), chapter 4.

39. *VM*, p. 23.

40. *Education of Daughters, Works*, Vol. 4, p. 24.

the heart that feeds it; and the purest effusions of benevolence, often rudely damped by man, must mount as a free-will offering to Him who gave them birth, whose bright image they faintly reflect."[41] Benevolence and its exercise through charity was the last divine mark left in human beings, and despite all she had to say against alms-giving when speaking of the social reality of her time, it was the principal medium she recommended to express humanity, for through it, natural benevolence could be sustained in children. Economizing in order to be able to "gratify benevolent wishes" was part of the farewell advice Mrs. Mason, Mary and Caroline's sometime teacher in *Original Stories*, gave the fourteen- and twelve-year-old in her charge.[42] In *A Vindication of the Rights of Woman*, Wollstonecraft further recommended that children be schooled together as being in the sole company of adults made them grow up too quickly and had a distorting effect on their bodily and mental faculties. Being with other children enabled them to learn to think for themselves and "open the heart to friendship and confidence, gradually leading to more expansive benevolence."[43]

She also suggested from her earliest works that they be made to empathize with animals, by raising awareness of them and extending our sensibility about them through stories.[44] The subject of the first three chapters of *Original Stories* was "The Treatment of Animals": "Do you know the meaning of the word Goodness? 'It is first, to avoid hurting any thing; and then, to contrive to give as much pleasure as you can.'"[45] Wollstonecraft was to insist on the importance of teaching children to be kind to animals again in *A Vindication of the Rights of Woman*, arguing that "[h]humanity to animals should be particularly inculcated

41. *VW*, p. 255.
42. *Works*, Vol. 6, p. 449.
43. *VW*, p. 251.
44. *Works*, Vol. 4, p. 44; see Botting, "Mary Wollstonecraft, Children's Human Rights, and Animal Ethics."
45. *Works*, Vol. 4, p. 368.

as a part of national education." She thought that cruelty to animals led to tyranny over other human beings in adulthood: "justice, or even benevolence, will not be a powerful spring of action unless it extend to the whole creation; nay, I believe that it may be delivered as an axiom, that those who can see pain, unmoved, will soon learn to inflict it."[46]

Interestingly, she thought the progress of civilization had made human beings less caring of animals. "For civilization," she explained, "prevents that intercourse which creates affection in the rude hut, or mud hovel." While in that passage of the *Vindication* she singled out the poor as exacting their revenge on animals for the humiliation they suffered at the hands of the rich, her *Original Stories* provided a vivid example of the mutual devotion between a destitute man and his dog, and the heartlessness of the rich toward both.[47] If the relationship between men and animals was corrupted by social injustice, it assumed a different perversion in women. They cared too much about their pets at the cost of caring for humanity or even their own children.[48] As we will discuss in subsequent chapters, Wollstonecraft was not alone in thinking that women's feelings were confined to a very limited number of living creatures, but she was one of the few to make it her business to challenge the circumstances that prevented the objects of their emotions from being enlarged. To be sure as we have seen already, she was well aware that feelings could be feigned; "[a]n affectation of humanity," she wrote in *The French Revolution* (1794), "is the affectation of the day; and men almost always affect to possess the virtue, or quality, that is rising into estimation."[49] In this as in other subjects, the question was how to improve and educate without the risk of generating artifice and falseness.

46. *VW*, p. 268.
47. *Works*, Vol. 4, pp. 371–379.
48. *VW*, p. 269.
49. *Works*, Vol. 6, p. 112.

In sum, while human beings had the potential to be compassionate and could, through acts of kindness, reveal their divine nature and small, but crucial, resemblance to their Creator, this capacity had to be developed. Moreover, while they were perfectible, human beings were by the same token corruptible and were mostly so in a society that distorted human relations through social and economic inequality and false values. All creatures had to be treated well and humans had to learn to do so from the earliest age. In addition to the need to recognize the unity of the species, Wollstonecraft believed in the supreme importance of treating all sentient beings well. Natural benevolence not only had to be nurtured; it had to be extended beyond the confines in which it found itself most easily exercised. This called for a particular education to which the imagination was handmaiden, serving it as no other faculty of the mind could.

The Imagination

If benevolence was the first of the virtues for Wollstonecraft, the imagination was the most formidable of the faculties. Reason and understanding could not but be important for an eighteenth-century intellectual such as Wollstonecraft, and she presented herself to her readers as the embodiment of rationality, especially when fighting male adversaries such as Burke or Rousseau. Nonetheless, the importance of imagination, which we have already noted in the creation of great art, was as central to her account of human moral development as it was for the moral philosophers she engaged with.[50] This is not to suggest that she thought men and women should be governed by the imagination. Which faculty ought to prevail at any one time very

50. As Barbara Taylor has rightly noted, Wollstonecraft tends to be presented as extolling reason to the exclusion of all other human capacities; following the publication of her *Mary Wollstonecraft and the Feminist Imagination*, this is no longer justifiable. See her *Mary Wollstonecraft and the Feminist Imagination*, especially pp. 58–94.

much depended on circumstances, the individual concerned, and their state of mind. It also depended on age, as she wrote in her *Vindication of the Rights of Men*: "though it is allowed that one man has by nature more fancy than another, in each individual there is a spring-tide when fancy should govern and amalgamate materials for the understanding; and a grave period, when those materials should be employed by the judgement."[51] Crucially, she did not think of reason and the imagination as being in opposition with each other. What mattered was a balanced mind. This was no mean feat as every period of civilization presented its own obstacles. To achieve the right balance might require adjustment and entail the prevalence of one or the other faculties at any one stage of an individual's life or at different stages in the development of society. What she thought the imagination was, what it actually did, how it operated, she did not say, although it does seem that she thought it was responsive to and possibly shaped by the emotions, on which it also had an impact.

Prefacing her anthology, *The Female Reader*, Wollstonecraft explained that "[in] this selection many tales and tables will be found, as it seems to be following the simple order of nature, to permit young people to peruse works addressed to the imagination, which tend to awaken the affections and fix good habits more firmly in the mind than cold arguments and mere declamation."[52] The imagination thus played a determinative role in the early stages of the growth of moral personality, and this had to be taken into account by parents and teachers. In an ideal childhood, education would be directed to nurturing the imagination, rather than reason, to ensure effective moral development. Unfortunately, this might not always be possible. In *Original Stories*, which Blake illustrated as already mentioned, she explained that the nature of the conversations and

51. *VM*, p. 58.
52. *Works*, Vol. 4, p. 56.

tales it contained had to be adapted to accommodate the present
state of society, which obliged her to seek methods for correct-
ing character defects and ignorance through reason. Teaching
by "precepts of reason" was far from ideal. "Good habits, imperceptibly fixed" were far preferable.[53] No less than other forms
of instruction, works of fancy, music and drawing, for instance,
refined the mind by entertaining it, Mrs. Mason told her pupils,
adding that they

> sharpen the ingenuity, and form insensibly the dawning of
> judgement. As the judgement gains strength, so do the pas-
> sions also; we have actions to weigh, and need that taste in
> conduct, that delicate sense of propriety, which gives grace
> to virtue.[54]

For Wollstonecraft, therefore, while the imagination had, or at
least should have, a very active role in human development, and
particularly so in childhood, it was best seen as one part of her
conception of the human mind, one in which each faculty rein-
forces and enriches the others. Thus, under the heading "Reading" in *Education of Daughters*, she claimed that "[r]eason strikes
most forcibly when illustrated by the brilliancy of fancy."[55] A
well-balanced mind was one in which the faculties aided rather
than opposed or subordinated one another, a view that can be
taken to reflect the influence, long noted by Sarah Hutton and
Barbara Taylor, that Platonists or Neo-Platonists had on her.[56]
Such an harmonious balance depended on a proper education
to be sure, but also on specific social conditions, as is made clear
in passages in which her reflections on the balance between the
faculties led her to think about their development historically.
Human beings were more imaginative in the unlimited freedom enjoyed in the state of nature, but the demands of society,

53. Ibid., p. 359.
54. Ibid., p. 415.
55. *Works*, Vol. 4, pp. 20–21.
56. See Tomaselli, "'Have Ye Not Heard That We Cannot Serve Two Masters?.'"

economic reality, and the exertions of specific civilizing forces, good or bad, made for the prevalence or atrophy of different parts of the intellect.

Although she was not entirely consistent on this topic, Wollstonecraft was concerned with the more general evolution of the human mind as well as the minds of individual men and women. In the very first *Letter* from her *Letters Written in Sweden, Norway, and Denmark*, she wrote that approaching a rather desolate area near Gothenburg, she was surprised that her presence did not elicit some curiosity among the few inhabitants: no one stared out of the windows or came outdoors to see them.[57] This lack of curiosity she attributed on this occasion to their being "so near brute creation." Explaining that those who could barely sustain themselves "have little or no imagination to call forth the curiosity necessary to fructify the faint glimmerings of mind which entitles them to rank as lords of creation,"[58] she contrasted these apathetic coastal Swedes to the Parisians she had recently observed whilst living in France under the Terror, saying

> recollecting the extreme fondness which the Parisians ever testify for novelty, their very curiosity appeared to me a proof of the progress they had made in refinement. Yes; in the art of living—in the art of escaping from the cares which embarrass the first steps towards the attainment of the pleasures of social life.[59]

If, in light of what we saw in chapter 1 of her views of the poetic nature of humanity in its infancy, Wollstonecraft's estimation of the unimaginativeness of these isolated Swedes comes as a surprise, it must be stressed that she was here contrasting men and

57. *Works*, Vol. 6, p. 245.
58. Ibid.
59. Ibid.

women fighting for subsistence to those, as she conceived the French, in an advanced stage of civilization.[60]

It would be wrong, however, to infer from this that the imagination only worked for the betterment of individuals and humanity within an advanced society or independently of particular circumstances in which communities or individuals found themselves. Far from this being the case, in a text to which we have already referred when discussing natural benevolence and which often casts a subversive light on one's assumptions about her views, *Letter on the Character of the French Nation*, the events she witnessed under the Terror led Wollstonecraft to think very ill of the imagination:

> The wants of reason are very few, and, were we to consider dispassionately the real value of most things, we should probably rest satisfied with simple gratification of our physical necessities, and be content with negative goodness; for tis frequently, only that wanton, the Imagination, with her artful coquetry, who lures us forward, and makes us run over a rough road, pushing aside every obstacle merely to catch a disappointment.[61]

Negative goodness is an interesting, if somewhat perplexing, concept. Contentment with the here and now and the satisfaction of having one's basic needs met are sentiments perhaps not readily associated with Wollstonecraft, as we will have further occasion to observe. To be sure, this pronouncement must be taken in the awful context in which she expressed it. Nevertheless, deploring the human propensity to risk forfeiting the certain happiness of the present for almost no less certain regrets was not a new departure for her caused by witnessing the Terror. Such sentiments had already found expression in *A Vindication*

60. This, however, is not to suggest that she was more immune to contradictions than anyone else.

61. *Works*, Vol. 6, p. 445.

of the Rights of Men three years earlier. There the imagination enlarged objects which the passions pursued, deluded and rejecting the evidence of the senses.[62] In her diatribe against Burke, Wollstonecraft presented him as possessed of an easily inflammable imagination.[63] By contrast, as we will see again below, she personified reason, calm in the act of reflection, dispassionate in its assessment of principle.

In that work, the imagination is presented as unpredictable and unruly. The language is palpably and intentionally gendered. Her depictions anticipate the wantonness she was to ascribe to it three years later in *A Letter on the Character of the French Nation*. Wollstonecraft spoke of it in rather extraordinary terms as, when referring to the opportunity presented by the early stages of the Revolution, she wrote that "the glorious *chance* that is now given to human nature of attaining more virtue and happiness than has hitherto blessed the globe, might have been sacrificed to a meteor of the imagination, a bubble of passion."[64] "A lively imagination," she wrote some pages later, "is ever in danger of being betrayed into error by favourite opinions, which it almost personifies, the more effectually to intoxicate the understanding."[65]

Yet, at the same time as she upbraided the unbridled imagination for the revolutionary excess she witnessed in France, she wrote to Imlay:

> Believe me, sage sir, you have not sufficient respect for the Imagination.—I could prove to you in a trice that it is the mother of sentiment, the great distinction of our nature, the only purifier of the passions.—Animals have a portion of Reason, and equal, if not more exquisite, senses, but no trace of Imagination, or her offspring Taste, appears in any

62. *VM*, p. 33.
63. Ibid., p. 46.
64. Ibid., p. 50.
65. Ibid., p. 57.

of their actions. The impulse of the senses—passions if you will—and the conclusions of Reason, draw men together but the Imagination is the true fire, stolen from heaven, to animate this cold creature of clay—producing all those fine sympathies that lead to rapture, rendering men more social by expanding their hearts, instead of leaving them leisure to calculate how many comforts society affords.[66]

Wollstonecraft might have been more consistent with her own views, mentioned earlier, about the importance of imagination to morality, if she had aligned herself with that faculty and identified Burke with a steadfast, unswerving, and uncreative reason. It was, after all, she and like-minded sympathizers with the Revolution who could be viewed as innovative and able to conceive of a better future. Burke, it could be thought, lacked the capacity to do so. Instead, she chose otherwise and, one might add, had to do so given the nature and extent of her attack of him in which she projected herself as his opposite. Under her pen and that of others who criticized his *Reflections*, he was the fickle, inconsistent, and irrational person, who supported the American cause against the Crown and Parliament in their call for representation and fair treatment as Englishmen, but not that of the French people in what could be construed as a comparable quest. Burke was emotionally erratic, inflamed, and self-contradictory. She presented herself as solidly anchored. She appropriated manly qualities and cast him in the frivolity of femininity, never hesitating to use gender and gendered language in waging her battles.

Even so, despite her sharp rhetoric and accusations that Burke lacked self-control, Wollstonecraft was unswerving in at least one respect, namely, in thinking that there was an appropriate strength of each of the faculties relative to each other at any given stage of life. "There are times and seasons for all

66. Letter to Imlay, cited in Richard Holmes, *Footsteps. Adventures of a Romantic Biographer* (New York: Vintage, 1985), p. 127.

things," she wrote in the midst of her *ad hominem* critique of
Burke, "and moralists appear to me to err, when they would con-
found the gaiety of youth with the seriousness of age; for the virtues of age look not only more imposing, but more natural, when
they appear rigid." Referring to Burke, she continued: "[h]e who
has not exercised his judgement to curb his imagination during
the meridian of life, becomes, in its decline, too often the prey of
childish feelings."[67] Burke's mind was unbalanced, not just like
a woman, more like a child. Nor was he alone. In *A Vindication
of the Rights of Woman*, Jean-Jacques Rousseau was described
as a man "whose imagination had been allowed to run wild," for
his account of what allegedly made men attractive to women
("if strength of body be, with some shew of reason, the boast of
men, why are women so infatuated as to be proud of a defect").[68]
"His imagination constantly prepared inflammable fewel," she
declared, "for his inflammable senses."[69] "Why was Rousseau's
life divided between ecstasy and misery?," she asked. To which
she answered:

> Can any other answer be given than this, that the effer-
> vescence of his imagination produced both; but had his
> fancy been allowed to cool, it is possible that he might have
> acquired more strength of mind. Still, if the purpose of life be
> to educate the intellectual part of man, all with respect to him
> was right; yet, had not death led to a nobler scene of action,
> it is probable that he would have enjoyed happiness on earth,
> and have felt the calm sensations of the man of nature instead

67. *VM*, p. 58.
68. *VW*, p. 111.
69. Ibid., p. 114. For more on Wollstonecraft and the imagination, see Schulman, "Gothic Piles and Endless Forests." For the politics of sense and sensibility
more generally, see Johnson, *Equivocal Beings*; see also Taylor, *Mary Wollstonecraft and the Feminist Imagination*; Gunther-Canada, "The politics of sense and
sensibility," pp. 126–147.

of being prepared for another stage of existence by nourishing passions which agitate the civilized man.[70]

In her diagnosis of Rousseau's condition, Wollstonecraft turned more Rousseauian than he. Her verdict on his life was that he had fallen prey to the very distorting psychological effects of modern civilization that he had so well described in both his *Discourses*. Had he reached old age, she thought, he might have had a chance to live to be true to his own natural self and his theory.[71]

Wollstonecraft could speak harshly of the imagination not only of particular men whose opinions she rejected, but more generally, as when she referred to the faculty as "debauch[ing]" or as "that lying, yet constantly trusted guide, the imagination."[72] Yet, even in so writing, she tended not to leave such comments unqualified: "[t]he imagination should not be allowed to debauch the understanding *before it gained strength*."[73] Nor did she herself forgo flights of fancy. She spoke of her own imagination darting forward in *A Vindication of the Rights of Woman*, and even in that non-fictional work, she invited her reader to join her in imagining in some detail "a woman of tolerable understanding," her marriage, widowhood, and motherhood up to her approaching death, indeed even "rising from the grave, may say—Behold, thou gavest me a talent—and here are five talents."[74] What is more, she thought of her most celebrated work as a magisterial creation of the imagination, writing in an effort to reassure her readers lest they think she wished to turn the world upside down: "But fair and softly, gentle reader, male or female, do not alarm thyself [. . .] I only created an imagination, fatigued by contemplating the vices and follies

70. *VW*, p. 172.
71. For more on the influence of Rousseau on Wollstonecraft's writings, see Laura Kirkley, "Jean-Jacques Rousseau."
72. *VW*, p. 257, p. 194.
73. Ibid., p. 257.
74. Ibid., p. 266; pp. 124–125.

[. . .] by supposing that society will some time or other be so constituted, that man must necessarily fulfil the duties of a citizen, and [. . .] his wife, also an active citizen, should be equally intent to manage her family, educate her children, and assist her neighbours."[75]

While potentially wayward if subjected to "superfluous nourishment" or "heated," the imagination when it operated within a right frame of mind was clearly essential to moral education and a moralist such as she.[76] It needed to be active in youth and develop in conjunction with the senses. Comparing the human body to a tree that "does not strengthen its fibres till it has reached its full growth," she added that the same was true of the mind:

> The senses and the imagination give form to the character, during childhood and youth; and the understanding, as life advances, gives firmness to the first fair purposes of sensibility—till virtue, arising rather from the clear conviction of reason than the impulse of the heart, morality is made to rest on a rock against which the storms of passions vainly beat.[77]

The work of the imagination did not end with the coming of age, however. It continued, not least in helping the mind accede where reason could not take her; "I may be thought fanciful," she wrote in the notes that were intended for an anticipated second volume to *A Vindication of the Rights of Woman*, "but it has continually occurred to me, that, though I allow, reason in this world is the mother of wisdom—yet some flights of the imagination seem to reach what wisdom cannot teach—and while they delude us here, afford glorious hope, if not a foretaste, of what we may expect hereafter."[78]

75. Ibid., p. 236.
76. *Hints*, p. 296; *VW*, p. 210.
77. *VW*, p. 198.
78. *Hints*, p. 300.

WHO ARE WE? WHAT ARE WE MADE OF? [91]

Such imaginary flights were not in everyone's gift, however; "[t]he generality of people cannot see or feel poetically, they want fancy." Here again we see that she did not think human beings to be of equal, in the sense of identical, nature or ability. Most people depended on those endowed with the capacity to bring their imagination to the process of acquiring and associating ideas: "[t]hose are the glowing minds that concentrate pictures for their fellow–creatures."[79] As we just noted, that is exactly what she sought to do in *A Vindication of the Rights of Woman*. Her mind could do what most could not and she saw it as her task, or perhaps her duty, to imagine a better world for them.

Memory

Like the imagination, memory could modify ideas and enhance past experiences.[80] Indeed, Wollstonecraft could write of it as being inventive: "In modern poetry, the understanding and memory often fabricate the pretended effusions of the heart, and romance destroys all simplicity."[81] Memory could also be distorting, contributing through its biases to a false construction of the self. Thus, it could be so highly selective as to choose to "treasure up" those past deeds that reflected well on the individuals themselves, thereby affording an unmerited good opinion of themselves.[82] Though she wrote relatively little of it, it seems that optimally, memory worked mechanically, collecting experiences and ideas, waiting for it to be called upon for use.[83]

As things stood, the loading of memory "with unintelligible words" was taken for education, whereas the "cultivation

79. *VW*, p. 201.
80. *VM*, p. 40.
81. Ibid., p. 29.
82. Ibid., p. 56; see Yousef, "Wollstonecraft, Rousseau and the Revision of Romantic Subjectivity."
83. *VW*, pp. 201 and 200.

of mind, [. . .] teaches young people how to begin to think."[84] Wollstonecraft was highly critical of education by rote, not least as it was often forced upon children by the selfishness of their parents. It was nothing short of "cruel" to cram the minds of the young with ideas incomprehensible to them. "Parents," she wrote, "are often led astray by the selfish desire of having a wonderful child exhibit; but these monsters very seldom make sensible men or women: the wheels are impaired by being set in motion before the time pointed out by nature, and both mind and body are ever after feeble."[85] If poems were to be remembered, they should not be repeated in public by children as such performances rendered them vain and affected as well as puppet-like. If memory needed to be exercised, Wollstonecraft recommended it be done in such a way as so avoid tedious repetition; judgment had to be formed in the process of committing something to memory.[86] Children were not to be treated as parrots. As we saw in relation to the arts, she disapproved of mindless imitation by children, not only on aesthetic grounds, but on psychological and moral ones.

Sensory Experience and the Association of Ideas

Wollstonecraft's unease about the potentially distortive capacity of memory or of its perverted development given contemporary pedagogical and parental practices and aspirations found a match in her discussion of the acquisition of knowledge through sensory experience. Although it was the principal source of knowledge, the ideas it produced required some scrutiny. She did not discuss the process of the association of ideas from the acquisition of singular sense impressions to the formation of

84. Ibid., p. 257; *Education of Daughters*, *Works*, Vol. 4, p. 12.
85. *The Female Reader*, *Works*, Vol. 4, p. 58. I am grateful to Eileen Hunt Botting for noting that this passage brings to mind Mary Shelley's novel, *Frankenstein*. See Botting, *Mary Shelley and the Rights of the Child*.
86. *The Female Reader*, *Works*, Vol. 4, p. 59.

abstract notions at great length, but she alluded to it on a number of occasions; indeed, she titled chapter 6 of *A Vindication of the Rights of Woman* "The Effect Which an Early Association of Ideas has Upon The Character." It contains her most explicit account of the operation of the mind in the acquisition of ideas, and distinguished two forms of associations of ideas: habitual, through repeated exposure to certain conjunctions of ideas, and instantaneous, that is, the immediate connection of ideas on their first occurrence. There was little possibility of controlling the latter. Much depended on the character of individual minds and their native composition. Spontaneity in the association of ideas was in some the source of creativity and exceptional insight. "The essence of genius" consisted in producing "in the most eminent degree the happy energy of associating thoughts that surprise, delight, and instruct."[87] As noted in relation to the imagination, those able to do so made the rest of the population feel and see what they would otherwise overlook.

This left habitual associations of ideas, which admitted a large degree of control and did not rest on being exceptionally gifted. It was the business of educators, be they parents or teachers of a sort, to ensure that they were correctly formed. Authors, such as Wollstonecraft, needed to enlighten their readers on the import of early associations of ideas and the processes involved in the acquisition of knowledge more generally. Understanding how the mind as a whole came to be formed and operated was essential, not least because the senses did not acquire ideas without the active involvement of the faculties; in other words, the mind was not passive in the process of perception. Reviewing a novel, she noted:

> On the contrary, the simplicity of truth is so happily united with that glow of imagination, which constitutes the grand charm of fiction, we do not find it difficult to credit the author's assertion, that he has closely adhered to his

87. *VW*, p. 201.

resolution not to repeat any hear-say accounts of opinions or customs; but only to note down, as facts, what he saw with his own eyes, and heard with his own ears.[88]

As with everything else, consideration had to be given to the development of the mind in its various stages:

> for the mind does not correct the mistakes of the senses till we have made the first step in science; and general ideas should be forcibly imprinted on the mind before particular modifications, much less abstract ideas, are mentioned.[89]

The mind had to be prepared for different kinds of knowledge from different sources. In addition, Wollstonecraft thought it essential to be aware ourselves of the context in which we acquired our impressions. An example of what she had in mind is provided by her opening remarks in an *Introductory to a Series of Letters on the Present Character of the French Nation*, written in Paris in mid-February 1793, thus in the midst of the Terror. There Wollstonecraft explained that "[i]t is necessary perhaps for an observer of mankind, to guard as carefully the remembrance of the first impression made by a nation, as by a countenance; because we imperceptibly lose sight of the national character, when we become more intimate with individuals."[90] Far from being wary of first impressions, they had to be preserved, though this is not to say that they did not need to be subject to scrutiny and revision.

In itself the acquisition of simple ideas neither constituted knowledge nor was exclusive to human beings. What differentiated the latter from animals was what Wollstonecraft termed "the power of generalizing ideas"; that was the power "of drawing conclusions from individual observations":

88. *Works*, Vol. 7, pp. 479–480.
89. *Analytical Review*, Vol. 25 (1797), *Works*, p. 382.
90. *Works*, Vol. 6, p. 443.

Merely to observe, without endeavouring to account for any thing, may (in a very incomplete manner) serve as the common sense of life; but where is the store laid up that is to clothe the soul when it leaves the body?[91]

According to some, this power had been denied women: "writers have insisted that it is inconsistent, with a few exceptions, with their sexual character," but Wollstonecraft believed it was up to these men to justify their assertions. She was only willing to concede one point, namely,

> That the power of generalizing ideas, to any great extent, is not very common amongst men or women. But this exercise is the true cultivation of the understanding; and every thing conspires to render the cultivation of the understanding more difficult in the female than in the male world.[92]

This was the subject of the fourth chapter of *A Vindication of the Rights of Woman*, and one might add the principal object of the work as whole. Women could generalize ideas, acquire knowledge, and develop their understanding or reason as well as men. Why neither sex was able to do so as fully as they were capable, and women not only condemned not to, but perceived to be incapable of so doing, was what she fought to challenge.

Reason

"Reason" and cognate terms, such as "the understanding," compete with "virtue" and "women" as some of Wollstonecraft's most frequently used words. She used the concept extensively and often normatively. Wollstonecraft feminized it as she did the imagination. This did not stop her from playing, as we have already seen, with stereotypical assumptions about masculine rationality and feminine want of it. She gave reason status,

91. *VW*, p. 128.
92. Ibid., p. 129.

endowing it with suzerainty. She spoke of the "sovereignty of reason" and "the *regal* stamp of reason" in the first *Vindication*.[93] At the onset of the work, she invited Burke to reason with her in an unashamedly patronizing manner.[94] In both her *Vindications*, she presented herself as rational, deploying reason, where he, Rousseau, and others didn't, wouldn't, or couldn't, overtaken as they were by unruly passions, fancifulness, vanity, or slavish adulation. She was the man! The master of herself, passions included!

Reason was God-given solely to human beings, though Wollstonecraft remarked in a Platonic note that animals might be granted reason in the next stage of life: if they are to mount in the scale of life, like men, by the medium of death, reason's development was "an arduous task."[95] Its more extensive cultivation, she claimed, would undeniably promote virtue.[96] She spoke of the cultivation of understanding in a comparable manner and, although she may have used the terms interchangeably, it is probably best to think of understanding as being the ultimate product of reason, though as has been stressed in relation to the imagination, it was not an activity undertaken independently of other parts of the mind. This said, Wollstonecraft's works do not offer, or attempt to offer, a systematic account of the nature of reason and its workings.

This is, in part, because she used "reason" as a battle axe against her opponents. This was especially true in her diatribes against Burke, whom she took, or pretended to take, as denying the importance of reason as the foundation of all knowledge—this view being based, as she presented it, on his criticisms of the French revolutionaries and their followers in Britain for attempting to reconstruct society and government based on reason. Care must therefore be taken when considering her pronouncements

93. *VM*, p. 27 and p. 30.
94. Ibid., p. 7.
95. *VM*, p. 31.
96. Ibid., p. 33.

about reason, rationality, and kindred concepts in the *Vindication of the Rights of Men* and also the *Vindication of the Rights
of Woman*, in which she likewise used the positive connotation
of "reason" as ammunition. Wrapping herself in it, whilst divest-
ing her opponents of it, be they Burke or Rousseau, made reason
appear the privileged faculty in both her *Vindications*, but this is
not the case when we consider her thought in the main.

Thus, while she believed in natural benevolence, she asserted
in the first *Vindication* that "I know not of any common nature
or common relation amongst men but what results from reason." "The common affections and passions," she continued,
"equally bind brutes together; and it is only the continuity of
those relations that entitles us to the denomination of rational
creatures; and this continuity arises from reflection—from the
operations of that reason which you [Burke] contemn [*sic*] with
flippant disrespect."[97] Here, we can presume her to be thinking
of society and government rather than more personal relations.
It was measured reflection on our social and political relations
that made for their continuity, in her view, a continuity absent
among animals. From this, Wollstonecraft went on to claim that
since reason improved as it was being exercised, so those who
used it most could be called upon in times of crisis to exercise
command over others; these were "the persons pointed out by
Nature to direct the society of which they make a part, on any
extraordinary emergency."[98] This offers us another instance of
Wollstonecraft's belief in a natural elite, one called forth to leadership in times of crises.

In *A Vindication of the Rights of Woman*, she contended that
children should be taught to submit to reason, by which she
meant reality, as early as possible. This did not reverse her position on the importance of the imagination in early education,
but rather it asserted the need to comprehend the nature of

97. Ibid., pp. 40–41.
98. Ibid., p. 41.

things and of God.[99] They had to learn to understand the world as it was. For this, reason needed to be exercised and fortified. It required strength and independence of mind to be exerted, something of which Wollstonecraft herself claimed to have been capable, enabling her to "view, with indignation, the mistaken notions that enslave my sex."[100] But if reason required independence, its right use alone made for independence from everything, "excepting unclouded Reason—'whose service is perfect freedom.'"[101] Thus, Wollstonecraft thought of God as perfect reason. "The stamen of immortality, if I may be allowed the phrase, is the perfectibility of human reason," she wrote in a surprising choice of botanical word, "[f]or, were man created perfect, or did a flood of knowledge break in upon him, when he arrived at maturity, that precluded error, I should doubt whether his existence would be continued after the dissolution of the body."[102]

Somewhat inexplicably, she continued by revealing that every unresolved difficulty in moral philosophy, everything that "baffles the investigation of profound thing, and the lightning glance of genius," contributed to her belief in the immortality of the soul.[103] This aside, she went on to define reason as "the simple power of improvement; or, more properly speaking, of discerning truth." Reiterating and qualifying in one stroke her view of the unity of mankind, she wrote:

> Every individual is in this respect a world in itself. More or less may be conspicuous in one being than another; but the nature of reason must be the same in all, if it be an emanation of divinity, the tie that connects the creature with the Creator; for, can that soul be stamped the heavenly image, that is not perfected by the exercise of its own reason.[104]

99. *VW*, p. 248.
100. Ibid., p. 107.
101. Ibid., p. 206.
102. Ibid., pp. 126–127.
103. Ibid., p. 127.
104. *VW*, pp. 126–127.

Thus, while reason was a faculty present in all human beings, every individual perfected it in a particular manner, depending on circumstances and experiences.

While she often wrote of the faculty as linking mankind to the divine, reason does not always emerge as particularly attractive from her work. Wollstonecraft spoke of it casting "her sober light."[105] Its arguments are said to be "cold" in contrast to the powers of the imagination.[106] "Modesty, temperance, and self-denial" are her "sober offspring," though later, in a *Vindication of the Rights of Woman*, the parentage of modesty includes sensibility tempered by reflection.[107] Reason labors to tame the passions, even Wollstonecraft's own.[108] It "destroys sublimity."[109] Associated with discipline and restraint, these depictions of reason need to be understood in the discursive contexts in which they occur. For a polemist like Wollstonecraft, the positive connotation "reason" had in many eighteenth-century debates made it a weapon of choice in her arsenal. As she well knew, it acquired added power for being yielded by a woman.

This said, the views Wollstonecraft expressed on reason are straightforwardly consistent. Allowing for the different circumstances in which she was writing, her objectives can be taken to demonstrate the need as well as the difficulties of acquiring a well-adjusted mind. She believed this required the development of reason, its power to generalize from individual sense experiences, and, of great importance, its operation with and alongside the other intellectual faculties, in a cooperative and balanced manner. In a perfected mind, reason would not act in isolation. Indeed, such a perfection also made demands of the body.

---

105. Ibid., pp. 106, 118.
106. *VM*, pp. 9, 48.
107. *VW*, p. 161 and pp. 207, 218.
108. Ibid., p. 225.
109. *Hints*, p. 300.

Mind, Body, and Soul

Under "Benevolence" in *Thoughts on the Education of Daughters* (1787), Wollstonecraft wrote of a time "when the soul is disentangled from the body, and should be prepared for the realms of love."[110] She used "mind" and "soul" interchangeably and appears never to have departed from a dualist position; she believed in the existence of two substances, a physical and an immaterial one. And while she spoke repeatedly of the soul departing from the body, she thought of the two substances in unison. Just as she talked of the different faculties, so she thought that the mind and the body should make for a harmonious whole in life; both had to be developed, that is, strengthened.

It was, however, essential that individuals not allow themselves to be entrapped by artifice and all those vain earthly matters that hindered intellectual development and a spiritual life: "Have ye not heard that we cannot serve two masters?" Mary Wollstonecraft exclaimed in *A Vindication of the Rights of Men*; "an immoderate desire to please," she continued, "contracts the faculties and immerges [*sic*], to borrow the idea of a great philosopher, the soul in matter, till it becomes unable to mount on the wing of contemplation."[111]

That she believed the body should mirror the mind is evidenced in *Original Stories* when Mrs. Mason, the educator, tells one of her charges, Caroline,

> good features, and a fine complexion, I term *bodily* beauty. The soul of beauty, my dear children, consists in the body gracefully exhibiting the emotions and variations of the informing mind. If truth, humanity and knowledge inhabit

110. *Works*, Vol. 4, p. 43.
111. *VW*, p. 23. The great philosopher is Plato. I have discussed Wollstonecraft's views on the immortality of the soul at greater length in "'Have Ye Not Heard That We Cannot Serve Two Masters?.'"

the breast, the eyes will beam with a mild lustre, modesty will suffuse the cheeks, and smiles of innocent joy play over all the features. At first sight, regularity and colour will attract, and have the advantage, because the hidden springs are not directly set in motion; but when internal goodness is reflected, every other kind of beauty, the shadow of it, wither away before it, as the sun obscures a lamp.

You are certainly handsome, Caroline; I mean, have good features; but you must improve your mind to give them a pleasing expression, or they will only serve to lead your understanding astray.[112]

If the mind needed to be reflected in the body, and its beauty transmitted to the body, its own strength rested on that of the body.[113] The body had to be exercised from youth, and Wollstonecraft deplored the fact that girls were not only not encouraged to exercise, but positively discouraged from doing so, owing to false conceptions of their nature and of beauty. In her view, weakened bodies presaged weakened minds and dependency.[114] It was her experience, Wollstonecraft wrote, that those women who had shown "any vigour of intellect, have accidentally been allowed to run wild," in other words, they were what is still often called "Tom boys."[115] She asked that girls "by being allowed to take the same exercise as boys, not only during infancy, but in youth, arrive at perfection of body, that we may know how far the natural superiority of man extends."[116] We might recall how much Wollstonecraft herself enjoyed exercise, particularly walking in the countryside. There is no doubt that she thought a strong mind required a strong body, and that the well-being

112. *Works*, Vol. 4, p. 390.
113. *VW*, p. 160.
114. Ibid., p. 165.
115. Ibid., p. 115.
116. Ibid., p. 165.

of the one was intrinsically connected to that of the other. If she had needed to be persuaded to write *A Vindication of the Rights of Woman*, the passage (which she quoted in *A Vindication of the Rights of Men*) in Burke's *A Philosophical Enquiry into the Origin of our Ideas of the Sublime and Beautiful* (1757) in which he described women "labour[ing] to be pretty, by counterfeiting weakness" would have been sufficient for her to set pen to paper. She would not suffer to see beauty and power so disassociated and was eager that women as well as men be rendered strong in body as well as mind from infancy. That ought to be the aim of education, and that was the education that she consistently proposed.

Here again Wollstonecraft thought on this historically. Reflecting on Grecian statues, and quite apart from her admiration of them as transcending a "servile copy of even beautiful nature," it bears repeating that she revealed that: "I believe that the human form must have been far more beautiful than it is at present, because extreme indolence, barbarous ligatures, and many causes, which forcibly act on it, in our luxurious state of society, did not retard its expansion, or render it deformed." The body, like the mind, also admitted of a historical perspective, according to Wollstonecraft.

The physical could however not be divorced from the rest of the person, even when considering beauty:

> Exercise and cleanliness appear to be not only the surest causes only considered; yet, this is not sufficient, moral ones must concur, or beauty will be merely of that rustic kind which blooms on the innocent, wholesome, countenances of some country people, whose minds have not been exercised. To render the person perfect, physical and moral beauty ought to be attained at the same time; each lending and receiving force by combination.[117]

117. *VW*, pp. 267–268.

That individuals had to be thought of as a totality of mind and body, not even just two parts working harmoniously, was one of the refrains in her writings, and of the greatest importance to her views on educational practice.

The Will

If by a free will, one understands (as is no doubt unlikely) a will unaffected by understanding, then Wollstonecraft did not believe the will was free. What little she wrote on the topic, which can be found principally in a small part of her review of Catharine Macaulay's *Letters on Education: with Observations on Religious and Metaphysical Subjects* (1790), left no doubt as to her impatience with the debate between those she called "Free-Willers" and "necessitarians." Education was the key to moral conduct.[118] Neither philosophical position could deny, in her view, the need to cultivate the mind and instill good habits, for neither could deny that education was necessary to discern good from evil, nor that familial and social environments were morally formative. Thus, she quoted Macaulay approvingly in her contention that "By the explanation of those different circumstances in the course of human life, which give rise to the two opposite necessities of doing good, or doing evil, it will appear, that bad governors, bad tutors, and bad company, are the primary authors of all the evil volitions of the species; and that ignorance is a foil in which no uniform virtue can take root and flourish."[119] Both women were insistent that neither philosophical school of thought could conceivably refute this in theory, let alone in practice.

118. On Macaulay, Wollstonecraft, and education, see Elizabeth Frazer, "Mary Wollstonecraft and Catharine Macaulay on Education," *Oxford Review of Education* 37, no. 5 (2011): 603–617; see also Gunther-Canada, "Cultivating Virtue"; Green and Weekes, "Catharine Macaulay on the Will."

119. Vol. 8 (1790), *Works*, Vol. 7, p. 321.

Brief though her discussion of the will may be, it ranks as one of her most fundamental tenets of her belief that habituation is key to character formation.[120] Human beings were what they were taught to be either explicitly by those educating them or through the imitation of the models, good or bad, before them. The will was shaped primarily by early training or indeed by lack of it, and to some degree by subsequent experience. A judicious education that made for the development of the faculties at appropriate times in the growth of the mind and body prepared human beings to act as they should in adult life. The lack of it made for individuals who could not control themselves. Wollstonecraft did not deny the will a place in an account of human action, but she did not underscore its presence. It was not a separate function of the self-command she so valued. The world, as she saw it, was divided between those who possessed self-control and those who did not. It was essential therefore that selves be such as to control themselves, that is, that they be formed to be able to do what they ought. Rightful habituation in early life did not, in her view, imply a subsequent life of perpetual imitation or preclude originality or genius. Quite the contrary, it allowed for the possibility of the making of character and individuality as foundations are to an architectural structure. This does not resolve the difficulties attending the philosophical problem of freedom of the will, but Wollstonecraft did go some way toward developing a theory of the mind and associated pedagogical theory that would help eradicate slavish adherence to unexamined beliefs and false needs and desires.

120. For an extensive discussion of the importance of education, particularly primary education for Wollstonecraft, see Botting, "Theories of Human Development: Wollstonecraft and Mill on Sex, Gender, and Education," in *Wollstonecraft, Mill, and Women's Human Rights.* For an account of Wollstonecraft as holding an Aristotelian conception of virtue, see Bergès, *Wollstonecraft's* A Vindication of the Rights of Woman.

The Passions, the Appetites, and Emotions

Wollstonecraft made frequent mention of passions and appetites, often as if they were so closely tied as to blur distinction. When she did separate them, the passions rose and the
appetites sank, and in at least one instance collapsed into one:
[p]assions are spurs to action, and open the mind; but they sink
into mere appetites, become personal and momentary gratification, when the object is gained, and the satisfied mind rests in
enjoyment."[121] On this view, love was a passion, lust (along with
hunger and thirst) an appetite, and the one could descend into
the other. Yet, whether emotional or biological, here again what
mattered was their being fashioned in the morally appropriate
form:

> Children are born ignorant, consequently innocent; the pas-
> sions, are neither good nor evil dispositions, till they receive
> a direction, and either bound over the feeble barrier raised
> by a faint glimmering of unexercised reason, called con-
> science, or strengthen her wavering dictates till sound princi-
> ples are deeply rooted, and able to cope with the headstrong
> passions that often assume her awful form. What moral
> purpose can be answered by extolling good dispositions, as
> they are called, when these good dispositions are described
> as instincts: for instinct moves in a direct line to its ultimate
> end, and asks not for guide or support. But if virtue is to be
> acquired by experience, or taught by example, reason, per-
> fected by reflection, must be the director of the whole host of
> passions, which produce a fructifying heat, but no light, that
> you would exalt into her place.—She must hold the rudder,
> or, let the wind blow which way it list, the vessel will never
> advance smoothly to its destined port; for the time lost in
> tracking about would dreadfully impede its progress.[122]

121. *VW*, p. 100.
122. *VM*, pp. 31–32.

Though this passage from the first *Vindication*, and, as discussed already, *A Vindication of the Rights of Woman* as a whole, portrays Wollstonecraft as wanting reason to dominate over the passions and indeed human beings in their entirety, it would be wrong to think these were her unqualified views and, by implication, that she desired the passions and appetites to be silenced. In considering her view of poetry, we saw she thought of it as the language of the passions working with the imagination and furthermore that "reason has no right to rein-in the imagination," adding, "if the passion is real, the head will not be ransacked for false tropes and cold rodomande."[123]

Speaking more particularly of the emotion of love, she insisted even in *A Vindication of the Rights of Woman* that those "who complain of the delusions of passion, do not recollect that they are exclaiming against a strong proof of the immortality of the soul." If feelings combined with the imagination to make heavenly love, the imagination "can then depict love with celestial charms, and dote on the grand ideal object—it can imagine a degree of mutual affection that shall refine the soul, and not expire when it has served as a 'scale to heavenly'; and, like devotion, make it absorb every meaner affection and desire."[124]

While there is no question that Wollstonecraft thought the passions and the appetites were morally hazardous in the absence of a sound education and the acquisition of good habits, she underscored their absolute necessity and reminded her readers to think of them in relation to different stages of human life. The intensity and kind of passions appropriate to the young were not so to those advanced in age. Passions were the spring to action, without them nothing would be achieved: "The youth should *act*; for had he the experience of a grey head he would be fitter for death than life, though his virtues, rather residing in his head than his heart, could produce nothing great, and his

123. Ibid., p. 28.
124. *VW*, p. 152.

understanding, prepared for this world, would not, by its noble flights, prove that it had a title to a better."[125] Quite apart from revealing that *A Vindication of the Rights of Woman* was far from having been written solely with women in mind, the section from which this passage comes demonstrates once again that Wollstonecraft thought of moral life as writers from Aristotle onward had, namely, as best conceived in its entirety and consisting of periods in which different emotions, experiences, and behavior were appropriate.[126] "Besides," she continued, "it is not possible to give a young person a just view of life; he must have struggled with his own passions before he can estimate the force of the temptation which betrayed his brother into vice." Adding: "Those who are entering life, and those who are departing, see the world from such very different points of view, that they can seldom think alike, unless the unfledged reason of the former never attempted a solitary flight."[127]

That Wollstonecraft's pronouncements on the mind and morality must be seen as relative to the stage of life of the individuals concerned together with the historical stage of their society is important in many respects, but particularly so in relation to her views on the condition of women, whom she saw as preserved in childhood, and a false one at that, throughout their lives. By contrast, she thought the education of men as it was being advocated by Rousseau's immensely feted *Émile* (1762) made the young old before their years. She expressed this most clearly in a review in August 1789 of the Rev. David Williams's *Lectures on Education. Read to a Society for promoting reasonable and humane Improvements in the Discipline and Instruction of Youth* (1789), which she thought took the best from Rousseau, leaving the paradoxes in his work on education behind:

125. Ibid., p. 195.
126. For a reading of Wollstonecraft that underscores the influence of Greek philosophers on her thinking, see N. F. Taylor, *The Rights of Woman as Chimera.*
127. *VW*, pp. 195–196.

Blinded by his prevailing idea, Rousseau, forgetting that he was a warm advocate for the immortality of the soul, endeavours to crowd into the spring-tide of youth, (when vivacity quickly throws off uneasy impressions) the important employment of riper years, the whole business of matured reason; he wished to make his pupil as perfect at the moment he launched into life, as men ought to be when they have finished their task, and nobly employed their faculties. He carefully, and arbitrarily, fixes the divisions of time, during the years dedicated to education, and overlooks the natural divisions of life into seasons, which may be reckoned distinct, though they smoothly unite without the storm he so poetically describes.[128]

Those were not Wollstonecraft's only objections to Rousseau's pedagogy. Her *Vindication of the Rights of Woman* contributed to making his views of the education of girls notorious. It is important to see that, while she generally approved of his philosophy of education for boys and would have wanted him not to exclude girls from it, she homed in on his inability, as she contentiously perceived it, to recognize that there was a time for everything, when it came to human development male as well as female, that is, a stage in the life of children and adults for the nurturing and flourishing of particular aspects of the mind and character.

Concluding Reflections

A chapter on Wollstonecraft's beliefs concerning human nature and the human mind should begin and end with God, the very last word of her *Vindication of the Rights of Men*. The preceding will have made apparent that neither He, nor spiritual life more generally, is ever far from any of Wollstonecraft's pages. As Todd has remarked, "Wollstonecraft thought about religion all

---

128. *Analytical Review*, Vol. 4 (1789), *Works*, Vol. 7, 141.

her life," though she thought about some aspects of it more so in some periods than others.[129] While she was no doubt mindful of her professedly Christian audience and never missed any opportunity to use the tenets of Christianity to support her arguments when she could do so, especially with what might be her more recalcitrant readers, she seemed to believe in a Providential order for much of her life and wrote within a Creationist framework.[130] She often spoke of the mind and the soul interchangeably and, on occasion, of its existence in an afterlife. Her anti-clericalism, to which she gave expression in *A Vindication of the Rights of Men*, and her repeated criticisms of religion in her subsequent works, especially but not solely of Catholicism, did not appear to eradicate her faith in a benevolent God. Even in that first *Vindication*, she affirmed that religion was part of her "idea of morality."[131] Her letters to her sisters and friends attest to this as they do to her wrangling with the question of the existence of evil in a divinely created universe. She quoted William Paley's *Principles of Moral and Political Philosophy* (1785) to her sister, Eliza, in June 1787, writing that she particularly admired his short definition of virtue: "Virtue is the doing of good to mankind, in obedience to the *will* of God, and for the sake of everlasting happiness."[132] In the last years of her life, she continued to think of herself as part of divine creation, as when she wrote from Hamburg in September 1795 to Imlay that

> [t]he tremendous power who formed this heart, must have foreseen that, in a world in which self-interest, in various shapes, is the principal mobile, I had little chance of escaping misery.—To the fiat of fate I submit. I am content to be wretched; but I will not be contemptible.[133]

129. *Letters*, p. 75, n.165.
130. See Sapiro, *A Vindication of Political Virtue*, pp. 45–52, 231–232.
131. *VM*, p. 7.
132. *Letters*, p. 130.
133. Ibid., p. 322.

And when she had cause to suffer again, this time from Godwin's attention to other women, she wrote in a similar vein on July 4, 1797, thus just a few months before her death: "I am absurd to look for the affection which I have only found in my own tormented heart; and how can you blame me for taken [*sic*] refuge in the idea of a God, when I despair of finding sincerity on earth."[134]

If she found consolation in faith, her writings did not exhort it in others. What they did from first to last was to underscore that life on earth, given the present condition of humanity, required strength of character and body. It demanded a harmonious operation of the faculties in a fit physique to be able to contend with the inevitable vicissitudes of life. What precisely made for such psychological harmony amongst the mind's parts and what their individual nature and function specifically were is not to be found in Wollstonecraft. Whether it is in the works of any of her contemporaries or later philosophers is an open question. What is without a doubt, if only judging by the content of her *Hints* toward what would have been a sequel to *A Vindication of the Rights of Woman*, is that she was not only deeply interested in the makeup of the mind throughout her short life as an author, but believed that a philosophy of mind or at the very least some consideration of it was prerequisite to any pedagogical, social, and political program.

The following chapters will return to the subjects discussed in the present one, which sought to stress Wollstonecraft's belief in the unity of mankind, its natural benevolence, and the importance of a balanced mind in which the faculties are educated to work with each other, differently at different periods of human individual development and at different stages of human history, but always in a robust body. In an ideal environment, education would ensure that boys and girls were habituated in the right manner, to recognize right from wrong, and be desirous of doing

134. Ibid., p. 428.

the one and not the other and treat all living creatures well. Such education would lead to the development of character and individuality, not hinder them. Youthful minds were pliable and "warm affections [were] easily wrought on."[135] A strong formation in the right milieu was essential: "[t]he most shining abilities, and the most amiable dispositions of the mind, require culture, and a proper situation, not only to ripen and improve them, but to guard them against the perversions of vice, and the contagious influence of bad examples."[136] Yet such was not the prevailing reality, especially not for girls. The young neither received the right education nor were they free of "bad examples." On the contrary, their environment had a distorting effect at every turn and elevated corrupting models to be followed mindlessly. While Wollstonecraft may not have joined a chorus of contemporary authors calling for a strengthening of religious faith, she certainly did endeavor to expose false idols.[137] In her *Vindication of the Rights of Woman*, a work that gave further expression to the anti-clericalism of her first *Vindication*, she strongly criticized the way in which religion was taught, especially at schools and colleges that retained "the relick of popery."[138] However, faith was a very different matter, and this is illustrated by her declaring: "That civilization, that the cultivation of the understanding, and refinement of the affections, naturally make a man religious, I am proud to acknowledge."[139] Something had clearly gone seriously amiss for society to be so far from the fair and equitable world that a benevolent humanity would be expected to have maintained.

135. *Education of Daughters, Works*, Vol. 4, p. 45.

136. Ibid.

137. See Harriet Guest, *Small Change: Women, Learning, Patriotism, 1750–1810* (London: University of Chicago Press, 2000).

138. *VW*, pp. 254–255.

139. *VM*, p. 40.

CHAPTER THREE

What Went Wrong?

THE WORLD AS IT WAS

AS WOLLSTONECRAFT LOOKED AROUND HER, she saw war, poverty, inequality, subjugation, ignorance, and enslavement. Humanity was divided between warring nations, the rich and poor, the envied and the scorned, the enlightened and the prejudiced. She sought to expose the actual condition of humanity and railed against its inequities and, as we saw most particularly so, against slavery. The language and images of enslavement infused her rhetoric as she deplored other types of subjugation: the subjugation of children to parents, of women to men, of men to one another, and the true to the false self. To be sure, her pronouncements on these, as on any other subjects, have to be taken in context; but she condemned all manner of domination and their attendant inequities, even as she was well-aware that some would be very difficult to eradicate. She valued independence and abhorred all forms of dependencies. Unsurprisingly, she had little, if any, acceptance of deference in her own life or writings, and while she does not come across consistently as a leveler of all social distinctions, she came close to that position, if only by implication, on occasion.

She saw the human species as marked by vanity. The desire to shine and thereby stand above others seemed to taint humanity. Burke, Rousseau, and Adam Smith among many contemporary authors also perceived it as such and did so in the wake of many predecessors, such as Hobbes, who described it using a variety of terms, most often "pride." Her condemnation of the domination of others, be it those of a different race, class, or gender, must not, however, obscure her efforts to highlight what might be called servitudes to the self, through false desires and beliefs, including delusions of superiority or inferiority to others. These she endeavored to expose and she ridiculed them in her writings. Racial, social, interpersonal subjugations and enslavement to one's own desires and pursuits were intricately related. No form of domination stood on its own, and oppressing others was part and parcel of a web of dependencies, including to false needs and psychological addictions. This makes unraveling her views on any one of these subjects in isolation somewhat challenging and on occasion problematic. While her opinions on these and related issues are recognizable, if not all fully voiced, in her first publications and early correspondence, they came together in her first *Vindication*, that on the rights of men, arguably her most thought-provoking work. They were then expanded in her second *Vindication*, where responding to Burke's *Reflections* prompted her to attempt to establish the sources of social and political distortions. *A Vindication of the Rights of Man, In a Letter to the Right Honourable Edmund Burke; occasioned by his reflections on the Revolution in France* therefore provides much of the basis of what follows, but one needs to also draw on her subsequent works, including her second *Vindication*, and those written during her time in revolutionary France and her travels in Northern Europe to obtain a better sense of her understanding of the course humanity had taken to arrive at the social order she knew and deplored.

Benevolence, we saw Wollstonecraft perceived as a natural human trait. Yet, she evidently did not think that contemporary society reflected this. It had to be nurtured to be sure, but why had it not been? What, in her view, was the root cause of what was wrong with the world: Social distinctions? Ancient institutions? Hereditary rule? Wealth? Scarcity? Men? Women? Aspects of human nature? However pronounced the wrongs might have been in her own time, Wollstonecraft did not consider the history of mankind as the tale of a fall from an idyllic first or so-called primitive society, least of all as she composed her later books. More often than not, she seemed to think that the rot had in essence set in from the start. Yet hers was not a view of humanity marked by original sin—quite the contrary, as Sapiro and other scholars have rightly argued.[1] Mankind as a whole was perfectible, as were individuals.

Evil and Perfection

By the last few years of her tragic life, Wollstonecraft thought better of civilization than she had ever done previously and certainly than she allowed herself to do at the time of her response to what she presented to her readers as Burke's unqualified defense of the status quo and ancient, or in her word "gothic," institutions. Yet, she had never entirely condemned it. "The more I see of the world," she was to write from Gothenburg in the early summer of 1795, "the more I am convinced that civilization is a blessing not sufficiently estimated by those who have not traced its progress; for it not only refines our enjoyments, but provides a variety which enables us to retain the primitive delicacy of our sensations."[2] Judged by her own standards, she was in an ideal position to appreciate civilization, having just traced its progress, prior to her setting off on her four-month journey through Northern Europe, in her *An Historical and*

1. Sapiro, *A Vindication of Political Virtue*, pp. 43–52.
2. *Letters Written during a Short Residence in Sweden, Norway, and Denmark*, *Works*, Vol. 6, p. 250.

Moral View of the Origin and Progress of the French Revolution; and the Effect It Has Produced in Europe. It is more than likely that composing that work led her to continue to reflect on the history of humanity and the nature of civilization while in Scandinavia.

Although her assessments of the civilizing process in her *The French Revolution* did not depart entirely from her earlier position on the subject, they were developed and modified to an extent. She had long quarreled with the view—generally associated with Rousseau since his *Discours sur l'origine et les fondements de l'inégalité parmi les hommes* (1754)—that the history of humanity was one of decline, let alone that this was inevitably so. As she had already memorably declared in *A Vindication of the Rights of Woman*: "Rousseau exerts himself to prove that all *was* right originally: a crowd of authors that all *is* now right: and I, that all will be right."[3] Rousseau's significance as one of Wollstonecraft's important interlocutors should not be overestimated relative to that of Burke, for instance; given the popularity of his pedagogical work, *Émile, ou De l'éducation* (1762), throughout Europe, Wollstonecraft could not but engage with it in *A Vindication of the Rights of Woman,* for although she shared its aspiration to raise independent men, she greatly deplored its aim to raise dependent women. The educational prescriptions it contained for women, namely that they should be both a creation for man's delight and dutiful mothers, epitomized everything she stood against. As we glimpsed already, she mocked or denigrated the man himself and praised him in near equal amounts, going beyond exposing the internal contradictions of the one work she sought to demolish, to deride Rousseau's other publications. She was well acquainted with his work, not least as a result of having reviewed two translations of *Les Pensées de J. J. Rousseau* (1763) in October 1788, publications on him, including one by Madame de Staël in May 1789, works that quoted him

3. *VW*, p. 82.

extensively, and in April 1790, the *Second Part of Confessions of J. J. Rousseau* (1784). Like Burke, Rousseau shaped part of Wollstonecraft's thinking, not because she agreed with him, but because clashing with him as she did with the author of *Reflections* forced her to engage on his intellectual terrain, the questions he had addressed, and the replies he gave to them. As a result, *A Vindication of the Rights of Woman* is so much more than it might have been. What could have been a straightforward treatise itemizing her recommendations for the education of girls became a complex critique of civilization, with reflections on its history mixed with quarrels both old and new with the principal theorists she chose as adversaries, and reflections on the moral and political topics that emerged as a result.

A Vindication of the Rights of Woman opens with what might be called "the civilization question," one that incorporated inquiries about its course, virtues, and failings as well as its engine, its beneficiaries, and its victims. Its introduction begins with the confession: "After considering the historic page, and viewing the living world with anxious solicitude, the most melancholy emotions of sorrowful indignation have depressed my spirits, and I have sighed when obliged to confess, that either nature has made a great difference between man and man, or that the civilization which has hitherto taken place in the world has been very partial."[4] In fact, although she would not own it outright, Wollstonecraft held both these views. She did to some degree think nature had made a great difference between man and man taken as individuals and believed unqualifiedly that civilization had been a very partial phenomenon. In the introduction, she chose to pursue the latter view, namely, that the civilizing process had been uneven. She went on to say that "the neglected education of my fellow-creatures is the grand source of the misery I deplore; and that women, in particular, are rendered weak and wretched

4. *VW*, p. 74.

by a variety of concurring causes."[5] Whatever progress had been achieved and however partial it might be, it had been enjoyed only by men—indeed, only by some men. History was effectively lopsided, a reading of the history of civilization that J. S. Mill was to share in *The Subjection of Women* (1869).[6] The minds of women were not in a healthy state, Wollstonecraft explained; returning to the motif of temporality we saw her emphasize in the previous chapter, she wrote: "for, like the flowers which are planted in too rich a soil, strength and usefulness are sacrificed to beauty; and the flaunting leaves, after having pleased a fastidious eye, fade, disregarded on the stalk, long before the season when they ought to have arrived at maturity."[7] One cause of this, she contended, was that females were treated as creatures whose sole aspiration was to inspire love rather than as autonomous rational human beings, "when they ought to cherish a nobler ambition, and by their abilities and virtues exact respect."[8] Although she specifically mentioned "the civilized women of the present century," there was nothing in the rest of the work, or indeed in *A Vindication of the Rights of Men*, to suggest that this condition was a relatively new occurrence, one without precedent in the history of humanity.

Was that it then? Was the civilization question to be solved by resolving the woman question? Would providing the right kind of education to women be the answer? Would it rectify the lopsided nature of civilization? If there had not been a revolution in France, and Wollstonecraft had not risen to the defense of the Rev. Richard Price in the face of Burke's attack on him in his *Reflections*, it is likely that the *Vindication of the Rights of Woman* would have redressed the wrong by educating the other half of humanity. To be sure, the second *Vindication* does that,

5. Ibid.

6. *The Subjection of Women*. See Botting, *Wollstonecraft, Mill, and Women's Human Rights*, chapter 3.

7. *VW*, p. 74.

8. Ibid.

but it is also much more than that precisely because of Wollstonecraft's reactions to Price, Burke, and the French Revolution.

Thus, the first chapter of *A Vindication of the Rights of Woman* tackles the civilization question and the nature of mankind with which the work as a whole begins. What distinguished man from the rest of animal creation was reason, Wollstonecraft maintained. The perfection of the species could be measured, she thought, in relation to its development. Wollstonecraft did not deny that it had indeed developed, but, not pointing to the condition of women in this instance, she claimed that most of mankind used their enhanced rational powers to defend prejudices and untruths. These would, of course, have included unsubstantiated notions about femininity and falsehoods about women, but instead of focusing on them, she returned to a subject raised by her engagement with Burke in her first *Vindication*. Reason had been and was being used against itself, to deprive men (or women) of their natural rights and to justify "the wretchedness that has flowed from hereditary honours, riches, and monarchy" as the "dispensations of providence," and thus seemingly rational arguments were presenting the evil in the world as the product of unalterable divine will.[9] She was throwing a punch in Burke's direction here, but she immediately launched one toward Rousseau as well. It should be noted from the onset, however, that the Rousseau with whom Wollstonecraft chose to wrestle was not the Rousseau a less combative reading would take him to be. He was not committed to the positions she attributed to him in relation to the state of nature, or at least not as she presented them.

So according to her interpretation of his work, by preferring the state of nature to civilization, Rousseau was also misusing reason. Based on the false hypothesis that man was a solitary animal by nature, his arguments, while "plausible," were "unsound"; it was "as unphilosophical as impious" to believe

9. *VW*, pp. 80–81.

that man had been created to live alone in a stationary state, for
how could an omnipotent, omniscient, and benevolent God have
made all things right, including mankind, and knowingly made
it evil and stationary. It was Wollstonecraft's belief that God had
willed the passions to unfold human reason, "because he could
see that present evil would produce future good."[10] That was
how she dealt with the problem of evil. It was indeed the product of a God-given human nature, but that same nature could,
and needed to, be perfected; its intellectual and moral character were perfectible through the activity of the passions, as He
willed it. The state of nature, even when rendered by Rousseau's
skillful argumentation, could not possibly be conceived "as a
state in which a single virtue took root."[11] That man had been
created to remain in a state in which he could not blossom as
a moral and rational being was a position wholly incompatible
with God's nature. It would mean that mankind had been created for no purpose other than to decorate His garden. As someone who believed (as she did) in the immortality of the soul,
Rousseau could not consistently think such a thing. In a series
of rhetorical questions she asked what God's purpose in creating
mankind could conceivably be thought to be if not to improve
ourselves through his "inestimable gift" and thus "to rise above
the state in which sensation produced brutal ease":

> For why should the gracious fountain of life give us passions,
> and the power of reflecting, only to imbitter our days and
> inspire us with mistaken notions of dignity? Why should he
> lead us from love of ourselves to the sublime emotions which
> the discovery of his wisdom and goodness excites, if these
> feelings were not set in motion to improve our nature, of
> which they make a part, and render us capable of enjoying a
> more godlike portion of happiness?

10. Ibid., p. 81.
11. Ibid.

By contrast to Rousseau, Wollstonecraft continued, she was "[f]irmly persuaded that no evil exists in the world that God did not design to take place," and she built this "belief on the perfection of God."[12]

Diverging forms of the belief in the perfectibility of man were widely held in the eighteenth century, including by Rousseau and Godwin. As she made clear, Wollstonecraft's was grounded in a Providential view of human nature. Though she was not to reiterate the point as she did so explicitly in *A Vindication of the Rights of Woman*, there is no reason to think that her trust in perfectibility was stubbed out in the latter part of her life, though the horrors she was to witness in France under the Terror made it falter. As suggested previously, she also appears to have retained her faith until the end of her life, though it too may have wavered at certain low points in her life. Where Rousseau had gone wrong, she contended, was to see only the evils attendant to every stage of society, without thinking of "tracing the gigantic mischief up to arbitrary power, up to hereditary distinctions that clash with the mental superiority that naturally raises a man above his fellows."[13] Having asserted this, Wollstonecraft went on to decry standing armies, the navy, and the clergy. Any profession that required subordination to rank as opposed to ability was necessarily "highly injurious to morality."[14] Given that she made a point of noting their indolence, she might also have added that any profession that allowed for periods of idleness, which standing armies and the navy invariably did, had a negative effect not only on the men themselves but also on the inhabitants, especially the women, of the communities in which they happened to be stationed. We will follow these thoughts further in this chapter. Insofar as her disagreement with Rousseau went, she concluded the first chapter of her second *Vindication* with

12. Ibid., p. 82. See Sapiro, *A Vindication of Political Virtue*, pp. 44–52.
13. *VW*, p. 83.
14. Ibid., p. 84.

the following: "had Rousseau mounted one step higher in his investigation, or could his eye have pierced through the foggy atmosphere, which he almost disdained to breathe, his active mind would have darted forward to contemplate the perfection of man in the establishment of true civilization, instead of taking his ferocious flight back to the night of sensual ignorance."[15] As Rousseau never claimed that such a return was either possible or desirable, though he was widely caricatured as doing so, not least by Voltaire, and as he endeavored to establish the conditions under which man could fulfil his nature in *Du Contrat Social* (1762), Wollstonecraft can hardly be said to be either a fair or attentive reader of his work, certainly not of that particular work, as Sapiro has rightly noted.[16] Fortunately, accurate Rousseauian scholarship was not Wollstonecraft's business. She was a combatant and sharpened her blade opportunistically. This is not to suggest that the disagreements she had with Rousseau, as she took him to be or presented him as being, were not genuine. However much she, like him, deplored artifice and artificiality, the progress of civilization was not, in her view, a tale of the unqualified alienation of man from nature, and certainly not the story of a secular fall.

Yet it took her sojourn in Northern Europe for Wollstonecraft to appreciate and value the advancement of civilization most fully. There she began to distinguish artificiality from civility and to soften the divide she had so sharply drawn in a *Vindication of the Rights of Men* and a *Vindication of the Rights of Woman* between morality and manners. Traveling through Scandinavia made her think better of the French and France than she ever had. That nation and its people had been associated in her mind with the dictates of superficial politeness and fashionable deportment. Far from such refinements, she ceased

15. Ibid., p. 86.
16. Sapiro, *A Vindication of Political Virtue*, p. 171.

to think of them as unqualified inauthenticity and affectedness, and the benefits of civilization rose in her opinion.

Writing the History of Civilization

While in Scandinavia, Wollstonecraft came to think that one could experience the progress of civilization directly by traveling through Europe. To do so, one had to proceed on a specific route, one that happened to be in the opposite direction of her own travel, and one that included nations normally not included in the Grand Tour: "If travelling, as the completion of a liberal education, were to be adopted on rational ground," she wrote from Copenhagen, "the northern states ought to be visited before the more polished parts of Europe, to serve as the elements even of the knowledge of manners, only to be acquired by tracing the various shades in different countries." However, it was important, she warned, not to let the hospitality one received on one's journey cloud one's judgment and become the gauge of their "virtues." Those she thought to be directly proportionate to "their scientific improvements."[17]

Yet Wollstonecraft did not put forward a systematic or consistent account of the progressive stages of civilization. Although she returned to the topic at various points in *The French Revolution* as well as subsequently, some of the longest unbroken treatment she offered on the subject can be found in Book IV Chapter I of that treatise, written while living in France. The study as a whole was intended to rise above the reactions triggered by the tumult and violence taking place in France, and thereby demonstrate that the revolution had not been caused "by the abilities or intrigues of a few individuals; nor the effect of sudden and short-lived enthusiasm; but the natural consequence of intellectual improvement, gradually proceeding to perfection in the advancement of communities, from a state of barbarism to that

---

17. *Letters Written in Sweden, Norway, and Denmark, Works*, Vol. 6, p. 327.

of polished society, till now arrived at the point when sincerity of principles seems to be hastening the overthrow of the tremendous empire of superstition and hypocrisy, erected up the ruins of gothic brutality and ignorance."[18] *The French Revolution* was essentially, but by no means solely, a resumption of the battle she had waged against Burke's *Reflections* four years earlier in *A Vindication of the Rights of Men*. She continued to engage with the judgment Burke had delivered on the revolution in its early stages as well as his reading of European history. She took him to venerate the past, to think age conferred legitimacy to laws and systems of government, that the status quo had to be preserved intact at all cost, and that he revered the aristocracy and was infatuated with Queen Marie Antoinette. She had other reasons to argue with him, as we have already seen, and would do so again, but those were the principal bones of contention she had with him in *The French Revolution*. It must be said, however, that she did not name him explicitly, quoting him only once, and that her tone in her dispute with him was now more muted.[19] Her appraisal of the English constitution was also more positive, and she became more visibly appreciative of the liberty enjoyed in her own country.

In the advertisement of what she then thought would be the first of two or three further volumes, Wollstonecraft explained that the work had grown under her hand as she needed to describe "manners and things" and had also been led into "several theoretical investigations, whilst marking the political effects that naturally flow from the progress of knowledge."[20] Prominent among these was the question of the origins of society and government, but as it was not her actual subject matter, her views on it are scattered through the text. Yet, her returning to it indicates that it was of obvious interest and importance to

18. *The French Revolution, Works*, vol. 6, pp. 6–7.
19. Ibid., p. 189.
20. Ibid., p. 5.

her and her project, as indeed it had been with renewed vigor since Hugo Grotius's and Thomas Hobbes's respective accounts of the state of nature and the advent of social and political institutions. Her intermittent discussion of the issue led to variations in her accounts that point to some genuine tensions in her thought about the deep cause of humankind's predicament, indeed its very nature.

The opening paragraph of *The French Revolution* described man in his infancy as being miserably weak, taken in isolation from other human beings, and as being crude in "his first notions respecting the nature of civil society," a rather surprising additional characterization, since one might have thought this would have been true of his first notions of anything at all.[21] This original crudeness was taken to explain why it had taken so long for the advent of political knowledge and why "public happiness" had been so slow in being generally diffused. From its onset, then, Wollstonecraft appeared to think that humanity had labored under a fundamental form of stupidity about the political. Although not directly contradictory, this claim did not sit entirely well with what we saw were Wollstonecraft's early reflections that humanity was at its most poetic and eloquent in the first period of its history; it was, she thought, the age in which the imagination flourished. How could the mind both be able to stretch imaginatively beyond its experiences and yet be so incomprehensibly limited? A possible answer is that human beings in the first stage of society had no cause to expect the political tribulations to come and their imaginations might have been exercised by other aspects of their life and environment. Leaving such speculation aside, like all other political theorists, what Wollstonecraft considered to be the state of nature and the first moments of social organization were determined by her own normative objectives. In order to be able to cast the French Revolution as an expression of social and political enlightenment,

21. Ibid., p. 15.

she chose to portray the past as marked by varying degrees of ignorance. In her account of the causes of the revolution, she wished to both stress the increased knowledge humankind had gradually gained over time and present the revolution as a monumental shedding of the false beliefs and prejudices humanity had assimilated in the course of its history. That proved more conceptually difficult than it might have initially appeared.

What she sought to achieve was complicated by the fact that she thought the principles embedded in the *Déclaration des Droits de L'Homme* (1789) to be self-evident truths, so this inevitably raised the question of why they had taken so long to be realized. Indeed, it seems that it was not even wholly evident to her that they were being realized in 1790s France. As we have seen in the preceding chapters, here too she seemed to think men were equal and yet not. She wanted to give an approving account of the forward march of history, while almost always reproving its constitutive features. Her history should have told of the gradual improvement of human understanding, but it did not.

Acknowledging that the Ancient Greeks and Romans had a highly developed culture posed one problem for a gradualist history of human improvement, but it was not the only difficulty. Wollstonecraft wished to show that the benefits of the arts and sciences had been the privileged enjoyment only of the elite, and in so doing seemed rather dismissive of the advantages of the development of the arts and sciences. Yet, while depicting the moral and political corruption of elites, she maintained that the arts and sciences were required for moral emancipation of humanity. But if the arts and sciences had been for the exclusive delight of the privileged, why had even this minority not profited from their morally edifying effects? Had elites been necessary to the flourishing of the arts and sciences or rather had social and political inequality been requisite for them to blossom? As other partly or mostly conjectural histories, hers raised many questions in the process of seeking to answer their chosen one.

It could be said that she wanted to achieve too much in too little time and in difficult personal circumstances, or that she sought to reconcile the intractable. Although some of the incongruities of what was after all entitled a "moral" as well as a "historical" view cannot easily be reconciled, her changing views should not be disregarded nor should their apparent inconsistencies be ignored. Wollstonecraft still proffers some interesting opinions on the state of nature and the subsequent changes mankind underwent before arriving at the stage of the society she lived in and that witnessed an unprecedented social and political revolution.

The State of Nature and First Societies

Wollstonecraft thought that humanity in its infancy was at its most poetic, its mind uncluttered and its imagination lively. If, as mentioned, the first age of man was one of political ignorance, it seems also to have been one of unhampered freedom, according to her. Indeed, Wollstonecraft's overall position might be given greater coherence if one supposes that it was precisely this freedom that made for the underdevelopment and redundancy of "political knowledge":

> Freedom is, indeed, the natural and imprescriptible right of man; without the enjoyment of which, it is impossible for him to become either a reasonable or dignified being. Freedom he enjoys in a natural state, in it's [*sic*] full extent: but formed by nature for a more intimate society, to unfold his intellectual power, it becomes necessary, for carrying into execution the main objects, which induces men to establish communities, that they should surrender a part of their natural privileges, more effectually to guard the most important.[22]

22. Ibid., p. 115.

Unlike Rousseau of the *Social Contract* (1762), Wollstonecraft followed social contract theorists, such as John Locke, in finding this trade-off, a surrender of some liberties to secure the rest, acceptable or at least not inherently unacceptable. She did not think that this in itself led to unfreedom. The creation of society was the product of the need to cooperate and the dependency to which it gave rise was, as we will see shortly, the only form of dependence she found unobjectionable. As stated in the quote above, the purpose of society was also "to unfold [mankind's] intellectual power." Though still enjoying a relatively high degree of freedom as well as imagination, humanity's ignorance in this period, she claimed, had facilitated the rise of domination:

> But from the ignorance of men, during the infancy of society, it was easy for their leaders, by frequent usurpations, to create despotism, which choking up the springs that would have invigorated their minds, they seem to have been insensible to the deprivations under which they lived; and existing like mere animals, the tyrants of the world have continued to treat them only as machines to promote their purposes.[23]

Beyond saying that ignorance facilitated its beginning, she did not, however, explain why such usurpation arose or hypothesize about the motivation behind the subsequent despotism. The assertion of power by one group over another might seem inevitable to an author who thought human beings inherently selfish or vainglorious, but Wollstonecraft believed them to be naturally benevolent. It might also have made some sense from an author who assumed that scarcity was the condition of the state of nature or became so in time, but Wollstonecraft did not make that assumption either. To understand how she might explain the fact that the domination of a few over the many became established at some point in the early history of humanity, one might need to go back to the discussion of her view of evil. Human beings

23. Ibid.

were created with passions, but with limited understanding. The latter had to be developed, she believed, to control, but not altogether overpower, the passions. What were these passions? They really came down to a single one, it would seem from her account in this context—the passion for "wealth or power" and the concomitant domination over others this entailed.

Freedom for Wollstonecraft is not best understood as freedom from the domination of others, even if it were arbitrary. Here I diverge from the readings of Wollstonecraft by Alan Coffee, Sandrine Bergès, and Lena Halldenius.[24] To be sure, she recoiled from the idea of domination by others and fought with all her rhetorical might against the brutal, psychological, and arbitrary domination of slavery, parents over children, men over women, and human beings over animals. The root of the problem for her was the passion for "wealth and power," and the solution for this could never be political in the first instance. No change of government could bring it about, as the dedication of the second edition of the *Vindication of the Rights of Woman* to Talleyrand sought to make clear. It could not be solved externally, however much social and institutional forces were at play in the issue. What was needed was a new order of self-understanding and comprehension of the history of society.[25]

With the advent of relations of power, the progress of humanity was at best uneven. It was the history of a fundamental

24. Lena Halldenius, *Mary Wollstonecraft and Feminist Republicanism* (London: Pickering & Chatto, 2015); Alan Coffee, "Independence as Relational Freedom," *Women Philosophers on Autonomy*, edited by Sandrine Bergès and Alberto Siani (New York and Abingdon, Oxon: Routledge, 2018), pp. 94–112; Alan Coffee, "Marie Wollstonecraft, Public Reason, and the Virtuous Republic," pp.183–200, and Sandrine Bergès, "The Republican Approaches to Motherhood of Mary Wollstonecraft and Sophie de Grouchy," pp. 200–217, in *The Social and Political Philosophy of Mary Wollstonecraft*, edited by Sandrine Bergès and Alan Coffee (Oxford: Oxford University Press, 2016).

25. Onora O'Neil makes a very interesting and comparable point when she argues that it is not so much that we need more trust in society, but that we need to make ourselves more trustworthy. See her *A Question of Trust: The BBC Reith Lectures 2002* (Cambridge: Cambridge University Press, 2002).

imbalance. This was not because the development of the understanding and increased learning of one tier of mankind was unparalleled in those they subordinated. That might have been true in some respects, but, although Wollstonecraft failed to make this clear, the ignorance, however general, was really that of the elites: it was they who failed to comprehend the true essence of political community.

Such a history of humanity was relatively easy to narrate, and that was the one that Wollstonecraft mostly chose to tell. It was the history of oppression, one that followed Rousseau's account of the creation of private property and its subsequent enshrine-ment in iniquitous laws, but differed from him in its very explicit and unqualified trust in political science:

> The first social systems were certainly founded by pas-sion; individuals wishing to fence around their own wealth or power, and make slaves of their brothers to prevent encroachment. Their descendants have ever been at work to solder the chains they forged, and render the usurpation of strength secure, by the fraud of partial laws; laws that can be abrogated only by the exertions of reason, emancipating mankind, by making government a science, instead of a craft, and civilizing the grand mass, by exercising their under-standings about the most important objects of inquiry.[26]

Wollstonecraft's explicit belief in the emancipatory powers of the science of politics is noteworthy here; she had already urged women to engage in it in it in *A Vindication of the Rights of Woman*, and interestingly for our present purpose, she claimed that it was essential for them to study it as an integral part of under-standing the history of man:

> They might, also, study politics, and settle their benevo-lence on the broadest basis, for the reading of history will

26. *The French Revolution, Works*, Vol. 6, p. 18.

scarcely be more useful than the perusal of romances, if read
as mere biography; if the character of the times, the political
improvements, arts, &c. be not observed. In short, if it be
not considered as the history of man; and not of particular
men, who filled a niche in the temple of fame, and dropped
into the black rolling stream of time, that silently sweeps all
before it, into the shapeless void called—eternity.[27]

The progress of political science was, in Wollstonecraft's view,
an index of the advancement of civilization, and her confidence
in the positive effect of the study of politics finds a number of
varying expressions in *The French Revolution*.[28] One of these
was that the incapacity to anticipate future contingencies, indeed
that the future might be different from the present, made the
laws of early societies inflexible and imperfect.[29] Past societies, she thought, could not have foreseen how social participation would unfold the faculties of mankind. The past had not
imagined the future and her present. This meant that past legal
systems could not have a hold on the present; their antiquity did
not, pace Burke, whom Wollstonecraft must have had in mind,
grant them any legitimacy—quite the opposite. The present
afforded radically new possibilities. The peoples of the past, and
especially those in power, had been unconscious of an essential
fact about the human condition which was the extent to which
their own well-being and that of others were interconnected:
"When society was first subjugated to laws, probably by the
ambition of some, and the desire of safety in all, it was natural
for men to be selfish, because they were ignorant how intimately
their own comfort was connected to that of others." This however was no longer necessarily the case; the end of such blind-
ness was now contemplatable: "But, when men once see, clear as
the light of heaven,—and I hail the glorious day from afar!—that

27. *VW*, p. 238.
28. *The French Revolution, Works*, Vol. 6, p. 225.
29. Ibid., p. 20.

on the general happiness depends their own, reason will give strength to the fluttering wings of passion, and men will '*do unto others, what they wish they should do unto them.*'"[30] Wollstonecraft thus envisaged a world in which the command found in Matthew 7:12 would finally be obeyed. She had the imaginative power, the genius, as we saw in the previous chapter, that few others had, to lead mankind toward a realistic utopia, to borrow a phrase from John Rawls.[31]

It must be stressed that Wollstonecraft thought man a quintessentially social being[32] and that she did not renege on her view that mankind was essentially benevolent. Indeed, she asserted that even the Terror did not undermine her ability "to prove that the people are essentially good."[33] Elsewhere in the text, she also put forward a somewhat different account of humanity's infancy, one that did not speak of domination of the few over the many. "Men in a savage state, without intellectual amusements, or even fields or vineyards to employ them, depending on the casual supply of the chace, seem continually to have made war, one with another, or nation with nation," she had contended in Book II, chapter III, adding "and the booty taken from their enemies formed the principal object of contest, because war was not, like industry, a kind of abridgement of their liberty."[34] It was what she next claimed that is most striking and original. Society was the product of a natural sociability allowed to flow in and through the process of the narration of stories by the elderly members of the group:

> But the social feelings of man, after having been exercised by a perilous life, flow over in long stories, when he reaches garrulous old age. Whilst his listening progeny wondering at

30. Ibid., p. 21.
31. Rawls, *The Laws of Peoples*.
32. *The French Revolution, Works*, Vol. 6, p. 223.
33. Ibid., p. 46.
34. Ibid., p. 146.

his feats, their hearts are fired with the ambition of equalling their sire. *His soul is warmed by sympathy, feeling the distresses of his fellow creatures, and particularly for the helpless state of decrepit age; he begins to contemplate, as desirable, associations of men, to prevent the inconveniences arising from loneliness and solitude. Hence little communities living together in the bonds of friendship, securing to them the accumulated powers of man, mark the origin of society: and tribes growing into nations, spreading themselves over the globe, form different languages, which producing different interests, and misunderstandings, excite distrust.*[35]

Here it would seem communities held together not by the domination of usurpers, but by companionship, was the original condition of society, and war occurred between nations unable to comprehend and trust each other. This too could have been developed into a narrative, but Wollstonecraft did not pursue it. It was however significant that she could conceive of such benign and cooperative existence among human beings, even at the beginning of their history, although it would seem by implication that the unintended consequence of such cooperative groupings was the cause of eventual conflicts. It was in this context that she explained that, with the invention of the arts, by which one can presume she meant agriculture and artisanal skills, humanity became more sedentary, and bellicose: "For whilst [the arts] were in their infancy his restless temper, and savage manners, still kept alive his passion for war and plunder." Once restlessness, "savage manners," and "ferocity" receded, "the right of property grew sacred." Social distinctions arose:

> The prowess or abilities of the leaders of barbarians gave them likewise an ascendency in their respective dynasties; which gaining strength in proportion to the ignorance of the age, produced the distinctions of men, from which the great

35. Ibid. My emphasis.

inequality of conditions has originated; and they have preserved long since the necessity has ceased to exist.[36]

It is also in this part of her discussion that we find her making
another significant point for the purposes of understanding her
vision for humanity, namely, about the purpose of government,
security, property, the development of agriculture and peace:

> Fortunately, in spite of the various impediments that have
> thwarted the advancement of knowledge, the blessings of
> society have been sufficiently experienced to convince us,
> that the only solid good to be expected from a government
> must result from the security of our persons and property.
> And domestic felicity has given a mild lustre to human hap-
> piness superior to the false glory of sanguinary devastation,
> or magnificent robberies. Our fields and vineyards have thus
> gradually become the principal objects of our care—and it
> is from this general sentiment governing the opinion of the
> civilized part of the world, that we are enabled to contem-
> plate, with some degree of certainty, the approaching age of
> peace.[37]

Thus, although we saw her attribute to the passion for wealth
and power the cause of the domination of some over others, she
also recognized the eventual benefits of the advent of government that protected the lives and property of its citizens when
compared to the ages of wars and devastation. Like Rousseau,
though not in the same sequence, she also believed that the
development of the arts and agriculture, and the growing sed-
entariness, led to the sacralization of property rights and their
enshrinement in law. This entrenched and accentuated social
inequalities, which ignorance helped maintain to this day.

Wollstonecraft's reflections on the origins of society, property, social distinctions, and governments were woven into her

36. Ibid., p. 147.
37. Ibid.

history of Europe, one that narrowed in scope as it proceeded to focus on France and its *Ancien Régime*. She did not follow the trajectory of stadial history which would have taken her conjectural history from hunting and gathering, the beginnings of herding, through agricultural, and finally to commercial, society. Although she spoke of agriculture as we just read, she turned instead and never entirely sequentially to conventionally demarcated periods of European history, those of the Ancient Greeks and Romans, of the barbaric invasions, chivalry, Renaissance Italy, the Reformation, and, finally, that of modern commercial society. In other words, she could be said to have interlaced episodes of European history between the two stages of a theoretical history of society—early society and modern commercial society. Yet, it was principally the state of nature and the beginnings of societies that provided the backdrop and context for her history of France and its revolution, and she returned to these topics repeatedly for explanatory purposes and to defend her pronouncements on the merit of civilization and demerit of some of its features, not least social distinctions.

Rank and Womanhood

Wollstonecraft did not envy the socially and economically privileged. In fact, she did not seem to think they were genuinely privileged at all. She mocked and ridiculed them, but her doing so did not expose what she termed "hissings of envy."[38] Rather, the expression of her scorn was tinged with pity. This did not make her idealize the poor either, though on occasion she did idealize rural life. The rich and the poor had their respective vices, "insincerity, want of natural affections, with all the specious train that luxury introduces" were "the polished vices of the rich," while the poor exercised their cruelty, as we saw above, on creatures below them, and had

38. *VW*, p. 223.

all those gross vices which the example of the rich, rudely copied, could produce. Envy built a wall of separation, that made the poor hate, whilst they bent to their superiors; who, on their part, stepped aside to avoid the loathsome sight of human misery.[39]

Nevertheless, though she declared her hands led her to be mistaken for a lady, Wollstonecraft was glad not to be a member of the nobility.[40] She seemed to have developed a particular dislike of that class as a whole, not least of its "ladies." Indeed, her conception of the upper classes was indelibly gendered, and its watermark was an image firmly etched in her mind by her stay in Ireland. Working as a governess for the Kingsborough family lent proof, if proof were needed, to whatever preconceptions she might have had before joining them in the Autumn of 1786. These preconceptions had already begun to find expression in her first publication, *Thoughts on the Education of Daughters*, written after the closure of her failed attempt to maintain a school on Newington Green forced her to take up the position of governess.

It is important to note that her assessment of the nobility and the poor did by no means make her an admirer of the middle ranks of society, especially as her experience widened. It is undeniable that she did state that *A Vindication of the Rights of Woman* was primarily addressed to that class, "because they appear to be in the most natural state."[41] This was not praise. It simply meant that they had not yet fully copied the "ladies" and the process of their doing so could conceivably be arrested by her words. The women she had overwhelmingly in mind were the "ladies," like Lady Kingsborough. In later years, when the French Revolution and her travels in Scandinavia gave her a glimpse of a bourgeois order and the ascendency of the middle

39. *VM*, p. 62.
40. *Letters Written in Sweden, Norway, and Denmark, Works*, Vol. 6, p. 246.
41. *VW*, p. 76.

class as well as closer encounters with merchants, she was led, as we shall see, to reconsider her assessment of aristocratic society. What is common to her critique of either class or indeed any group of people is her evaluation of the psychological impact their activity, or lack thereof, had on the individual members of that class: the more their pursuits stripped them of fellow feelings, the worse she thought of the pursuits and the class of people engaged in them.

To be sure, with regard to her comments on the nobility, it is not easy to disentangle her disappointment or anxiety at finding herself in Ireland, a governess aged twenty-seven, from her account of the character and habits of Lord and Lady Kingsborough and their circle. Uprooted and strangely alienated, Wollstonecraft found her reaction to her situation confusing even to her. Of her unhappiness, however, there can be little doubt. In a letter dated October 30, 1786, to her sister, Everina, she described her arrival at Mitchelstown castle in the following terms: "[t]here was such solemn kind of stupidity about this place as froze my blood—I entered the great gates with the same kind of feeling as I should if I was going to the Bastile [sic]."[42] Her spirits sank. This was not due to any overt mistreatment. She wrote shortly before Christmas 1786: "I am a GREAT favorite in this family";[43] and by her own earliest account, she was "treated like a gentlewoman by every part of the family," adding most significantly for our purposes, "but the forms and parade of high life suit not my mind."[44]

What appalled her, and was made explicit in *A Vindication of the Rights of Woman* some six years later, were what she took to be aristocrats' values, their attitudes toward matrimony, to themselves, each other, and above all to their children. Recalling her abhorrence of blind imitation, it is understandable that

42. *Letters*, p. 84.
43. Ibid., p. 97.
44. Ibid., p. 85. For a succinct and insightful account of this period in Wollstonecraft's life, see Todd, *Mary Wollstonecraft: A Revolutionary Life*, pp. 87–116.

the fact that this privileged class might be held up as a model to the rest of society was irksome. Her contempt for it was encapsulated in the same letter to Everina, in which, quite apart from everything else, she worried that she might not be "up to the task" (an important turn of phrase to which we shall return) but her fear that her French be deemed inadequate for a governess did not stand in the way of her derision:

> Lady K. is a shrewd clever woman a great talker—I have not seen much of her as she is confined to her room by a sore throat—but I have seen half dozen of her companions—I mean not her children, but her dogs—To see a woman without any softness in her manners caressing animals, and using infantine expression—is you may conceive very absurd and ludicrous—but a fine Lady is new species to me of animals.[45]

Notwithstanding what we saw in the preceding chapter of Wollstonecraft's own consideration for animals and her belief that learning to treat them well was central to human development, that sort of rapport with pets was morally abhorrent to her. As Todd remarks, "[t]his passion for dogs marks the portrait of the trivial mother in *Mary, A Fiction* (ch. 1) and the unmaternal fashionable lady in *A Vindication of the Rights of Woman* (ch. 12)."[46] Lady Kingsborough epitomized a kind of woman Wollstonecraft did not want to be or have others become. Though her ladyship was not the sole target of Wollstonecraft's rejection of a certain conception of womanhood, she and her female relations were to play a very important role in the theorist's social and political imaginary, and provided much of the background of her discussion of marriage, love, and parenthood in both her *Vindications*.

It should be noted that Wollstonecraft did not think Lady Kingsborough unkind or stupid, or even particularly ignorant,

45. *Letters*, p. 87.
46. Ibid., n.188.

unless one believes emotional deficiency to be a kind of moral ignorance.[47] What she lacked was even a modicum of devotion to her children, and a hint of the kind of selflessness that Wollstonecraft valued then and would do more so with the years. Lady Kingsborough was the center of her own attention; even her dogs seemed no more than an extension of herself. Her world was one of appearances: "She rouges." "Lady K's animal passion fills up the hours which are not spent in dressing," Wollstonecraft reported.[48] When her children were ill with a severe fever, she had visited them "in a formal way—though their situation called forth my tenderness," yet she "lavished awkward fondness on her dogs." Wollstonecraft was witnessing what she had described already in the very first paragraph of her first publication:

> As I conceive it to be the duty of every rational creature to attend to its offspring, I am sorry to observe, that reason and duty together have not so powerful an influence over human conduct, as instinct has in the brute creation. Indolence, and thoughtless disregard to every thing, except the present indulgence, make many mothers, who may have momentary starts of tenderness, neglect their children. They follow a pleasing impulse [. . .] I mean vanity and self-love.[49]

Vanity and self-love constituted humanity's Achilles' heel. They were part of human nature, but not essentially so. We saw earlier how Wollstonecraft's conception of education as character formation was one that made for personalities that resisted that "pleasing impulse." And while it was a natural tendency it produced unnatural results, notably, the "unnatural fashionable" mother, to draw on Todd's phrase again.

47. Ibid., pp. 81–82.
48. Ibid., p. 91.
49. *Education of Daughter, Works*, Vol. 4, p. 7.

Lady Kingsborough, her friends, relations. and daughters exemplified the very opposite of the ideals *Thoughts on the Education of Daughters* sought to instill. That pedagogical work not only celebrated the duties of motherhood, of the care that should be taken of providing children with a strong constitution and self-discipline and of developing their sense of benevolence, but also ridiculed makeup and the like, commending simplicity of dress together with unaffected manners. These are manners that, Wollstonecraft claimed, "demand respect, and will be admired by people of taste, even when love is out of the question."[50]

Thus, while she already entertained some such thoughts prior to her time in Ireland, what she saw of the lives of the Kingsboroughs led her years later to conjoin the idea of aristocracy or of the rich with an idea of femininity that she was to deride. It was by no means the only similitude she drew; as mentioned previously, she was frequently to liken women to slaves in her second *Vindication*, and it was a very important comparison.

When Wollstonecraft searched through Burke's *A Philosophical Enquiry into the Origin of our Ideas of the Sublime and Beautiful* for ammunition to attack him all the better for his *Reflections on the Revolution in France*, Lady Kingsborough must have come to mind, not least because Wollstonecraft had deployed some of the same language to describe her as Burke used in his early work to describe the ways of women. Wollstonecraft told her sister: "I think now I hear her infantine *lisp*"; the "lisp of the nursery" was something that she had warned against in *Thoughts on the Education of Daughters*.[51] She was to berate Burke for claiming that because the idea of beauty in women carried with it that of "weakness and imperfection," women "learn to lisp, to totter in their walk, to counterfeit

50. Ibid., p. 17.
51. *Letters*, p. 91, my italics; and *Works*, Vol. 4, p. 10.

weakness, and even sickness."[52] Given her stance on the importance of physical strength, this could only have triggered anger in Wollstonecraft. Although Burke presented his view as a reflection of an alleged reality, she wrote as if he had single-handedly persuaded women to behave in this preposterous manner: "You may have convinced them that *littleness* and *weakness* are the very essence of beauty."[53] Continuing in what is one of her most memorable passages:

> And that the Supreme Being, in giving women beauty in the most supereminent degree, seemed to command them, by the powerful voice of Nature, not to cultivate the moral virtues that might chance to excite respect, and interfere with the pleasing sensations they were created to inspire. Thus confining truth, fortitude, and humanity, within the rigid pate of manly morals, they might justly argue that to be loved, woman's high end and great distinction! They should "learn to lisp, to totter in their walk, and nick-name God's creatures."[54]

This last quotation owed more to *Hamlet* ("You jig and amble, you lisp, you nickname God's creatures and make your wantonness your ignore," III.i.146–148) than it did to Burke, who may have been inspired by it, but it is not improbable that Wollstonecraft was especially pricked by those comments, because their truth was confirmed by her own observations.

The letters from Ireland thus presage some of the arguments of her political works, not least the account given of contemporary attitudes to marriage described in the *Vindication of the Rights of Men*, a little more than three years later. "You cannot conceive my dear Girl," she wrote to Everina in mid-May 1787,

52. Burke, *A Philosophical Enquiry*, p. 110.
53. *VM*, p. 47.
54. Ibid.

"the dissipated lives the woman of quality lead." "When I am in spirits I will give you a faithful picture," she promised, adding:

> In many respects the *Great* and *little* vulgar resemble and in none more than the motives which induce them to marry. They look not for a companion and are seldom alone together but in bed—The husband, perhaps drunk and the wife's head full of the *pretty* compliment that some creature, that Nature designed for a Man—paid her at the card table.[55]

Wollstonecraft was much disturbed by the mercenary approach to marriage disclosed in the conversations she witnessed:

> Confined to the society of a set of silly females, I have no social converse [. . .] The topics of matrimony and dress take their turns—Not in a very *sentimental* style—alas poor sentiment it has no residence here—I almost wish the girls were novels readers and romantic, I declare false refinement is better than none, at all; but these girls understand several languages, and have read cart-loads of history, for their mother was a prudent woman.[56]

As we will see again in subsequent sections, she believed that marriage and personal relationships, more generally, should be anchored in genuine feelings for the persons themselves and, above all, in mutual respect. Treating people as a means was profoundly wrong. Treating people as property or the conduit to its acquisition or accumulation shocked her; indeed, so much so that she raised the subject somewhat out of the blue in her rebuttal to Burke's *Reflections*. Such instrumental conceptions of marriage led to a world in which both men and women were things, a world that was all the worse for women, a world that Burke not only seemed to her to defend but to extoll in his *Reflections*. Its publication made her articulate her rejection of every

55. *Letters*, p.125.
56. Ibid., p. 91.

inch of that world and its deeply embedded and overwhelming selfishness.

Burke's Reflections

One might have expected *A Vindication of the Rights of Men, in a Letter to The Right Honourable Edmund Burke; Occasioned by his Reflections on the Revolution in France*, Wollstonecraft's first major intervention in politics, to be a straightforward political tract, a meticulous critique, say, of Burke's interpretation of the nature of the events in France up to November 1790, or even a conscientious defense of the Rev. Richard Price and his *A Discourse on the Love of our Country, delivered on Nov. 4, 1789, at the Meeting-House in the Old Jewry, to the Society for Commemorating the Revolution in Great Britain*. Insofar as it approximated any or all of these things, it was arguably surpassed by other ripostes, but it was the first.[57]

The *Reflections* had appeared on November 1. Wollstonecraft's *Vindication*, dashed off in less than a month, the pages printed almost as fast as she was able to write them, was first published anonymously on November 29, and again, this time bearing her name, on December 18. It is not the most famous of the replies Burke's *Reflections* elicited, much less is it the most widely read. That title goes to Thomas Paine's *Rights of Man: Being an Answer to Mr. Burke's Attack on the French Revolution* (1791). Nor was it the only response by a woman. Catherine Macaulay's *Observations on the Reflections of the Right Hon. Edmund Burke, on the Revolution in France* (1790) was at least one other; there might have been others among the anonymous publications. A fraction of the length of Burke's *Reflections*, let alone of Paine's two-part work (*Rights of Man. Part the Second.*

---

57. On Wollstonecraft as a critic of Burke, see Conniff, "Edmund Burke and His Critics"; Bromwich, "Wollstonecraft as a Critic of Burke"; and de Bruyn, "Edmund Burke."

Combining Principles and Practice appeared in 1792), Wollstonecraft's *Vindication* does not offer a single flowing argument and, while the various points it makes are each undoubtedly comprehensible, what they constitute as whole cannot be said to be systematic. It is not a measured rebuttal building on specific points sequentially, unlike James Macintosh's initially very successful *Vindiciae Gallicae: A Defence of the French Revolution and its English Admirers* (1791). Indeed, one of its striking features is that it does not really even live up to its title: *A Vindication of the Rights of Men* is not is a vindication of the rights of men in the sense that it provides a theoretical defense of the existence of these rights. It asserts most forcefully that men have God-given rights but does not set out to deliver an argument for their existence, if by "argument" one means a discursive practice that could, at least in principle, convince the incredulous. As far as rights are concerned it preaches to the converted, though as Botting has argued, its effect in this respect should not be underestimated.[58] To search for such a defense would be to mistake its tone and spirit. It is not a vindication even of those involved in the events that had taken place in France up to the time of its composition. The best such defense is found in Wollstonecraft's later work, *The French Revolution* (1794). Nor does it truly endeavor to justify Richard Price and the Revolution Society, the other chief targets besides the revolutionaries themselves, of Burke's *Reflections*. It does criticize Burke for the manner of his censure of Price, whom the former had condemned for abusing the power of the pulpit. While she conceded that the pulpit was not the place for political discussions, she thought the occasion, namely, the commemoration of 1688, excused the nature of Price's sermon, and noted that "no stated duty was encroached upon."[59] Mostly, however, she chastised Burke for the lack of

58. See her introduction to *The Vindication of the Rights of Woman* (New Haven, CT and London: Yale University Press, 2014), as well her *Wollstonecraft, Mill, and Women's Human Rights*, chapters 1 and 2.

59. *VM*, p. 17.

respect he had shown an elderly preacher and admired figure. She thought Burke "[i]n reprobating Dr. Price's opinions [. . .] might have spared the man," although she herself did not hold back in her attack on Burke. To the degree that hers is a vindication at all, it is a vindication of itself, of the need to challenge Burke and all he appeared to be standing for on the publication of the *Reflections*. It is an attack, a vilification of Burke, as a politician and theorist; it is an attack that ventures beyond his *Reflections*, on what Wollstonecraft takes to be his conceptual framework and assumptions, on his style, on his own attacks, and more. It questions his analytical and moral competence, his independence, morality, and patriotism. It questions his very self, and most significantly, his masculinity.

The length to which Wollstonecraft went in so doing makes the work stand out. *A Vindication* distinguishes itself from the other retorts to the *Reflections*, because it deploys a discourse that broke down any barrier one might have assumed existed between the public and the domestic, the political and the moral, and brought into the mix of an already complex debate the condition of women as well as the slave trade, the nature of earthly and divine love as well as the distribution of property, and aesthetic as well as moral considerations. From its earliest stage, Burke believed that what was taking place in France was not merely a political revolution, in the same vein as the Glorious Revolution of 1688 and the American Revolution, as the Reverend Richard Price had argued, but a civilizational one with neither precedent nor equal, one that would entirely transform every aspect of European societies, down to the relations between the sexes.[60] Wollstonecraft thought that this was precisely what needed to happen for the revolution to achieve what she took to be its central aim, liberty. Thus, what makes Wollstonecraft's an exceptional text is that it rather unexpectedly

60. See Pocock, "The Political Economy of Burke's Analysis of the French Revolution," and "'Introduction' to Edmund Burke."

spoke in some detail of interpersonal relationships and the way they were distorted by power and property ownership. It related the personal to the political. It treated the two as one. What is more, it also provided a stage on which to present herself: it is a diptych. In depicting him, she depicted herself. She presented herself to the world through it and asserted herself as she diminished him.

As its full title makes clear, *A Vindication of the Rights of Men, in a Letter to the Right Honourable Edmund Burke; Occasioned by his Reflections on the Revolution in France*, was a direct epistolary address to Burke. Its three very short paragraphs, "Advertisement," explained the increasing "indignation" that Burke's "sophistical arguments" had produced in her as they had been presented "in the questionable shape of natural feelings and common sense" by him. What had been mere "effusions of the moment" grew and became the publication that has come down to us, thanks to the encouragement of Joseph Johnson, her publisher. Wollstonecraft further explained that she had confined her critique "to the grand principles at which he has levelled many ingenious arguments in a very specious garb."[61]

This was at best seriously misleading, in fact, plainly untrue. She came close to admitting so herself, as we shall see in the next section. Whatever else it contained, Wollstonecraft's text was a very personal attack on Burke and its reach extended, as mentioned already, beyond his *Reflections*, and as far back as *A Philosophical Enquiry into the Origin of our Ideas of the Sublime and Beautiful*. The merit of Wollstonecraft's reply rests in large part on her being one of Burke's "closest readers," who, as his eminent intellectual biographer, David Bromwich, has remarked, "had no doubt that the *Sublime and Beautiful* had left its mark on *Reflections on the Revolution in France*."[62] In so doing, she was led to speak of love, friendship, marriage, and women, none

---

61. *VM*, p. 3.
62. Bromwich, *The Intellectual Life of Edmund Burke*, p. 83.

of which can be said to be found in the *Reflections* or in other
contemporary responses to it. To be sure, Burke did speak of
women in it. He referred in the most derogatory terms to the
women who partook in the debates as well as the violence of
the first stage of the revolution, and in the most laudatory tone
about queens, Marie Antoinette in particular, in other words of
women at both ends of the social spectrum. In so doing, he conjured an idea of femininity defiled by the revolutionary women
themselves and a violation of civilization in the vandalism of
the royal bedchamber and the attack on the queen of France.
He evoked the demise of chivalry, the marker of the progress of
civility, but he did not speak of friendship, marriage, and love
as Wollstonecraft was to, although he did implicitly do so about
respect. While it should be clear from the preceding that she had
given these subjects some consideration prior to her rebuttal to
his *Reflections*, her outrage toward his work caused her to knit
them together and think well beyond the framework of the issue
at hand.[63]

Burke, Wollstonecraft, Appearing and Being

From the very first sentence of her *Letter to the Right Honourable Edmund Burke*, Wollstonecraft drew a line in the sand. She
was not about to indulge in the customary, but false, courtesies
with which a reply such as hers might be expected to open. Even
the choice of "A Vindication" as her title gives a taste of the ironic
tone to come. In echoing Burke's own early satirical work, *A Vindication of Natural Society: or, A View of the Miseries and Evils
arising to Mankind from every Species of Artificial Society. In a
letter to Lord ****By a late Noble Writer* (1756), she was evoking
a text that had been so very effective in denouncing the misery of

---

63. For a nuanced analysis of Burke, honor, and government, see Bourke,
"Edmund Burke and Enlightenment Sociability"; on Burke and chivalry, see de
Bruyn, "Edmund Burke the Political Quixote"; on the debate between Burke and
Wollstonecraft, see O'Neill, *The Burke-Wollstonecraft Debate*.

the poor, their dreadful working conditions to satisfy the absurd vanity of the rich, and the absurdity of modern society, that in the preface to the second edition in 1757 Burke had to spell out its satirical nature and explain his purpose: to show how the kind of critical light that Lord Bolingbroke had shone on the Christian religion could just as easily be turned to expose the inanity of the social order.[64] Burke had been ruthless in his parody of Bolingbroke and in showing up society. Now he seemed to be defending that same society with all the rhetorical might he had previously used to attack it or simulate such an attack.

Possibly taking her cue from what had been Burke's mercilessness in his *Vindication*, Wollstonecraft would neither offer apologies for taking up his time nor profess it an honor to engage with him. She would not desist from expressing "contempt, and even indignation." Placing herself firmly on the side of truth, she also conjured up his *Sublime and Beautiful*, declaring: "for truth, in morals, has ever appeared to me the essence of the sublime; and in taste, simplicity the only criterion of the beautiful."[65] She would speak as she felt. Describing herself as "[r]everencing the rights of humanity," she would assert them fearlessly. She would write as she was. There was only one Mary Wollstonecraft.

Not so Burke. She peeled off the private person she detected beneath his public persona, but was kind to neither one, judging him to be "a good, though vain man." She described him as a superficial and ambitious wit, and "the weather-cock of unrestrained feelings." This was the kind of inconsistency associated

---

64. Burke's title was itself echoing the titles of works published in the 1750s in reaction to John Bolingbroke's attack on the tenets of established Christian religion, e.g., Robert Clayton, *A Vindication of the Histories of the Old and new Testament, in Answer to the Objections of the Late Lord Bolingbroke* (1752), and Peter Whalley, *A Vindication of the Evidences and Authenticity of the Gospels from the Objections of the Late Lord Bolingbroke* (1753). See *The Writings and Speeches of Edmund Burke*, Vol. 1, p. 129 n.7.

65. *VM*, p. 5.

with women. He was fanciful, weak, and manipulative.[66] Given all this, and more, it was unsurprising that when he argued, he "would become impassioned" and his imagination inflamed.[67]

Thus, from the very beginning of her *Vindication* she garlanded Burke with the terms of fickle femininity. By implication, and as was to become more evident as her assault unfolded, she garbed herself in masculinity. Who but herself had she in mind when writing that "truly sublime is the character that acts from principle, and governs the inferior springs of activity without slackening their vigour; whose feelings give vital heat to his resolves, but never hurry him into feverish eccentricities."?[68] She stood for simplicity, vitality, and authenticity. She was true to herself. She was consistent. She was rational. Hers was a character strengthened by principle. She was the independent agent. She made him her opposite, and it was a presentation of herself as much as it sought to expose him.

Dependence

One of the most interesting aspects of this first *Vindication* is the opportunity that it offered Wollstonecraft to display a nuanced understanding of the psychological impact of depending on others for wealth, power, employment, or good opinion. The kind of subjection it generated distorted human relations and dug deeply into the character of those on both sides of the dependency. She had much to say on the subject, but one example is particularly revealing. Though its presence in her *Vindication* was due to her seeking to undermine a point Burke made about the importance of an independent Church, the way she took him up on this point is nonetheless surprising. He had written of the importance of the pedagogical role played by the

66. Ibid., pp. 5–6.
67. Ibid., p. 7.
68. Ibid., p. 6.

clergy and illustrated it in part by alluding to the *Grand Tour,* when clerics accompanied their noble charge on their journey through Europe. Far from dismissing what was after all but a rather incidental example, Wollstonecraft dug into it, thinking through the likely nature of the companionship.

On November 2, 1789, the land and property of the Catholic Church was seized by the French National Assembly, and *assignats* were issued as paper currency in December. Then on July 12, 1790, the Civil Constitution of the Clergy subordinated the Church to the state. Burke vented his outrage at this unprecedented attack on the Church at some length and detailed its multifaceted significance for society as well as argued for the importance of religion to the maintenance of the state. He declared religion to be the basis of civil society.[69] Wollstonecraft, though she did not say so explicitly, would not have quarreled with that or disputed the importance of faith to individuals and society as a whole. Whether that entailed an organized religion, and the Catholic Church in particular, is another matter, as she was strongly anti-papist and High Church more generally in that period. Burke also said that God "willed the state."[70] It is just conceivable that she also might have agreed with that, though not without copious qualifications, and it is clear that she would not have thought that God had willed anything remotely like the *Ancien Régime.* There is more to say on this topic in the next chapter, but the point for the moment is that the target of her critique of that part of Burke's *Reflection* was different; she homed in on the illustration he provided in support of his belief in the essential task the clergy performed in society. As Burke developed his argument for the indissolubility of the link between Church and State in the minds of the people of England, he wrote:

> Our education is in a manner wholly in the hands of ecclesiastics, and in all stages from infancy to manhood. Even in

69. *Reflections,* p. 141.
70. Ibid., p. 148.

our youth, leaving schools and universities, enter that most important period of life which begins to link experience and study together, and when with that view they visit other countries, instead of old domestics whom we have seen as governors to principal men from other parts, three-fourths of those who go abroad with our young nobility and gentlemen are ecclesiastics; not as austere masters, nor as mere followers; but as friends and companions of a graver character, and not seldom persons as well born as themselves. With them, as relations, they most commonly keep up a close connexion through life. By this connexion we conceive that we attach our gentlemen to the Church; and we liberalise the church by intercourse with the leading characters of the country.[71]

The passage warrants quotation in full as, along with that from *The Sublime and the Beautiful* claiming that women "learn to lisp, to totter in their walk, and nick-name God's creatures," it constitutes one of the greatest influences on the shape and content of the *Vindication of the Rights of Men* and Wollstonecraft's subsequent thoughts on affective relations. In rejecting it, she came to articulate one of her principal beliefs, namely, that "Among unequals there can be no society;—giving a manly meaning to the term; from such intimacies friendship can never grow; if the basis of friendship is mutual respect, and not a commercial treaty."[72] Far from denying the omnipresence of the clergy in education or of resisting the view that this engendered long-lasting links in the minds of the young, Wollstonecraft's retort to what she read as Burke's maudlin account of the tutor/pupil association on the *Grand Tour* was to remind him and her readers of the distribution of power in such relationships. Burke's belief that the clergy could exercise moral authority over those on whom they depended for preferment was ludicrous: "How, indeed, could they venture to reprove for his vices their

71. Ibid., pp. 149–150.
72. *VM*, p. 39.

patron: the clergy only give the true feudal emphasis to this word."[73] Proximity to the nobility corrupted the clergy, Wollstonecraft claimed; it made clerics both more servile to their superiors and more tyrannical toward their inferiors.[74] As for "our young men of fashion, by a common, though erroneous, association of ideas," they "conceived a contempt for religion, as they sucked in with their milk a contempt for the clergy."[75]

Whereas Burke saw in the property of the established Church in France or England the source of its independence and moral authority over the rich and powerful, Wollstonecraft highlighted the dependency of the individual members of the clergy on the latter's good will. Ironically, she and Burke were in agreement. He wanted the clergy to have means and thus to be more on a par socially and financially with the rich and powerful they had to guide spiritually and morally. He knew that the respect they were owed hung on their not having been seen as servants.[76] For Wollstonecraft, the reality was that individual clergymen could not escape the conditions set by patronage. From her perspective, nothing healthy could come out of this kind of relation. That kind of dependence vitiated all it touched.

It is therefore not altogether surprising that she sought to add to her relentless denigration of Burke in casting him as a dependent, as himself prey to relations of clientage by virtue of being in receipt of a government pension, which he in fact was only to receive in the summer of 1794.[77] Early in the *Vindication* she questioned his moral integrity; she asked Burke to examine his heart and ask himself

> how it is consistent with the vulgar notions of honesty, and the foundation of morality—truth; for a man to boast of

---

73. Ibid.

74. Mr. Collins in Jane Austin's *Pride and Prejudice* (1813) comes to mind.

75. *VM*, p. 39.

76. *Reflections*, p. 152.

77. Bourke, *Empire and Revolution*, pp. 846–847.

his virtue and independence, when he cannot forget that he is at the moment enjoying the wages of falsehood; and that, in a sulking, *unmanly* way, he has secured himself a pension of fifteen hundred pounds per annum on the Irish establishment?[78]

Dependence unmanned. Women were dependent. Children were dependent. Women remained so for life. The implicit contrast with her situation ran through her attack on the *Reflections* and was made explicit in the opening paragraph of her dedication of *A Vindication of the Rights of Woman* to M. Talleyrand-Périgord, Late Bishop of Autun: "Independence I have long considered as the grand blessing of life, the basis of every virtue—and independence I will ever secure by contracting my wants, though I were to live on a barren health."[79] Wollstonecraft wanted this grand blessing to be extended to all human beings, and not, as we will see in the next chapter, thanks to the asceticism of extreme poverty. It would necessitate a total transformation of humanity from its conceptions of children to its view of wealth, in fact, an end to misconceptions. As things were, "[t]he child is not left a moment to its own direction, particularly a girl, and thus rendered dependent is called natural."[80] The dependence that Wollstonecraft did think natural, unavoidable, and indeed desirable was the interdependence that arose and engendered genuine cooperation. She made this clear in her *Original Stories*, one of her earliest publications, but there is no reason to suppose that she departed from the view. Crucially, it did not entail either inferiority or superiority in those engaged in it. Indeed, that kind of dependence was the sphere in which virtues were developed.[81] That, of course, was as it ought to be, not

---

78. *VM*, p. 12. My emphasis.

79. *VW*, p. 67.

80. Ibid., p. 113.

81. *Original Stories, Works*, Vol. 4, pp. 412 and 432.

as it was; as it was, subservience in one form or another was the watermark of society.

The Many Consequences of Inheritance

The first distortions in human relations occurred at birth. Before even those brought about by education, male primogeniture meant that inequality was at the very heart of the family the instant infants came out of the womb, as Wollstonecraft and her siblings knew only too well.[82] A fixed system of inheritance tended to warp what ought to be the purest relationship, namely, that between parents and children as well as between brothers and sisters, and within family members more widely. The fact that she brings up the subject and its ramifications is one of the most striking features of Wollstonecraft's riposte to the *Reflections*. It followed from her contention that "[t]he perpetuation of property in our families is one of the privileges you most warmly contend for," to which she added, "yet it would not be very difficult to prove that the mind must have a very limited range that thus confines its benevolence to such a narrow circle, which, with great propriety, may be included in the sordid calculations of blind self-love."[83] Identifying Burke as the champion of property rather than of liberty, as he had been generally considered prior to the publication of his *Reflections*, brought her to focus on inherited wealth and that led her to what she clearly conceived of as closely related topics, even though they were unusual in a combative political pamphlet, namely, marriage and love.

The desire to maintain property within a family, and indeed to increase it through arranged marriages, made tyrants of parents and cowed their children, who were made to break promises

82. For an account of inheritance in her family, see Todd, *Mary Wollstonecraft: A Revolutionary Life*, pp. xxi and 3.
83. *VM*, p. 21.

to those they imprudently loved, and forced "to do violence to a natural impulse, and run into legal prostitution."[84] "Who can recount." she asked, "all the unnatural crimes which the *laudable, interesting* desire of perpetuating a name has produced?"[85] At its root was a false sense of pride perverting "that first source of civilization, natural parental affection, that make no difference between child and child, but what reason justifies by pointing out superior merit."[86] What is more, this ambition to secure "good" unions prevented early marriages, Wollstonecraft argued, thereby making for a world in which "young men become coxcombs" and seducers; such a world debauched them as well as their conquests. It wrecked the making of "sober manliness of thought, and orderly behaviour," essential to the character of a "master of a family, a husband, and a father."[87] Nor were women spared from the consequences of a matrimonial system driven by property. On the contrary, it made them aspire to form an advantageous alliance, which once sealed enabled them to engage freely with the aforementioned coxcombs. Only (presumably rich) widows and the poor married for love.

The adultery such a marriage market engendered made wives neglectful mothers. However, rather than dwelling on the impact this had on children, as one might have expected of Wollstonecraft given her early writings on education, she remained on the subject of women, thinking of their moral standing and their view of themselves and of life. These were not respectable.[88] This was not so much on account of their adulterousness, but their slavish devotion to their physical appearance. Henceforth Wollstonecraft appeared to generalize. Women worshiped

84. Ibid.
85. Ibid.
86. Ibid., p. 22. At this point, Wollstonecraft, seemed to slip self-contradictorily into allowing for preference of one child over another, something her pronouncements here and elsewhere would not permit.
87. Ibid.
88. See Tomaselli, "Reflections on Inequality, Respect, and Love," pp. 4–33.

their own looks: "A woman never forgets to adorn herself to make an impression on the senses of the other sex, and to extort homage which it is gallant to pay, and yet we wonder that they have such confined understandings!"[89] Shifting from speaking about them, women, as "they," as if she were not of the same sex, Wollstonecraft addressed women directly in one of the most significant paragraphs of this *Vindication* and, one might add, of her writings in their entirety: "Have ye not heard that we cannot serve two masters? an immoderate desire to please contracts the faculties, and immerges, to borrow the idea of a great philosopher, the soul in matter, till it becomes unable to mount on the wing of contemplation."[90] "But, till hereditary possessions are spread abroad," Wollstonecraft claimed, "how can we expect men to be proud of virtue? And, till they are, women will govern them by the most direct means, neglecting their dull domestic duties to catch the pleasure that sits lightly on the wing of time."[91]

Property and Appearance

Thus, property seemed to have a lot to answer for. It was to blame for the web of appearance that Wollstonecraft so decried as she saw most, if not all, members of her society irretrievably caught in it. It made people seek to appear richer than they were. It made the middle ranks imitate the upper one. It made all strive to be other than they were and live outside themselves. It was however not property as such that was the evil. Its unequal distribution was the wrong: "Property, I do not scruple to aver it, should be fluctuating, which would be the case, if it were more equally divided amongst all the children of a family; else it is an everlasting rampart, in consequence of a barbarous feudal

89. *VM*, pp. 22–23.

90. Ibid., p. 23. We will return to this passage below. See also Tomaselli, "'Have Ye Not Heard That We Cannot Serve Two Masters?.'"

91. *VW*, pp. 140–141.

institution, that enables the elder son to overpower talents and depress virtue."[92] Creating such a rampart was precisely what Burke valued in the accumulation of property in some families. He realized it to be the necessary condition for the creation of a political class in the country of his birth and education, Ireland. And it was exactly what the English sought to prevent by disallowing primogeniture among Catholic families and thereby preserving the Protestant ascendancy.[93] His critique of the penal laws against the Catholics, known as *Tracts on the Popery Laws* and drafted in 1762–1765, remonstrated against their injustice, arguing they violated natural justice, and he exposed them as the cause of the depressed state of the country. They stood in the way of economic recovery and "frustrated Catholics 'in every road of industry,' threw 'almost all sorts of obstacles in their way': and not merely, but industry devoted to developing their property."[94] It remained unpublished in his lifetime and there is no reason to think that Wollstonecraft would have been aware of it, though Burke was not the only person to decry the injustice of the penal laws. Yet, juxtaposing their respective stance on primogeniture and inherited property shows that for all the differences between the two authors, both thought of the subjects in terms of natural justice and industriousness.

Wollstonecraft did not call for the abolition of private property. Ownership was not in itself a wrong to be eradicated. In fact, it was authorized by nature, a term that Wollstonecraft often used interchangeably with "God."[95] Its legitimacy was conditional on the manner of its acquisition: "The only security of property that nature authorizes and reason sanctions is, the right a man has to enjoy the acquisitions which his talents

92. *VM*, p. 23.
93. "Introduction," *Tracts on the Popery Laws*, in Burke, *Pre-Revolutionary Writings*, pp. 88–93.
94. Ibid., p. 91.
95. *VW*, p. 99: "Nature, or, to speak with strict propriety, God, has made all things right."

and industry have acquired."[96] Paradoxically, legacies and therefore the process of inheriting were far from excluded in this account of what stood for legitimate private ownership, since Wollstonecraft added: "and to bequeath them to whom he chooses."[97] While there is no doubt a potential tension at the very least between this definition of justly acquired property and the description we saw her give of inheritance's nefarious influence on families, marriages, and human personality, Wollstonecraft may have assumed that, given the freedom, legacies would be left to those deserving them. This she might be taken to imply when she wrote of the "natural parental affection, that makes no difference between child and child, but what reason justifies by pointing out superior merit."[98] What she meant by "superior merit" in this instance is not explained; given what we know from the tenor of her writings, one might surmise that she meant some form of moral or intellectual achievement, possibly like hers.[99] When in *A Vindication of the Rights of Woman*, she described how all aim to obtain respect through their property, she did say that "and property, once gained, will procure the respect due only to talents and virtue."[100]

Wollstonecraft did not only advance an account of admissibly acquired property, but also ventured some proposals for partial redistribution of lands, both from private and common ownership. "Why cannot large estates be divided into small farms?," she asked, adding,

> These dwellings would indeed grace our land. Why are huge forests still allowed to stretch out with idle pomp and all

96. *VM*, pp. 23–24.
97. Ibid., p. 24.
98. *Ibid.*, p. 22.
99. Male primogeniture and frustrated or failed expectations of inheritance made itself felt in her own family. See Todd, *Mary Wollstonecraft: A Revolutionary Life*, pp. 25–26.
100. *VW*, p. 230. We can only guess whether she thought she was more deserving of her grandfather's legacy than her oldest brother.

the indolence of Eastern grandeur? Why does the brown waste meet the traveller's view, when men want to work? But commons cannot be enclosed without acts of parliament to increase the property of the rich! Why might not the industrious peasant be allowed to steal a farm from the Heath?[101]

Though she was prone to romanticize rural life, she could also see it as if from the windows of a great house. In her characteristically frank manner, Wollstonecraft owned that there was "something disgusting in the distresses of poverty, at which the imagination revolts, and starts back to exercise itself in more attractive Arcadia of fiction." She could imagine how one might be led to create vast and sumptuous gardens around the halls and mansions of the wealthy, adding however:

> [e]very thing on the estate is cherished but man; yet, to contribute to the happiness of man, is the most sublime of all enjoyments. But if, instead of sweeping pleasure-grounds, obelisks, temples, and elegant cottages, as objects for the eye, the heart was allowed to beat true to nature, decent farms would be scattered over the estate, and plenty smile around. Instead of the poor being subject to the griping hand of an avaricious steward, they would be watched over with fatherly solicitude, by the man whose duty and pleasure it was to guard their happiness, and shield from rapacity the beings who, by the sweat of their brow, exalted him above his fellows.[102]

Landscapes could be re-conceived, she argued, conjuring up a tableau of a clean, industrious, and no less aesthetically pleasing rural idyll. A fairer distribution of the land would be as visually appealing to the proprietor as his current gardens, and he would be a much happier man for it. Whether for the sake of winning them over or out of sheer realism, Wollstonecraft contended for

101. *VM*, pp. 60–61.
102. Ibid., p. 59.

greater distributive justice on the basis of its spiritual benefits
to the rich, on their well-being, not by appeals to equality. Even
when more radical in tone, the perspective reveals itself, in the
end, to be as much that of the privileged as of the subjugated.
She did not lose sight of either end of the spectrum:

> This sight I have seen;—the cow that supported the children
> grazed near the hut, and the cheerful poultry were fed by
> the chubby babes, who breathed the bracing air, far from the
> diseases and the vices of the cities. Domination blasts out
> all these prospects; virtue can only flourish amongst equals,
> and the man who submits to a fellow-creature, because it
> promotes his worldly well-being, and he who relieves only
> because it is his duty to lay up a treasure in heaven, are much
> on a par, for both are radically degraded by the habits of their
> life.[103]

A world in which property was more evenly divided would be
one in which virtue could prevail. Inequality stood in the way of
virtue as it did the possibility of friendship.

The indictment of inherited property that Wollstonecraft
delivered in her first *Vindication* continued with the same level
of virulence in her second. She devoted the entirety of chapter 9
to "The Pernicious Effects Which Arise from the Unnatural Distinctions Established in Society." Its opening sentence reads:
"From the respect paid to property flow, as from a poisoned
fountain, most of the evils and vices which render this world
such a dreary scene to the contemplative mind." Outdoing even
her own rhetorical heights, Wollstonecraft continued: "For it is
in the most polished society that noisome reptiles and venom-
ous serpents lurk under the rank herbage; and there is volup-
tuousness pampered by the still sultry air, which relaxes every
good disposition before it ripens into virtue."[104] The yearning for

103. Ibid., pp. 60–61. My emphasis.
104. *VW*, p. 230.

wealth and the respect it conferred led to the neglect of duties, the division between morality and religion, and "a den of sharpers or oppressors."[105] It fostered idleness. Though Wollstonecraft never missed an opportunity to decry it as a vice, its mention here is particularly striking given the serpentine imagery of her opening gambit. The image could not but evoke Adam and Eve's ejection from the Garden of Eden and the Divine condemnation of mankind to labor. Rather than associating freedom from labor with a paradisiacal condition, Wollstonecraft chose to make the want of it sinful.

Idleness

That Wollstonecraft valued activity and labor is clear from all her works. Both mind and body had to be exercised. Neither could be fully developed without exercise. Obviously, the same was true of virtue: it could only be acquired through the discharge of duties.[106] Necessity, the need for activity to meet needs, was required to motivate exertion of mind, body, and morality. Inherited wealth annulled this kind of necessity. It even stood in the way of true education: "[i]s it among the list of possibilities that a man of rank and fortune *can* have received a good education."[107] "How can he discover that he is a man," she continued, "when all his wants are instantly supplied, and invention is never sharpened by necessity?" Inherited wealth paid for others to provide for the needs of its possessors, and, in so doing, stifled the flourishing of all. In Wollstonecraft's conception of human fulfillment, the importance of striving and effort, indeed of struggle, cannot be overestimated. It shaped her thoughts on every subject. She believed that "every thing valuable must be the fruit of laborious exertions."[108] Whether

105. Ibid.
106. Ibid.
107. *VM*, p. 43.
108. Ibid., p. 44.

she thought indolence was one of humanity's natural traits or socially induced is not entirely clear, but, whatever its origins or cause, there is no doubt that she was convinced that it had to be overcome. This is exemplified in the Preface to her *Female Reader*:

> As we are created accountable creatures we must run the race ourselves, and by our own exertions acquire virtue: the utmost our friends can do is to point out the right road, and clear away some of the loose rubbish which might at first retard our progress.—If, conquering indolence, and a desire of present enjoyment, we push forward, not only the tranquil joy of an approving conscience will cheer us here, but we shall anticipate in some degree, which we advance to it, that happiness of which we can form no conception in our present state, except when we have some faint glimpse from the pleasures arising from benevolence, and the hope of attaining more perfect knowledge.—We are indeed all children educated by a beneficent Father for his kingdom—some are nearer the awful close than others, to their advice the young should listen—for respectable is the hoary head when found in the path of virtue.[109]

In the present condition of mankind, labor was degraded as well as unrewarded. Pleasure was falsely associated with leisureliness. This was "enervating pleasure" and inverted "the order of nature, which has ever made true pleasure the reward of labour."[110] Lady Kingsborough, and her circle, certainly had left their mark on Wollstonecraft. This said, Wollstonecraft was not entirely closed to the possibility that a degree of idleness might be conducive to the sophistication the French exhibited. In seeking to understand *The Origin and Progress of the French Revolution*, she wrote that "it is perhaps, in a state of

109. "Preface," *The Female Reader*, *Works*, Vol. 4, p. 60.
110. *VW*, p. 140.

comparative idleness—pursuing employments not absolutely necessary to support life, that the finest polish is given to the mind, and those personal graces, which are instantly felt, but cannot be described." She did express the hope, however, "that the labour of acquiring the substantial virtues, necessary to maintain freedom, will not render the french [*sic*] less pleasing, when they become more respectable."[111]

Inequality or Vanity?

Wollstonecraft vented her abhorrence of many features of modern society. Much of what she despised was the consequence of inequality, unequal power that generated dependency, which itself was the result of unequal property, aggravated by unequal inheritance. Given that material inequality was the source of so much misery and denaturation, did she look to equality as the greater corrector of the wrongs of the world? Did her belief in the unity of mankind commit her to the equality of human beings? Inequality plays a very large role in her indictment of society, but it does not quite find a match in calls for equality to rectify it. Despite her repeated contention that "[a]mong unequals there can be no society,"[112] her arguments, be they decrying injustices or asserting the rights of men and women, were not firmly grounded on claims about the equality of men, much less on the equality between men and women. She did on rare occasions refer to "the natural equality of man" or imply it, but it was not the foundation of her condemnation of the ills of society or her vision of a better future.[113] She does in

111. *The French Revolution, Works,* Vol. 6, p. 148.
112. *VM,* p. 39.
113. For an insightful reading of Wollstonecraft's liberal critique of social distinctions and inequality, see Sapiro, *A Vindication of Political Virtue,* esp. pp. 77–166. Taylor, *Eve and the New Jerusalem*; and Taylor, *Mary Wollstonecraft and the Feminist Imagination* also underline Wollstonecraft's attacks on inequality but locates her in the radical egalitarian tradition of the 1790s and beyond.

other instances speak of the natural inequality between people
and, more important still, of the role of government in relation
to it:

> Nature having made men unequal, by giving stronger bodily
> and mental powers to one than to another, the end of gov-
> ernment ought to be, to destroy this inequality by protecting
> the weak. Instead of which, it has always leaned the opposite
> side, wearing itself out by disregarding the first principle of
> it's [*sic*] organization.[114]

She did not believe it to be the business of governments to oblit-
erate inequalities so much as she thought that it ought to pro-
tect "the weak." Eradication of the consequences of innate differences was neither possible nor possibly even desirable:

> That there is a superiority of natural genius among men does
> not admit of dispute; and that in countries the most free
> there will always be distinctions proceeding from superiority
> of judgment, and the power of acquiring more delicacy of
> taste, which may be the effect of the peculiar organization,
> or whatever cause produces it, is an incontestable truth. But
> it is a palpable errour [*sic*] to suppose, that men of every
> class are not equally susceptible of common improvement:
> if therefore it be the contrivance of any government, to pre-
> clude from a chance of improvement the greater part of the
> citizens of the state, it can be considered in no other light
> than as monstrous tyranny, a barbarous oppression, equally
> injurious to the two parties, though in different ways. For
> all the advantages of civilization cannot be felt, unless it
> pervades the whole mass, humanizing every description of
> men—and then it is the first blessing, the true perfection of
> man.[115]

114. *The French Revolution, Works*, Vol. 6, p. 17.
115. Ibid., p. 220.

Thus, what Wollstonecraft expected of governments and society more generally was the end of conditions that prevented any citizen from having the chance to flourish and excel. Greatness was not the monopoly of any one class. While she did not appeal for any form of leveling, she wanted barriers to individual developments to be removed. Interestingly, Wollstonecraft did not turn to governments for the changes that were needed. Whether she thought governments unwilling or incapable of effecting them is not entirely clear, though one might surmise that she believed both to be the case. Her address was to individual men and women or society more generally. Only they could undertake the momentous transformation she envisaged. For, while she held property responsible for much of the wretchedness in the world, property alone would not have led to the current state of affairs were it not for certain features of human nature. More specifically, were it not for the fact that human beings measured their worth and the worthiness of their lives by the esteem acquired through ownership, no ill would come out of property. In an ideal world, the desire for property would be, if not entirely limited, then more closely related to meeting the needs of self-preservation. For all her condemnation of the inequality of property-holding, its impact on industry and injustice, Wollstonecraft never let go of the central plank of her moral critique, that it was vanity and the craving for self-worth through the admiration in the gaze of others that was the root of all evil.

Concluding Reflections

It is principally thanks to her clash with Burke over his attack on Price that Wollstonecraft gave her thoughts about inequality and its attendant consequences greater philosophical depth. It was he who, more than anyone else, brought her to ponder the relationships of power, the master/pupil relation, that between rich and poor, men and women, and, consequently, also love and respect. Plundering Burke's writings to better belittle his

Reflections, she read or re-read his first major publication, *A Philosophical Enquiry into the Origin of our Ideas of the Sublime and Beautiful.* Replying to him made her angry, perhaps even angrier than she had been, about the perverted relationships between human beings at every level and in every sphere, which she believed a society based on inequality created. Such a society was sustained by as well as bred ignorance, and that, ultimately, was the greatest obstacle to a better one.

CHAPTER FOUR

What She Wished
and Wanted

Writing for Society as It Is and
for Society as It Ought to Be

Wollstonecraft repeatedly evoked an ideal society that might exist in what sometimes seemed a very far-off and very different future. The disparity between the world as it was and the world as she wanted it to be presented Wollstonecraft with a dilemma: to write for the world that was or to write for the world as it ought to be. Mostly, the two kinds of perspective were intertwined in her writings. On most occasions, it is a matter of the reader's overall sense of what Wollstonecraft stood for, which of the two vantage points one takes her to be speaking from at any one time. While some questions of interpretation might not be easily resolved, an awareness that she wrote at times for the present state of things and at others for that of an ideal to come, helps to disentangle her many, sometimes seemingly conflicting, pronouncements. She appears to have been conscious herself of her double identity as ameliorator and transformer. She offered a glimpse of this when she wrote, as we saw in the introduction, of the difficulty she faced explicitly in relation to her aspirations and hopes for her infant daughter, Fanny, in a letter to the baby's father, Imlay. You know that as a female I am particularly attached to her," she divulged, adding

> I feel more than a mother's fondness and anxiety, when I reflect on the dependent and oppressed state of her sex. I dread lest she should be forced to sacrifice her heart to her principles, or principles to her heart. With trembling hand I shall cultivate her sensibility, and cherish delicacy of senti-ment, lest, whilst I lend fresh lushes to the rose, I sharpen the thorns that will wound the breast I would fain guard—I dread to unfold her mind, lest it should render her unfit for the world she is to inhabit—Hapless woman! What a fate is thine![1]

Was a mother to prepare her daughter for the world or bring her up as she should be and try to create the world one would wish for one's daughter? Whether writing for the present or an imag-inable future, however, what mattered for Wollstonecraft were ideas, not because she was indifferent to practice, but because she was intent on delivering it. How one conceptualized the world and everything in it set limits to what was possible within it, in her view. Conversely, a critical examination of our most important categories could open up new prospects and thus transform social reality.

A New Idea of Woman, but Also of Man

The dedicatory preface of the second edition of *A Vindication of the Rights of Woman* takes the form of a letter addressed to Charles-Maurice de Talleyrand-Périgord (1754–1838), whom she had met during his diplomatic visit to England in the summer of 1792. She dedicates the second edition to him, as a leading

---

1. *Letters Written during a Short Residence in Sweden, Norway, and Den-mark, Works*, Vol. 6, p. 269.

member of the Revolution in its early stages and the author of *Rapport sur l'instruction publique, fait au nom du Comité de constitution à l'Assemblée nationale, les 10, 11, et 19 septembre 1791,* and speaks of her hope that her ideas might be tested and disseminated throughout the whole of France. In her concluding paragraph, she entreated Talleyrand with the following words:

> I wish, Sir, to set some investigations of this kind afloat in France; and should they lead to a confirmation of my principles, when your constitution is revised the Rights of Woman may be respected, if it be fully proved that reason calls for this respect, and loudly demands JUSTICE for one half of the human race.[2]

Exactly how France was to become the testing ground for her principles, she did not specify. It was, after all, only a dedicatory letter. She did, however, offer at least some practical suggestions in terms of early schooling, hints that she admitted borrowing from Talleyrand's own work on education, as shall be discussed below.[3] Nonetheless, the strategy the letter itself revealed should not be overlooked. Wollstonecraft sought to convince an emissary of the Constituent Assembly and author of a report on public education for both the sexes to consider her arguments, allow them to be tested by implementation, one presumes, and, upon their confirmation, to ensure that the rights of women be enshrined in a revised constitution. What her letter indicates, and her *Vindication* confirms, is that however much justice for one-half of the human race called for the constitutional assertion of that half's rights, what was needed for those rights to be proclaimed and protected was a conceptual shift in the general understanding of what a woman was.

Woman, Wollstonecraft made clear, was not simply a physical form. For as long as she was perceived as such, progress, by

2. *VW*, p. 70.
3. Ibid., p. 263 n.5.

which she meant moral progress in the widest sense, would be halted. However, woman was also not to be conceived as a mere body to which a few affective and intellectual attributes were added, begrudgingly or not, by various individual authors or societies at large. She was one human creature.[4] "I shall first," she wrote in her introduction, "consider women in the grand light of human creatures, who, in common with men, are placed on this earth to unfold their faculties."[5] Once she was seen as such by men and women, her rights would be observed as a clear matter of justice. Difficult as it was to make those in power accede to women's rights, even equal rights, the greater challenge was to alter their conception of women. Following Wollstonecraft's recasting, as it were, of women as human beings, she would "more particularly point out their peculiar designation."[6]

Before all else, Wollstonecraft had to assuage Talleyrand's fears and indeed those of all men and of many women, that to think of women as human beings, to treat them as such, would lead to the collapse of the social order. She chose to do this by arguing that it was the present condition that was morally bankrupt, and that it was largely so because women were misconceived as bodies for men's pleasure and reproduction. Most of Wollstonecraft's argument rested on exposing the contradictions in the world as it was. She took the overt aims of society, the assumptions as to what was required for its maintenance and continuity over time, and held a mirror to it. What was wanted were good citizens and parents, who would in turn engender good citizens and parents, but society produced neither. To do so, society had to make both, and for this to happen, both the sexes had to be reconceived, as did the relationship between them and that of society to children and the young. "The conclusion which I wish to draw," she wrote toward the end of *A Vindication of the*

4. Ibid., p. 74.
5. Ibid., p. 75.
6. Ibid.

Rights of Woman, "is obvious; make women rational creatures, and free citizens, and they will quickly become good wives, and mothers; that is—if men do not neglect the duties of husbands and fathers."[7]

Good citizens, parents, and children were those who performed their duty *qua* citizens, parents, and children. This was what Wollstonecraft took to be the accepted understanding, and it reflected social expectations. At present, Wollstonecraft explained in her first *Vindication*, these expectations could not be met given the conflicting norms prevalent in contemporary society, which treated marriage as a conduit to the acquisition and consolidation of property and therefore as a market in which men and women were traded by their families. We considered in chapter 3 some of the consequences of this practice and its attendant, primogeniture: it warped "natural parental affection, that makes no difference between child and child," placed an "insuperable bar [. . .] in the way of early marriages," made "young men become selfish coxcombs," "weaken[ed] both mind and body, before either has arrived at maturity," and produced "a finical man of taste, who is only anxious to secure his own private gratifications and to maintain his rank in society." As for girls, they were either "sacrificed to family convenience, or else marry to settle themselves in a superior rank, and coquet, without restraint, with the fine gentleman" just described.[8]

None of this produced dutiful fathers and mothers, nor citizens: "[t]he character of a master of family, a husband, and a father, form the citizen imperceptibly, by producing a sober manliness of thought, and orderly behaviour."[9] Duties were interconnected and mutually reinforcing, in her view. "The being who discharges the duties of its station is independent," she claimed, "and, speaking of women at large, their first duty

7. Ibid., p. 275.
8. *VM*, p. 22.
9. Ibid.

is to themselves as rational creatures, and the next, in point of importance, as citizens, is that, which includes so many, of a mother."[10] Duty made the woman as well as the man. That was independence. That was freedom. For both the sexes it was the performance of familial duties that made the citizen; it laid the ground for true citizenship. Their fulfillment as individual human creatures depended to a great extent on the realization of their duties as social beings, in Wollstonecraft's view. We shall see further how she might have envisioned such a family and the parents within it. But such understanding was not the way of the times. Women neglected children for lovers, devoting themselves instead to their self-adornment, and "to coquet, the grand business of genteel life, with a number of admirers, and thus to flutter the spring of life away, without laying store for the winter of age, or being of any use to society."[11] And so the world continued. And spread. It spread from one class to another,[12] and with it a general culture that did not respect women, because, in truth, they were not worthy of respect.[13]

Among other things, but essential to her other wishes, Wollstonecraft wanted marriage to be based on respect and, for this to happen, both men and women had to be different from the way they were currently made. They had to be in a position to be deserving of respect.

Her view was firmly anchored in what had developed in the eighteenth century into a near commonplace, that "[t]he two sexes mutually corrupt and improve each other."[14] Certainly, Wollstonecraft wished, indeed, demanded (given that she was in no doubt that her reasoning was sound and that the experiment she proposed in France would prove it) justice for one-half of the human race—women. But this was not about rectifying

10. *VW*, p. 235.
11. *VM*, pp. 22–23.
12. Ibid., p. 23.
13. Ibid., p. 22.
14. *VW*, p. 229.

an imbalance by raising women to the level of men, by granting the one sex the rights that were being affirmed in law in France by and for the other sex. Wollstonecraft wanted women and men to be remodeled into a different type of women and men. She wanted them to consider and think of themselves as human beings "placed on this earth to unfold their faculties," as we have just seen her say. She wanted the revolution to go much further than it appeared to be going at that stage and was likely to venture, given its self-imposed limitations of rights for man and not woman, that is, beyond being a civil and political phenomenon to one leading to a moral metamorphosis of humanity. What she wished for was an entirely new way of thinking about women and men as wholesome beings, and this necessitated an entirely new way of thinking about everything else.

Stressing her independence and "disinterested spirit," she explained that she wrote for her sex, not herself, and did so out of "an affection for the whole human race." Her motive was "the cause of virtue," and this led her to "earnestly wish to see woman placed in a station in which she would advance, instead of retarding, the progress of those glorious principles that give a substance to morality."[15] Wollstonecraft wished for moral progress, and for it to take place necessitated more than the Declaration of the Rights of Man (1789) to be recast as the Declaration of the Rights of Man and Woman.

Neither *A Vindication of the Rights of Men* nor *A Vindication of the Rights of Woman* are aptly named. The first was so named ironically, we saw, to remind Burke of his own *Vindication*, in which he had so aptly laid bare the dreadful inequities of contemporary society that he was now upholding, in Wollstonecraft's and his many critics' view. The second title was likely to have been chosen as a match to her first. More than campaigning for rights or making a case for them, both of Wollstonecraft's *Vindications* argue against those whom she took to be implicitly

15. Ibid., p. 67.

or explicitly denying men and women their rights to liberty, security, and property. However, both depart from what their labels might lead one to expect to make much more extensive assessments of civilization. This is not to say that Wollstonecraft was indifferent to the cause to which her titles committed her. In the Advertisement heading *A Vindication of the Rights of Woman*, but following the Letter to Talleyrand in the second edition, Wollstonecraft stated that

> [w]hen I began to write this work, I divided it into three parts, supposing that one volume would contain a full discussion of the arguments which seemed to me to rise naturally from a few simple principles; but fresh illustrations occurring as I advanced, I now present only the first part to the public.
>
> Many subjects, however, which I have cursorily alluded to, call for particular investigation, especially the laws relative to women, and the consideration of their peculiar duties. These will furnish ample matter for a second volume, which in due time will be published, to elucidate some of the sentiments, and complete many of the sketches begun in the first.[16]

Since she only mentioned a second volume in relation to the existing first, it is not entirely clear what might have been the three parts into which the initial project was to be divided.[17] It is not improbable that she meant the first two parts to consist, as we just saw her saying, to show woman as a human creature, and next to consider her "peculiar designation." In the event, it proved difficult to keep the two entirely apart. Her *Hints*, which are taken to have been notes toward a sequel to the *Vindication*, are, it must be said, more in line with such topics as the

16. Ibid., p. 71.
17. Ibid., p. 235.

imagination, the sublime, imitation, and character than they are with law.

The Declaration of the Rights of Woman, Patriotism, and the Progress of Civilization

Inasmuch as Wollstonecraft contended for the rights of woman, she was not alone. Most notably, Olympe de Gouges (1748–1793) had composed her *Déclaration des Droits de la Femme et de la Citoyenne* in September 1791. Its twenty-seven articles called for equality between the sexes, including full legal and political rights as well as the division of power, the end of celibacy of priests, and argued for a constitutional monarchy in an addendum. The two authors shared many convictions, including the abhorrence of slavery and domination more generally. In making their case for the rights of women, both campaigners sought to allay any possible fear that this would undermine morals. Far from leading to sexual depravity, both stressed, as many others would well into the following centuries, it would have the opposite effect and strengthen morality and benefit society. For all the similarities in their stance of rights and morality, however, Wollstonecraft and Gouges differed in at least one major respect, that is, that the Englishwoman was not seeking to incorporate women into a man's world, even a reformed one. Hers was part of a developing, but extensive, critique of civilization. It is possible that Gouges's might also have become one, or more clearly so if it be taken to constitute one in embryo, had she not been guillotined by the Jacobins on November 3, 1793.

Asserting first that there was "a more general diffusion of knowledge" in France "than in any part of Europe," which Wollstonecraft attributed to "the social intercourse which had long subsisted" there, she then proceeded to speak freely and, indeed it is hard to deny, insulted the French. She thought them under the empire of "a kind of sentimental lust," the French character endowed of a "sinister sort of sagacity," due to the duplicitous nature of their political and civil government, which they termed "finesse," and their polished manner drove sincerity out of society.[18] French women were even more immodest than their English counterparts, and despised the pillars of modesty, that is, the "personal reserve, and sacred respect for cleanliness and delicacy in domestic life."[19] If patriotism had at all touched them, Wollstonecraft urged, "they should labour to improve the moral of their fellow-citizens, by teaching men, not only to respect modesty in women, but to acquire it themselves, as the only way to merit their esteem."[20] Wollstonecraft did not seem to know of Gouges's work, and almost certainly not the price the French playwright and political actor paid for her endeavoring to do just what her English counterpart urged.

Woman, Wollstonecraft continued, would hamper the progress of knowledge and virtue for as long as she was left unprepared by education to become man's genuine companion. The revolution would ultimately fail, if women were not granted freedom to develop their reason in order to understand wherein their duty lay. The "true principle of patriotism," as she called it, could only be taught by a mother who was a true patriot herself. That by "the true principle of patriotism," Wollstonecraft had the love of humanity in mind is clear from what she next declared: "the love of mankind, from which an orderly train of virtues spring, can only be produced by considering the moral and civil interest of mankind; but the education and situation of woman, at present, shuts her out from such investigations."[21] Thus mixed with Wollstonecraft's national characterization, of which these comments on French women, and her *Letter on the Present Character of the French Nation* are but two examples, was an expression of a cosmopolitanism that can be detected in earlier writings.

18. Ibid., pp. 67–68.
19. Ibid., p. 68.
20. Ibid.
21. Ibid.

That true patriotism knew no boundary was Price's view and argument. This was the love of country that he had extolled in his 1789 *Discourse on the Love of our Country*, which was the subject of much of Burke's *Reflections*. The latter work had by no means been her first encounter with the Newington Green's minister's sermon. In the December 1789 issue of the *Analytical Review*, she had reviewed the Dissenting Minister's address, delivered on November 4, 1789 to the Revolution Society, which had first celebrated the Glorious Revolution on its centenary the previous year. In 1788, Three Resolutions had been passed which Price effectively reiterated and Wollstonecraft had highlighted in her review article. After applauding Price's unaffected style and sincerity, she focused on his account of patriotism, saying: "Dr P. gives us a forcible definition of that love which we ought to cherish for our country; love, the result of reason, not the undirected impulse of nature, ever tending to selfish extremes.[22] True patriotism, rather than being incompatible with the love of humanity, was thus a particular expression of a more expansive love. She reproduced his defense of Christianity's prescription of universal benevolence against those who argued such sentiment to be incompatible with the love of one's country. On his view, and Wollstonecraft's who quoted him to an unusual length in her review, Christianity "recommended that UNIVERSAL BENEVOLENCE which is an unspeakably nobler principle than any partial affection." She noted his claim that "[t]he noblest principle in our nature is the regard to general justice, and that good-will which embraces all the world." From this, it followed on his view, one that Wollstonecraft seemed to share: "Our first concern, as lovers of our country, must be to *enlighten* it."[23]

Given her perception of herself, this made her a patriot, but what of the rest of her sex? The difficulty was that women were

22. *Analytical Review*, Vol. 5, December 1789, *Works*, Vol. 7, p. 185.
23. Ibid.

generally thought to be capable neither of patriotism nor of loving mankind, and much less so of both, that is, of true patriotism, as she, following Price, conceived the matter. Indeed, as we have had occasion to see already, Wollstonecraft herself did not think the majority of women capable of anything much beyond the narrowest conception of self-love. This had to be changed. She wanted it to change for the sake of women themselves and very much also for that of humanity. The progress of the species hung on it.

A Vindication of the Rights of Woman detailed the condition of women, how they had come to be as they were, and how they were so very far from what they ought and needed to be. Much of her indictment of their condition had already been spelled out in her first *Vindication*. In a world in which people were defined and defined themselves by what they owned and the status this accorded them, marriages were used instrumentally, with the results just described. This contributed to the commodification of women, who in turn treated themselves as objects of desire, making their physical appearance the center of the universe. Wollstonecraft would not have minded half as much had that appearance been one of health and strength. Indeed, not only would it not have mattered, she would have celebrated such a concern. In her view, we saw, men were not at all exempt from the consequences of the materialism of society, but they did not labor under an imposed ideal of fragility and weakness. Some, if not all, could, at least in principle, strive to reach their full potential as human beings. If this was true only of an elite of men, and had been so for much of history, the French Revolution seemed in its first years to extend that possibility at least in principle to all men by granting them civil and political rights. No such prospect was visible for women. Yet without it the revolution would only perpetuate the world as it had found it. Wollstonecraft envisioned a different future, one that necessitated a more radical political revolution, as well as a social and economic one, and above all a moral one.

The Limits of Education

It would be true to say that what Wollstonecraft wanted was
the undoing of all that we previously indicated she did not like
about women as well as men. She wanted an end to feebleness,
idleness, dependence, inequality, prejudice, narrowminded-
ness, ignorance, and more. In other words, she wanted to undo
what had gone wrong with the world, rather puzzlingly so given
mankind's natural benevolence. It is also true that she called for
rights for women as well as men. Whether she thought that civil
and political rights were sufficient means to achieve much of
what she hoped for humanity as a whole is doubtful, but what is
undoubtable is that she spoke of rights as intrinsically linked to
duties and duties to rights: "without rights there cannot be any
incumbent duties."[24] What is no less clear is that in the world as
it was, rights were indispensable. They were indispensable as the
means to accede to the knowledge of one's duties to oneself and
others and to the means of discharging these duties.

Education stood out among the rights Wollstonecraft
demanded for her sex. Duties had to be known, of course,
but their performance also needed to be made desirable. The
century produced many proposals for women's education. She
herself acknowledged that much and said that these pedagogical works could not be ignored. Much of *A Vindication of the
Rights of Woman* consists of reviews and critiques of proposals
for the education of women, and of men. Thus, she wrote that
"[t]aking a view of the different works which have been written
on education, Lord Chesterfield's Letters [*to His Son on the Art
of Becoming a Man of the World and a Gentleman* (1774)] must
not be silently passed over." [25] She did not mean, as she immediately made clear, "to analyze his unmanly, immoral system,
or even to cull any of the useful, shrewd remarks which occur

24. *VW*, p. 235.
25. Ibid., p. 188.

in his epistles." What she wanted instead was to challenge the pedagogic philosophy permeating the epistolary collection in its entirety, namely, preparing the young for the world as early as possible.[26] This was anathema because she did believe, as we saw earlier, that "[f]or everything, [. . .] there is a season." She thought of education as needing to be appropriate for the age of children and the young. She thought it unnatural to hasten development, and far better for the young to come into the adult world full of ideals rather than with none, with illusions rather than being deluded and corrupted.[27] She had much to say on this and other aspects of education, and, it must be stressed, a great deal about that of boys as well as girls, as discussed in later sections.

By a suitable education Wollstonecraft did not just mean the three Rs—reading, writing, and arithmetic—not even one with the addition of the classical education boys and young men enjoyed in schools and universities. What she wanted was an education that would take women out of themselves in the sense of defying what she took to be the prevailing extreme form of self-centeredness. Yet, it was to be an education that would also turn them inward in the sense of taking them away from the searching for validation in the gaze of others, away from the mirrors of appearances, away from parading themselves. For this, women had to be enlightened, and so did men.

Enlightenment called for the breakdown of oppositions. While Wollstonecraft herself made copious polemical use of them, especially, but not just, in her first *Vindication*, opposing nature to artifice, morality to manners, virtue to politeness, native to foreign and so forth, she was eager to break down many of these for philosophical reasons. Particularly nefarious, in her view, were those oppositions clustered around the idea of femininity and masculinity, such as that of weakness and strength.

26. Ibid., pp. 188–189.
27. See Botting, *Mary Shelley and the Rights of the Child*, pp. 63–88.

To be enlightened was to be made to realize the nonsense of identifying femininity with beauty, beauty with fragility and weakness, and thus seeing the beautiful in contrast to the sublime, the powerful, the strong, and masculinity. Although Wollstonecraft did not want women to be thought of in merely physical terms, she was adamant that women's bodies had to be made strong, as we saw her argue more generally in chapter 3. Education had to ensure that they develop a robust physique. As her own life and that of those around her evidenced, physical endurance was essential. Everything was contingent on this, not least strength of mind, indeed even financial independence, which Wollstonecraft so valued:

> Men have superiour [*sic*] strength of body; but were it not for mistaken notions of beauty, women would acquire sufficient to enable them to earn their own subsistence, the true definition of independence; and to bear those bodily inconveniences and exertions that are requisite to strengthen the mind.[28]

Men might be considered physically stronger on average, but that did not mean that women had to be denied physical development. On the contrary, Wollstonecraft made it a requirement of girls' education from early childhood onward, as well as for boys, to ensure parity of attention to physical development:

> Let us then, by being allowed to take the same exercise as boys, not only during infancy, but youth, arrive at that perfection of body, that we may know how far the natural superiority of man extends. For what reason or virtue can be expected from a creature when the seed-time of life is neglected?[29]

Wollstonecraft's reflections must always be understood, as noted at the onset of this chapter, either for the world as it is or for one as it should be. This is made evident when she writes that

28. *VW*, p. 165.
29. Ibid.

Men and women must be educated, in a great degree, by the opinions and manners of the society they live in. In every age there has been a stream of popular opinion that has carried all before it, and given a family character, as it were, to the century. It may then fairly be inferred, that, till society is differently constituted, much cannot be expected from education.[30]

One had to be realistic. Education, both in the narrow and the wider sense, reflected the spirit of the age. That spirit was one that reigned in a hall of mirrors. Appearances were everything, and they were driven by and exacerbated by the desire for material goods. The age was marked by the seemingly endless growth of luxury consumption, as many had noted from François Fénelon (1651–1715), Bernard Mandeville (1670–1733), Rousseau, and Adam Smith. If Wollstonecraft agreed with them and others about the Zeitgeist, she was more sober than most pedagogues of the time about the hopes to be placed in the education of individuals. It could not transcend "the opinions and manners of the society they live in." These had to be challenged directly, as she was endeavoring to do in all her writings.

This said, something could be done. The education of women could, and had to, go beyond mere "accomplishments." Both the sexes could be drawn out of ignorance. Borrowing "some hints from a very sensible pamphlet, written by the late bishop of Autun on Public Education," Wollstonecraft provided some idea of what she had in mind in terms of testing her ideas in France:

Let an enlightened nation then try what effect reason would have to bring [women] back to nature, and their duty; and allowing them to share the advantages of education and government with man, see whether they will become better, as they grow wiser and become free. They cannot be injured by

30. Ibid., p. 89.

the experiment; for it is not in the power of man to render them more insignificant than they are at present.

"To render this practicable," she added,

> Day schools, for particular ages, should be established by government, in which boys and girls might be educated together. The school for the younger children, from five to nine years of age, ought to be absolutely free and open to all classes. A sufficient number of masters should also be chosen by a select committee, in each parish, to whom any complaint of negligence, &c. might be made, if signed by six of the children's parents.[31]

There was to be no subordinate authority, no ushers, as seeing them being treated as servants by teachers would be "injurious to the morals of youth." Rich and poor were to be taught together, dressed alike, and subject to the same discipline. Given her insistence on the importance of physical exercise, it isn't surprising to find Wollstonecraft specifying that the schoolroom be situated within a large ground, so as to ensure that children have hourly exercise and to give them the opportunity to learn botany, mechanics, and astronomy through observation. They were to learn the three Rs as well as natural history and sciences, but this "should never encroach on gymnastic plays in the open air." The Socratic or conversational form should be used to teach "[t]he elements of religion, history, the history of man, and politics."[32] If we recall the importance she gave to the good treatment of animals, it is to be expected that she maintained that "[h]humanity to animals should be particularly inculcated as a part of national education."[33]

---

31. Ibid., p. 263. In a note, Wollstonecraft acknowledged her debt to Talleyrand's *Rapport*.

32. Ibid., pp. 263–264.

33. Ibid., p. 268.

Specialization, on this scheme, would come after the age of nine, when "girls and boys, intended for domestic employments, or mechanical trades, ought to be removed to other schools, and receive instruction, in some measure suited to the destination of each individual, the two sexes being still together in the morning; but in the afternoon, the girls should attend a school, where plain-work, mantua-making, millinery, &c. would be their employment."[34] The more academic or wealthier young people would then be taught ancient and modern languages, and continue with their study of sciences, history, politics ,and even "polite literature."[35]

From this point on, if not earlier, Wollstonecraft's proposals seem to pertain more to the world as she was wishing it to be than the world as it was. She seemed to realize this herself, and anticipating the fears her plan for mixed education might induce in her readers, she conceded:

> Girls and boys still together? I hear some readers ask: yes. And I should not fear any other consequence than that some early attachment might take place; which, whilst it had the best effect on the moral character of the young people, might not perfectly agree with the views of the parents, for it will be a long time, I fear, before the world will be so far enlightened that parents, only anxious to render their children virtuous, shall allow them to choose companions for life themselves.[36]

Although her pedagogical schema, if put into practice in revolutionary France, as she was suggesting (in the first instance, one presumes), would have made for very different citizens over time, the enlightened world she evoked in the above passage required more than the education of rich and poor, male and female in common.

34. Ibid., p. 264.
35. Ibid.
36. Ibid.

The Enlightened World of the Future

In the as yet distant world Wollstonecraft imagined, there would be neither rich nor poor. Some would be richer or poorer than others, but not markedly so, or at least not to the extent experienced in late eighteenth-century society. There would be private property. She did reveal that "under whatever point of view I consider society, it appears, to me, that an adoration of property is the root of all evil."[37] Yet, Wollstonecraft not only did not call for its abolition, but thought ownership of property a natural and good thing. Moreover, she indicated that "in spite of the various impediments that have thwarted the advancement of knowledge, the blessings of society have been sufficiently experienced to convince us, that the only solid good to be expected from a government must result from the security of our persons and property."[38] Labor was the rightful means for the acquisition of property. "The only security of property that nature authorizes and reason sanctions is," she had told Burke, "the right a man has to enjoy the acquisitions which his talents and industry have acquired, and to bequeath them to whom he chooses."[39] Still overtly addressing him, she had asked in her first *Vindication*, "Why cannot large estates be divided into small farms? These dwellings would indeed grace our land."[40] Likewise, some of the commons might be given to industrious peasants to cultivate.[41] In other words, property, which she conceived mostly as land, should be more evenly distributed, in her view. Providing the means of subsistence to all would mark the end of both idleness, which we know she so deplored, and poverty. It would be wrong, however, to infer from this that she believed the problem facing modern society was reducible to the poverty question.

37. *Letters Written in Sweden, Norway, and Denmark, Works*, Vol. 6, p. 325.
38. *The French Revolution, Works*, Vol. 6, p. 147.
39. *VM*, pp. 23–24.
40. Ibid., p. 60.
41. Ibid., p. 61.

Much was needed to solve it and much more to usher in an enlightened society. The lives of men and women would have to be altogether unlike that of Wollstonecraft's contemporaries. They would have to have other conceptions of themselves, each other, and the purpose of their being. While she did not draw anything like a blueprint of such a society, taking together some of her hints, expressed desires, and critical comments goes some way toward producing a sketch of her ideal. That ideal was not utopian, if by this one means denying the issue of scarcity and assuming human beings to be angels or near angels. It was also not a return to an imagined or historical past. It might be deemed unrealistic or, indeed undesirable, and therefore uto-pian in a derisory sense, but that is a different matter.

Commerce and the Division of Labor

We can infer from Wollstonecraft's profound critique of com-merce that the society of the future would have little of it. She decried the impact commerce had on those engaged in it. This was particularly pronounced during her last few years. It became evident in the later part of her *French Revolution* and her *Let-ters from Sweden, Norway, and Denmark*. The rising commer-cial class was a source of concern for her. They were both cause and symptom of a growing social phenomenon that augured ill for all.

> The destructive influence of commerce, it is true, carried on by men who are eager by overgrown riches to partake of the respect paid to nobility, is felt in a variety of ways. The most pernicious, perhaps, is it's [*sic*] producing an aristocracy of wealth, which degrades mankind, by making them only exchange savageness for tame servility, instead of acquiring the urbanity of improved reason.[42]

42. *French Revolution, Works*, Vol. 6, p. 233.

She was so affected by what she saw of business in her travels that it made her think better of the past:

> During my present journey, and whilst residing in France, I have had an opportunity of peeping behind the scenes of what are vulgarly termed great affairs, only to discover the mean machinery which has directed many transaction of the moment. The sword has been merciful, compared with depredations made on human life by contractors, and by the swarm of locusts who have battened on the pestilence they spread abroad. These men, like the owners of negro ships, never smell on their money the blood by which it has been gained, but sleep quietly in their beds, terming such occupations *lawful callings*; yet the lightning marks not their roofs, to thunder conviction on them, "and to justify the ways of God to man."[43]

Similarly, in one of her final reviews, she wrote of the "rapacious whites, from whose bosoms [*sic*] commerce has eradicated every human feelings."[44] "You may think me too severe on commerce," she wrote to Imlay, "but from the manner it is at present carried on, little can be advanced in favour of a pursuit that wears out the most sacred principles of humanity and rectitude."[45] Indeed, she even told him (unaware of his past business in the slave trade) that his character had been affected by engaging in it: "Ah! Shall I whisper to you—that you—yourself, are strangely altered, since you have entered deeply into commerce—more than you are aware of—never allowing yourself to reflect, and keeping your mind, or rather passions, in a continual state of agitation."[46]

Commerce generated demographic changes and with it a shift from agriculture to manufacturing: "Commerce also,

43. *Letters Written in Sweden, Norway, and Denmark*, *Works*, Vol. 6, p. 344. The reference is to *Paradise Lost*, I, 26.
44. *Analytical Review*, Vol. 25 (1797), *Works*, Vol. 7, p. 480.
45. *Letters Written in Sweden, Norway, and Denmark*, *Works*, Vol. 6, p. 304.
46. Ibid., pp. 340–341.

overstocking a country with people, obliges the majority to become manufacturers rather than husbandmen."[47] Both the most secure and "the least arduous road to pre-eminence," commerce "turned [vast numbers of men] into machines, to enable a keen speculator to become wealthy; and every noble principle of nature is eradicated by making a man pass his life in stretching wire, pointing a pin, heading a nail, or spreading a sheet of paper on a plain surface." She thus deplored how "the division of labour, solely to enrich the proprietor, renders the mind entirely inactive."[48] She was drawing on Adam Smith's description of the psychological impact of the division of labor in *Wealth of Nations*, and she went on to paraphrase him as follows:

> The time which, a celebrated writer says, is sauntered away, in going from one part of an employment to another, is the very time that preserves the man from degenerating into a brute; for every one must have observed how much more intelligent are the blacksmiths, carpenters, and masons in the country, than the journeymen in great towns; and, respecting morals, there is no making a comparison.[49]

Given her emphasis on the unity of mind and body, it is to be expected that she thought the respective physiques of those employed in monotonous manufacturing labor and those of craft workers said all: "[t]he very gait of the man, who is his own master, is so much more steady than the slouching step of the servant of a servant, that it is unnecessary to ask which proves by his actions he has the most independence of character."

As her insistence on the importance of a healthy and strong body together with her desire to foster all that makes for "independence of character," we can assume that her enlightened society of the future would not have an economy that was marked

47. Ibid.
48. Ibid.
49. Ibid., pp. 233–234.

by an intense, let alone intensifying, division of labor. Rather, it would be artisanal and agricultural. The very last pages of her *French Revolution* provide further clues as to how she envisioned work. "Besides, it is allowed," she claimed,

> That all associations of men render them sensual, and consequently selfish; and whilst lazy friars are driven out of the cells as stagnate bodies that corrupt society, it may admit of a doubt whether large work-shops do not contain men equally tending to impede that gradual progress of improvement, which leads to the perfection of reason, and the establishment of a rational equality.[50]

We can infer from this that a forthcoming world of "rational equality" would be devoid of large single-sex working units. This, together with what we saw of her pedagogical recommendations, would mean that men and women would be educated, work, and therefore remain together throughout life.

Rank and Luxury

What the concluding pages of Wollstonecraft's *French Revolution* also indicate and can be garnered from nearly all her works is that the enlightened society of tomorrow would not be differentiated by rank or driven by the desire for luxury. We saw just how it was "men who are eager by overgrown riches to partake of the respect paid to nobility" who entered into commerce, triggering the baneful consequences she outlined. Besides the dim view she had of the nobility, acquired or reinforced by her work as a governess for the Kingsboroughs, she deplored the way in which the middle ranks sought to appear richer than they were and endeavored to mimic their social superiors, copying the manners and all that the latter made fashionable: "[t]he vanity of leading the fashions, in the higher orders of society, is not

50. Ibid., p. 234.

the smallest weakness produced by the sluggishness into which people of quality naturally [fall]."[51] The deplorable results this produced were more particularly fueled by royal courts:

> Since the existence of courts, whose aggrandisement has been conspicuous in the same degree as the miseries of the debased people have accumulated, the convenience and comfort of men have been sacrificed to the ostentatious display of pomp and ridiculous pageantry. For every order of men, from the beggar to the king, has tended to introduce that extravagance into society, which equally blasts domestic virtue and happiness. The prevailing custom of living beyond their income has had the most baneful effect on the independence of individuals of every class in England, as well as in France; so that whilst they have lived in the habits of idleness, they have been drawn into excesses, which, proving ruinous, produced consequences equally pernicious to the community, and degrading to the private character.[52]

All ranks and every individual were thus adversely affected by the luxury consumption of monarchs and the aristocracy attending them at court, not excluding the courtiers themselves: "[e]xtravagance forces the peer to prostitute his talents and influence for a place, to repair his broken fortune; and the country gentleman becomes venal in the senate, to enable himself to live on a par with him, or reimburse himself for the expenses of electioneering, into which he was led by sheer vanity." All followed suit: the professions becoming "equally unprincipled," and the merchants "selling any thing for a price far beyond that necessary to ensure a just profits, from sheer dishonesty, aggravated by hardheartedness, when it is to take advantage of the necessities of the indigent." [53]

---

51. Ibid., p. 225.
52. Ibid., p. 233.
53. Ibid.

The trickle-down effect, Wollstonecraft described, was not one of wealth or comfort, but of economic, moral, and psychological degradation. Unlike Adam Smith, with whose *Theory of Moral Sentiments* (1759) and *Wealth of Nations* she was well acquainted, she did not take comfort from any aspect of commercial society. She shared his concern for the effects of repetitive labor on the character of workers and he was explicit about the gullibility displayed in acquisitiveness: neither he nor she believed it could conceivably secure happiness or even be a conduit to it. Smith, however, thought that for all its nefarious consequences, the division of labor and luxury economy could in the long term mean that the poor would be better off in absolute terms than in a more equal society. Wollstonecraft did not. Even when she had cause to reconsider her views about luxury during her travels in Scandinavia, there is no evidence that it led her to revise her position about its economic, not to mention moral, effect. If there was a consolation prize for modern commercial society, it was not measured in the improved condition of the laboring poor.

Had rank been what it once was, it may well not have incurred the opprobrium that Wollstonecraft leveled at it. Wollstonecraft noted earlier in her account of the history of France how offices had been sold under "the insidious Mazarine," who had thereby broken the "independent spirit of the nation," and how under Louis XIV, by drawing the nobles and "concentrating the pleasures and wealth of the kingdom in Paris, the luxury of the court become commensurate to the product of the nation." To this she added:

> Besides, the encouragement given to enervating pleasures, and the venality of titles, purchased either with money, or ignoble service, soon rendered the nobility as notorious for effeminacy as they had been illustrious for heroism in the days of the gallant Henry.[54]

54. Ibid., p. 225. She is referring to the French King Henry IV.

Effeminacy was, of course, not confined to France or its nobility. Like many other eighteenth-century authors concerned with
its seeming preponderance, Wollstonecraft saw it as one with
luxury.[55] For more reasons than one, therefore, in addition to a
limited division of labor and level of commerce, an ideal society
would know neither rank, nor luxury.

Effeminacy and Vanity

Effeminacy was not only linked to luxury but associated with,
and the product of, a number of varied practices and institutions
in Wollstonecraft's writings. Thus she claimed contra Burke that
the newly assembled members of the French National Assembly
"knew more of the human heart and legislation than the prof-
ligates of rank, emasculated by hereditary effeminacy."[56] She
thought, for instance, that educating boys at home would result
in making them "become vain and effeminate."[57] This comment was part of a discussion of the relative merits of boarding
and home schooling. She admitted that she "should, in fact, be
averse to boarding-schools, if it were for no other reason than
the unsettled state of mind which expectation of the vacations
produce."[58] The reason she was not outrightly against them was
because at home they would acquire too high a sense of their own
importance, through tyrannizing servants, and "from the anxiety expressed by most mothers, on the score of manners, who,
eager to teach the accomplishment of a gentleman, stifle, in their
birth the virtues of a man." They would then be brought into
adult company by their mothers, and "treated like men when
they are still boys," which was, as we saw, a great pedagogical

55. *VM*, p. 24.
56. Ibid., p. 41.
57. *VW*, p. 252.
58. Ibid.

error in Wollstonecraft's view, and which would make them vain and effeminate.[59]

Vanity and effeminacy were mutually reinforcing and facets of the same persona. As we have seen, "effeminacy," "unman-liness," and cognate words were all featured negatively in her register. She used "unmanly," for instance, as a term of abuse in upbraiding Burke,[60] or referred to the "unmanly servility" that primogeniture generated.[61] By contrast, she appropriated masculinity when she addressed him: "And, Sir, let me ask you, with manly plainness."[62] However, she wrote that she refused to speak of Catharine Macaulay as having "a masculine under-standing, because I admit not of such an arrogant assumption of reason; but I contend that it was a sound one, and that her judgement, the matured fruit of profound thinking, was a proof that a woman can acquire judgement, in the full extent of the word."[63] Speaking to the fears that the arguments of *A Vindication of the Rights of Woman* would engender "masculine women," she rejoined:

If by this appellation men mean to inveigh against their ardour in hunting, shooting, and gaming, I shall most cor-dially join in the cry; but if it be against the imitation of manly virtues, or more properly speaking, the attainment of those talents and virtues, the exercise of which ennobles the human character, and which raises the females in the scale of animal being, when they are comprehensively termed mankind;—all those who view them with a philosophic eye must, I should think, wish with me, that they may every day grow more and more masculine.[64]

59. Ibid.
60. *VM*, p. 12.
61. Ibid., p. 23.
62. Ibid., p. 36.
63. *VW*, p. 188.
64. Ibid., p. 75.

We can surmise then that in the ideal world, men and women would not be effeminate, but manly. They would not be vain or feeble, but pursue the same virtues the attainment of which a just education would prepare them. This would be an education that fostered natural benevolence, which we saw in chapter 2, was a potential that needed to be cultivated in human beings, as did all virtues.

The Virtues

Wollstonecraft contrasted modesty with chastity, though the two were ultimately mutually reinforcing. The effect of the latter was a "purity of mind" whereas the former was a "simplicity of character that leads us to form a just opinion of ourselves, equally distant from vanity or presumptions, though by no means incompatible with a lofty consciousness of our own dignity." "Modesty," she added, "is that soberness of mind which teaches a man not to think more highly of himself than he ought to think, and should be distinguished from humility, because humility is a kind of self-debasement." Thus, General George Washington was not immodest in accepting the command of the American forces, she thought, because "[a] modest man often conceives a great plan, and tenaciously adheres to it, conscious of his own strength."[65]

What Wollstonecraft strongly balked at was the kind of sexual modesty, that is chastity, demanded of women; but she did not object to either being regarded as virtues as long as they were deemed so for both the sexes.[66] Indeed, to expect any virtue of one sex and not the other counted as one of the most

65. Ibid., p. 207.
66. Ibid., pp. 78, 213, 226–228. See Crafton, "'Insipid Decency'"; and Simon Swift, "Mary Wollstonecraft and the 'Reserve of Reason,'" *Studies in Romanticism* 45, no. 1 (2006): 3–24. *JSTOR*, www.jstor.org/stable/25602032; Catriona MacKenzie, "Reason and Sensibility: The Ideal of Women's Self-Governance in the Writings of Mary Wollstonecraft," *Hypatia* 8, no. 4 (1993): 35–55.

significant contradictions within the culture of her day. In truth, the wantonness of men was far more consequential in her view than it would be of women, as we shall see. Abhorrent to her, however, was not sexuality, but the lasciviousness to which she thought unequal and distorted human relations inevitable led, and which in turn poisoned marriages. A culture in which a woman, raped, lost her honor and bore the shame that ought to have covered the rapist was absurd beyond absurdity:

> When Richardson makes Clarissa tell Lovelace that he had robbed her of her honour, he must have had strange notions of honour and virtue. For, miserable beyond all names of misery is the condition of a being, who could be degraded without its own consent![67]

A society that made chastity and virginity a sexual attribute that added, or, when failing, took away the value of a woman as an object of desire or marriage was one that Wollstonecraft wanted to leave behind. So too was a world in which neither man nor woman was "rendered amiable by the force of those exalted qualities, fortitude, justice, wisdom and truth."[68] She wanted women to pursue and be enabled to pursue the same virtues as men, even if one were to grant (*which she did not*) that females might not "attain the same degree of strength of mind, perseverance, and fortitude."[69]

Of each of "those exalted qualities, fortitude, justice, wisdom and truth," she wrote explicitly only to varying degrees. The body of her work makes it clear however that she thought of these virtues as inseparable and mutually necessary. In the closing sentence of chapter 23 of her early work, *Original Stories*, which

67. *VW*, p. 150; see Dorothy McBride Stetson, "Women's Rights and Human Rights: Intersection and Conflict," in *Feminist Interpretations of Mary Wollstonecraft*, edited by Maria J. Falco (University Park: Pennsylvania State University Press, 1996), pp. 172–176.

68. *VM*, p. 47.

69. *VW*, p. 106.

appeared in three London editions in her lifetime,[70] Wollstonecraft said of justice that it was the foundation of all virtues. She
was to make a similarly strong claim about truth in her post-
humously published novel, *The Wrongs of Woman: or, Maria.*[71]
Both works were fictional, both moralizing, and Wollstonecraft
wrote little explicitly about either justice or truth. Yet, her entire
corpus might be said to have been about both, either through
her descriptions of the injustices of the world or in the ways individuals could seek to counter it or alleviate some of its disastrous
consequences. She generally conceived justice as social justice
and by highlighting specific injustices. In *Original Stories*, it
was in relation to the "Mischievous Consequences of delaying
Payment" of debts, the title of the chapter in which the claim of
the foundational nature of justice occurs. That brief chapter also
made a point regarding bartering about which Mrs. Mason tells
her young charges, "[b]argains I never seek, for I wish every one
to [receive] the just value of their goods."[72] What is clear is that
in her view, to be disposed to undertake any social and political
redress on whatever scale, minor or large, one needed to be compassionate and sensitive to the conditions of others. One also
had to be able to recognize justice and injustice. In other words,
one needed the kind of character that was sensitive to injustices,
and this required knowledge and to see the truth as it stood.
This explains why she conceived of justice as the cornerstone
of the virtues in her early intellectual life and of truth holding
that position in later life. Psychological disposition and knowledge were fundamental to the exercise of all the virtues. Thus,
she explained that justice called on self-command: "[e]conomy
and self-denial are necessary in every station, to enable us to
be generous, and [to] act conformably to the rules of justice."[73]
Ideally, charity, we saw in chapter 2, would not be needed, but

70. *Prefatory Note, Works,* Vol. 6, p. 354.
71. *Wrongs of Woman, Works,* Vol. 1, p. 145.
72. *Original Stories, Works,* Vol. 6, p. 441.
73. Ibid., p. 445.

in an unjust society it was. Writing with respect to girls deemed "*ruined*," in the language and view of her day, she rejected the practice of placing women in "Asylums and Magdalens," explaining: "It is justice, not charity, that is wanting in the world!"[74]

Of fortitude Wollstonecraft spoke in the highest terms.[75] It was in her view what "distinguishes steadiness of conduct from the obstinate perverseness of weakness"; along with physical and mental exercise, she thought of it as essential to the maternal, and one can assume also paternal, character; those without it, especially the "indolent, become rigorous, and to save themselves trouble, punish with severity faults that the patient fortitude of reason might have presented."[76] Fortitude was necessary to the pursuit of happiness.[77] It presupposed strength of mind, and that could only be acquired by a rational education that developed the faculties gradually in the order appropriate to the age, thereby fostering independent judgment.

With age another virtue should become apparent: forbearance. Together with liberality of sentiment, it was a virtue of maturity.[78] Children, she believed, should not "be taught to make allowance for the fault of their parents, because every such allowance weakens the force of reason in their minds, and makes them still more indulgent of their own." The reverse was true of adults: "[i]t is one of the most sublime virtues of maturity that leads us to be severe with respect to ourselves, and forbearing of others."[79] She believed that forbearance was intimately linked to benevolence and wrote of it in religious terms in her first publication under an essay on "The Benefits which arise from Disappointments":

> The Author of all good continually calls himself, a God long-suffering, and those most resemble him who practice

74. *VW*, p. 149.
75. Ibid., p. 96.
76. Ibid., p. 275.
77. *Wrongs of Woman, Works*, Vol. 1, p. 123.
78. *Education of Daughters, Works*, p. 43.
79. *VW*, p. 250.

forbearance. Love and compassion are the most delightful feelings of the soul, and to exert them all that breathes is the wish of the benevolent heart.[80]

Wollstonecraft was to do so again in *Original Stories* in a passage that ties together a number of her beliefs discussed in chapter 2:

> When Mrs. Mason returned, she mildly addressed Mary. I have often told you that every dispensation of Providence tender to our improvement, if we do not adversely act contrary to our interest. One being is made dependent on another, that love and forbearance may [soften the human heart, the whole family on earth might have a fellow-feeling for each other]. By these means we improve [one another]; but there is no real inferiority.

In a possible future, humanity would be at one with itself, with individuals understanding their dependence on the rest and thereby their true self-interest. For that future to be realized, individuals needed to be made virtuous. As she thought "[s]tealing, whoring, and drunkenness [as] gross vices" and "over-reaching, adultery, and coquetry" but "venial offences, though they reduce virtue to an empty name, and make wisdom consist in saving appearances," one can assume that none would be prevalent in an age to come.[81] Nor would "adulterous lust."[82]

Marriage, Sex, and Friendship

While Wollstonecraft did not renege on the need to recognize human mutual interdependence, she did not wish to undermine the importance of eliminating some forms of dependency. Above all, whether in the present or in an ideal future, women had to

---

80. *Education of Daughters*, *Works*, pp. 36–37.
81. *VM*, p. 24.
82. *VW*, p. 292.

be free not to marry and they should never have to marry out of financial need. They therefore had to be able to earn a living, and more especially so if they wished to remain single or not to remarry in widowhood. However, the independence Wollstonecraft wanted for women (and indeed men) went far beyond financial or even social independence. She wanted women and men to remain individual persons within a marriage.[83] The distinctiveness of individual identity was something she valued. Marriage did not dissolve two people into one, in contrast to the way Novalis (1772–1801) or Georg Wilhelm Friedrich Hegel (1770–1831), for instance, were to conceive of it.

For marriages to be "the parent of those endearing charities which draw man from the brutal herd," men had to be chaste before matrimony. The reason for this was that promiscuous men had little respect for women. Additionally, male promiscuity had very baneful consequences on the physical relationship between the married pair:

> To adulterous lust the most sacred duties are sacrificed, because before marriage, men by a promiscuous intimacy with women, learned to consider love as a selfish gratification—learned to separate it not only from esteem, but from the affection merely built on habit, which mixes a little humanity with it.[84]

For Wollstonecraft, philanderers were selfish even in the act of sex itself. Moreover, sex without affection between both parties was bestial. But this was not all. It had to be the right feeling, it had to be sexual desire. Sex, Wollstonecraft contended in the novel she began a year before her death, was not elevated, but degraded, by lack of passion, by frigidity:

> When novelists or moralists praise as a virtue, a woman's coldness of constitution, and want of passion; and make her

83. Ibid., p. 232.
84. Ibid., p. 292.

yield to the ardour of her lover out of sheer compassion, or
to promote a frigid plant of future comfort, I am disgusted.
They may be good women, in the ordinary acceptation of
the phrase, and do no harm; but they appear to me not to
have those "finely fashioned nerves," which render the sense
exquisite. They may possess tenderness; but they want that
fire of the imagination, which produces active sensibility, and
positive virtue.[85]

She may have had in mind Rousseau's phenomenally successful
epistolary novel, *Julie, ou la nouvelle Héloïse* (1761), in which
Julie marries the older man her family chose for her, despite her
love for her younger tutor. What was one to think of a woman,
she continued, "who marries one man, with a heart and imagination devoted to another?" Wollstonecraft's point went beyond
this kind of scenario:

> Is she not an object of pity or contempt, when sacrilegiously
> violating the purity of her own feelings? Nay, it is as indeli-
> cate, when she is indifferent, unless she be constitutionally
> insensible; then indeed it is a mere affair of barter; and I
> have nothing to do with the secrets of trade.[86]

Sex called not only on the right feelings, but importantly also
the mind: "understanding is necessary to give variety and interest to sensual enjoyments, for low, indeed, in the intellectual
scale, is the mind that can continue to love when neither virtue
nor sense give a human appearance to an animal appetite."[87]
Thus, physicality had to be rendered human and sexual intercourse never remotely come close to rape, neither outside nor
inside marriage. For this, the totality of the person had to desire
it, and as it would be put today, consent to it. To be untrue to
one's feelings of whatever kind, including physical attraction or

85. *Wrongs of Woman, Works*, Vol. 6, p. 144.
86. Ibid., p. 145.
87. *VW*, p. 271.

revulsion, could never be virtuous, according to Wollstonecraft. "Truth is the only basis of virtue," she declared, "and we cannot, without depraving our minds, endeavour to please a lover or husband, but in proportion as he pleases us." It could be that men to "enslave" women inculcated a "partial morality," making sex a duty regardless of women's true desires, but this was symptomatic of what could not be, that is, attributing specific duties to specific groups of people. Virtues applied to all or none, as for physical desire, she urged: "let us not blush for nature without a cause!"[88] This said, Wollstonecraft looked forward to a time when desires lined up with the morally good and away from the vicious. She had already expressed such a wish, unaware of what her own future desires were to be: "Supposing, however, for a moment, that women, were, in some future revolution of time, to become, what I sincerely wish them to be, even love would acquire more serious dignity, and be purified in its own fires; and virtue giving delicacy to their affections, they would turn with disgust from a rake."[89] Whether this was a possible world, given the often-ineffable natures of physical desire and love, remains an open question, but it is one that Wollstonecraft seemed to have wrestled with.[90]

She wanted marriages to be grounded in mutual respect and esteem in addition to, as we just saw, physical attraction.[91] The latter might well pass and the nature of love change over time. "To seek for a secret that would render it constant," she contended, "would be as wild a search as for the philosopher's stone, or rather grand panacea." More than this, the discovery of this secret would not only be useless but "pernicious to mankind." "The most holy band of society," she believed, "was friendship."[92] It was in the context of this discussion in *A Vindication of the*

88. *Wrongs of Woman, Works*, Vol. 6, p. 145.
89. *VW*, p. 204.
90. See Tomaselli, "Reflections on Inequality, Respect and Love."
91. See Kendrick, "Wollstonecraft on Marriage," pp. 34–49.
92. *VW*, p. 99.

Rights of Woman that Wollstonecraft uttered what she knew would be shocking, namely, that "an unhappy marriage is often very advantageous to a family, and that the neglected wife is, in general, the best mother."[93] This is best understood by stressing that this statement came just after her assertion that "[i]n order to fulfil the duties of life, and to be able to pursue with vigour the various employments which form the moral character, a master and mistress of a family ought not to continue to love each other with passion."[94] Her point, as she explained herself, was that a fixation on one single object, in this case one person, was mentally and morally enfeebling. There were stages in a relationship, as there were in a human life more generally, we recall her having argued, and indeed also in the history of humanity.

The most sublime of all affections, friendship, unlike love, strengthened with time.[95] True friendship itself was, however, not easily found. Indeed, quoting François de La Rochefoucauld's (1613–1680) *Réflexions ou sentences et maximes morales* (1665), Wollstonecraft admitted it might be rarer still than true love.[96] Importantly, she was not unaware of the inherent tension between maintaining the distance between individuals which respect for their integrity commanded and the total intimacy that her view of true sexual desire and sex itself no less commanded. Sex and friendship seemed to pull in different directions.[97]

And yet, the ground for friendship needed to be laid. That it could not exist between unequals, she insisted in a *Vindication of the Rights of Men*. Besides equality, it required respect, which in turn demanded a shared sense of the nature of virtue and its pursuit. It called for education, which we have seen should be of

93. Ibid., p. 100.
94. Ibid.
95. Ibid., p. 151.
96. Ibid., p. 99.
97. This is discussed at greater length in Tomaselli, "Reflections on Inequality, Respect and Love," n.471.

both the sexes together, and impart knowledge of the world and an interest in its affairs. Husbands and wives needed to be able to converse and to flourish as human beings within the context of marriage, if it "be the cement of society."[98] They needed to be equally necessary and independent of each other, because each fulfilled the respective duties of their station, possessed all that life could give."[99] By this, it must be stressed, Wollstonecraft did not mean that women's duties were those of parenting and men's those of citizenship. As we have seen repeatedly, Wollstonecraft was insistent that both should be parent *and* citizen, but parenting as well as citizenship could take on different forms. Men did not breastfeed, which Wollstonecraft along with many others in the eighteenth century strongly advocated. Women did not usually fight in wars, but they died giving birth to the next generation of citizens more often than men did defending their country on the battlefield. If self-sacrifice was the measure, women more than earned their civic entitlement.[100]

Yet neither women nor men should be made to marry. Indeed, Wollstonecraft quoted Francis Bacon's (1561–1626) *The Essaies* (1612) that "the best works, and of the greatest merit for the public, have proceeded from the unmarried or childless men"; she thought the same was true of great women.[101] She added, however: "the welfare of society is not built on extraordinary exertions; and were it more reasonably organized, there would be still less need of great ability, or heroic virtues."[102] Thus, here as elsewhere, Wollstonecraft was thinking on two levels simultaneously, that of the world as it was, and that as it ought to be. In the world as it was, seducers should be legally obliged to maintain both the women they seduced and the children they

98. *VW*, p. 261.
99. Ibid., p. 232.
100. See Tomaselli, "The Most Public Sphere of All: The Family."
101. *VW*, p. 140.
102. Ibid.

fathered.[103] In the future, they would either not exist or, if they did, women would not fall for them; indeed, they would choose "the calm satisfaction of friendship, and the tender confidence of habitual esteem" over the unequal prerogatives of love.[104] While she did not overtly call for divorce to be facilitated, she had her characters note or reveal the inequity of the laws regarding matrimony and divorce, but noted how in Sweden divorce could be obtained by either party.[105] In the here and now, laws could be and needed to be changed.

In a more equitable society, not only adults but children would be freed from unjustified restrictions on their flourishing. They could be and needed to be unfettered from the shackles of false conceptions. For this, they would have to be educated so they could exercise their reason and come in due course to an understanding of the grounds behind parental instructions: "but, till society is very differently constituted, parents, I fear, will still insist on being obeyed, because they will be obeyed, and constantly endeavour to settle that power on a Divine right which will not bear the investigation of reason."[106] New ways of thinking were necessary. Fixed association of ideas had to be reconfigured.

In Sum

While she did not refrain from deploying them, Wollstonecraft wanted to break down dichotomies, such as those between wit and judgment,[107] manners and morals, and the beautiful and the sublime. Of these, the last pair was probably the most critical one to demolish or fundamentally realign. Important though

103. Ibid., p. 148.
104. Ibid., p. 186.
105. *Wrongs of Woman, Works*, Vol. 1, pp. 172, 178–179, and 181; *Letters Written in Sweden, Norway, and Denmark, Works*, Vol. 6, pp. 317–318.
106. *VW*, p. 250.
107. *VM*, p. 57.

the discussion of these two concepts were in eighteenth-century Europe, particularly in Britain and Germany, Wollstonecraft was more especially drawn to their opposition as a result of reading or re-reading Burke's *A Philosophical Enquiry into the Origin of Our Ideas of the Sublime and Beautiful* (1757) in battle with him for his *Reflections*. Had he not associated the sublime with the strong, the admirable, respect, perfection, and the masculine, and the beautiful with the weak, the pitiful, love, imperfection, and the feminine, Wollstonecraft might have overlooked the work entirely. As it was, it infuriated her. There were theological reasons for her to be so angered, as well as dismayed. As Wollstonecraft saw it, the primary consequence of Burke's severance of the beautiful and love from the sublime and respect in what had become a highly influential work throughout Europe when she turned to it, would be that "Plato and Milton were grossly mistaken in asserting that human love led to heavenly, and was only an exaltation of the same affections; for the love of the Deity, which is mixed with the most profound reverence, must be love of perfection, and not compassion for weakness." Great though it was, her concern, as she was quick to add, was not only for her sex for its being identified with the pathetic and fragile, but also for men: "[t]o say the truth, I not only tremble for the souls of women, but for the good natured man, whom everyone loves. The *amiable* weakness of his mind is a strong argument against its immateriality, and seems to prove that beauty relaxes the *solids* of the soul as well as the body."[108] On Burke's view, she argued, respect and love were "antagonist principles" and beauty would have to be eradicated from civil society lest it diminished virtue among men. As can be observed from the preceding chapters, both her *Vindications* and much of her work more generally endeavored to tear apart those associations and solder together the ideas of beauty and strength, love and respect, femininity and fortitude and the "manly virtues." She

108. Ibid., p. 48.

wanted a future in which men and women were respected, and for this they had to be made respectable. That, in turn, required that they be educated into new beings in a new society.

The World to Come

The world that Wollstonecraft called for would not be a return to a golden age of the past. In *The French Revolution*, she wrote of being "confident of being able to prove, that the people are essentially good, and that knowledge is rapidly advancing to that degree of perfectibility, when the proud distinctions of sophisticated fools will be eclipsed by the mid rays of philosophy, and man be considered as man—acting with the dignity of an intelligent being."[109] In her subsequent *Letters Written in Sweden, Norway, and Denmark*, she explained that she had not hitherto thought as much as she now did about the "advantages obtained by human industry." "The world require[d]," she thought, "the hand of man to perfect it; and as this task naturally unfolds the faculties he exercises, it is physically impossible that should have remained in Rousseau's golden age of stupidity."[110] Happiness could not consist in ignorance, and she went so far as to follow that thought with the opinion that "[t]he increasing population of the earth must necessarily tend to its improvement, as the means of existence are multiplied by invention."[111] As we saw in the first two chapters, the early history of mankind was not devoid of attraction, in her view. It was the age of imagination and poetry, and it may be that she believed some of this might be recaptured once the world was set right, stripped of false illusions, affectations, and delusions about the true end of life.[112]

In an ideal world, girls and boys would be raised together, and their bodies, senses, imagination, and understanding would

109. *The French Revolution, Works*, Vol. 6, p. 46.
110. *Letters Written in Sweden, Norway, and Denmark, Works*, Vol. 6, p. 288.
111. Ibid.
112. *Hints*, 25, pp. 300–301.

be educated to different extents appropriate to their ages in such a way as to make them physically strong and psychologically resilient, and thus prepared to perform their duties as citizens, husbands and wives, and parents in due course. Spouses would be freely chosen and those who did not wish to marry would be free not to do so. All would be equipped to support themselves as all would have a skill or profession to secure employment. All would have inner resources and know the pleasures of the mind as well as such pleasures as can be had roaming the countryside. Property rights would be protected, but economic inequality minimal. It would be a decentralized society in order to avoid risking the kind of vanity and display that could be seen in courts and capitals such as Paris, with a division of labor that would stop short of the kind we saw her decry, one that involved stupefying mechanical repetitive work. Having been educated together, the sexes would also work together in farms, shops, and small-scale workshops. Both parents would discharge their duties as parents.

It would be a world in which the erroneous and nefarious oppositions of the sublime and the beautiful, respect and love, indeed sex and respect, would long have been dissolved. One in which men and women would be prepared and expected to exercise the same virtues and judged by the same moral and legal standards. They would be friends, once passion subsided. It would be a world graced with the fairest virtues, those of benevolence and generosity, one can also presume.[113]

Would there be wars? If any, only defensive ones, "the only justifiable war[s]."[114] And she did say that "[o]ur fields and vineyards have thus gradually become the principal objects of our care—and it is from this general sentiment governing the opinion of the civilized part of the world, that we are enabled to contemplate, with some degree of certainty, the approaching

113. *VM*, p. 23.
114. *VW*, p. 236.

age of peace."[115] Would there be punishments? Probably not very many, as there would be fewer crimes, given the changed relations between people and relative economic equality, but almost certainly not solitary confinement (except possibly in the case of murder),[116] and certainly not capital punishment, least of all public executions, which depraved spectators.[117] Would there be religion? Perhaps, though probably not clerics, not as she saw them in the world as it was at any rate, though if some, if they resembled the Rev. Dr Richard Price; from what we saw of her invoking God throughout her writings, there would certainly be faith. Virtue would be pursued for its own sake and never in fear of Divine retribution, as she thought the idea of retributive punishment incompatible with God's nature. In an enlightened world, only reformative punishment would be deemed legitimate and in accordance with the attributes of God.[118] In "the next stage of existence," she indicated in her notes toward a second volume of her *Vindication of the Rights of Woman*, there would not be punishment, but only amplified happiness. Those, such as the first Roman emperor, Augustus, whose vices, acquired to retain his power, "must have tainted his soul," would not enjoy this augmented happiness.[119] But, of course, the earthly society of the future would be free of figures like Augustus.

At the end of the penultimate chapter of her *Vindication of the Rights of Woman*, Wollstonecraft explained that in her discussion of the advantages to be had from the education she proposed:

> I have dwelt most on such as are particularly relative to the female world, because I think the female world oppressed; yet, the gangrene, which the vices engendered by oppression

115. *The French Revolution*, Vol. 6, p. 147.
116. *Analytical Review*, Vol. 13 (1792), *Works*, Vol, 7, p. 442.
117. *Letters Written in Sweden, Norway, and Denmark*, *Works*, Vol. 6, p. 323.
118. *Hints*, 17–21, p. 299.
119. Ibid., 21, pp. 299–300.

have produced, is not confined to the morbid part, but pervades society at large: so that when I wish to see my sex become more like moral agents, my heart bounds with the anticipation of the general diffusion of that sublime contentment which only morality can diffuse.[120]

This passage alone underscores the importance of reading her most famous text as part and parcel of a comprehensive view of the human condition, society, and its history. Pace Godwin, Wollstonecraft should not be thought of as the famous author of the *Vindication of the Rights of Woman*. However much that work contributed to her fame, it can easily be taken to contain but one aspect of her assessment of civilization. It should not eclipse the rest of her corpus, nor can it be fully appreciated outside of it. Its critical nature might also lead one to think of her as one of the greatest nay-sayers. She was no such person. As the opening chapter indicated, she enjoyed and loved many things, and was eager to share those she did. For true happiness to be within reach of all, however, the closing chapters have shown that nothing short of a moral revolution would do. While not consistently optimistic (who can be?), her "heart [did] bound with the anticipation of the general diffusion of that sublime contentment which only morality can diffuse." As the ill was general and profound, so the remedy had to be general and profound. Women and men had to change to change the world together.

120. *VW*, p. 275.

CHAPTER FIVE

A Life Unfinished

OFTEN DESCRIBED AS THE first English feminist, Wollstone-craft has been considered in a variety of different political lights. Seen as a liberal by some or a utopian socialist, republican, neo-republican or as a combination of these by others, Wollstonecraft continues to defy categorization and her pronouncements or expressed views continue to resonate with various contemporary or subsequent political doctrines.[1] How could it be otherwise when she wrote perceptively about so very many subjects from the inner self, sexuality, the soul, and divinity to the unity of the human species, and lived in and responded to a rapidly changing political landscape? How could this be otherwise when she sub-jected her own views to revision and qualification as she resided in France under the Terror or traveled to such contrasting places as Portugal and Sweden were in the eighteenth century? What is more, she wrote in several different genres, from reviews to nov-els, the last of which, *The Wrongs of Woman: or, Maria*, written a year before her death, was left unfinished, and published post-humously, though with faint sketches of alternative endings that

1. Among the many assessments, Susan Ferguson's remains an outstanding discussion. See Ferguson, "The Radical Ideas of Mary Wollstonecraft."

make for alternative readings.[2] This open-endedness is what her life, sadly shortened by septicemia on September 10, 1797, following the birth of her daughter Mary, imposes on us.

Teaching Wollstonecraft over the years, I have urged students to refrain from grading her as a feminist or a radical, or as not enough of a this or too much of a that, and to endeavor to let her speak for herself for as long as is possible within her own personal, intellectual, social, and political contexts, before labeling her, if labeling be necessary. Likewise, I have cautioned against ranking her works in relation to each other on various ideological scales. No one can stop Wollstonecraft being appropriated by any one school of thought or ideological party, but it is best not to approach her with preconceptions of what she ought to be or with a view to classifying her in one box or other. In the preceding pages, I have presented some of the important building blocks that made up her view of the world as it was and the world as it might be, her conception of imitation and originality, the mind, its ideas and their associations, of nature, beauty, humanity, its history, and its arts and artefacts.

Different generations and the individuals within them draw different insights from her works, and this is how it should be.[3] She has inspired a wide range of thinkers and campaigners in many countries.[4] Flora Tristan (1803–1844), author of the *Worker's Union* (1843), acclaimed her, writing that *A*

2. For an important assessment of this work in its political context, see Crafton, *Transgressive Theatricality, Romanticism, and Mary Wollstonecraft.*

3. Such a point is well made by Cora Kaplan, "Mary Wollstonecraft's 'Reception and Legacy,'" in *The Cambridge Companion to Mary Wollstonecraft*, edited by Claudia L. Johnson (Cambridge: Cambridge University Press, 2002), p. 268, and more generally, pp. 246–270. For more on Wollstonecraft's reception over the generations, see Johnson, "Early Critical Reception," Botting, "Nineteenth-Century Critical Reception," Murray, "1970s Critical Reception," and O'Brien, "Recent Critical Reception," in *Mary Wollstonecraft in Context*, edited by Nancy E. Johnson and Paul Keen (Cambridge: Cambridge University Press, 2020), pp. 41–49, 50–56, 57–63, and 64–72, respectively.

4. See Botting, "Wollstonecraft in Europe, 1792–1904."

Vindication of the Rights of Woman was "an indestructible work," explaining that: "[i]t is indestructible because the happiness of the human race is tied to the triumph of the cause that supports the *vindication of woman*."[5] In a 1929 essay on Wollstonecraft, Virginia Woolf spoke of her "form of immortality": "she is alive and active, she argues and experiments, we hear her voice and trace her influence even now among the living."[6] Emma Goldman identified with Wollstonecraft as one of humanity's great rebels, whom she depicted as follows:

> The Pioneers of human progress are like the Seagulls, they be-hold new coasts, new spheres of daring thought, when their co-voyagers see only the endless stretch of water. They send joyous greetings to the distant lands. Intense, yearning, burning faith pierces the clouds of doubt, because the sharp ears of the harbingers of life discern from the maddening roar of the waves, the new message, the new symbol for humanity.[7]

Amartya Sen considers Wollstonecraft as having, along with Thomas Paine, powerfully explored "the reach and range of ethical understanding of rights, based on the value of human freedom," not least in relation to slavery, where he sees her contra Burke, as "arguing for a universalist perspective that would overcome positional prejudice and sectional favouritism."[8]

In recalling the far-reaching implications Wollstonecraft's philosophical and political views have, and continue to have, it is important not to lose sight of all we saw her say about individual relations and indeed our relation to our own self and

5. Tristan, *Flora Tristan*, p. 100.

6. *Nations and Athenaeum*, October 5, 1929, and *New York Herald Tribune*, October 20, 1929, quoted in Cora Kaplan, "Mary Wollstonecraft's 'Reception and Legacy,'" in *The Cambridge Companion to Mary Wollstonecraft*, edited by Claudia L. Johnson (Cambridge: Cambridge University Press, 2002), p. 246.

7. Wexler and Goldman, "Emma Goldman on Mary Wollstonecraft."

8. Sen, *The Idea of Justice*, pp. 362–363 and 161.

sense of identity. Wollstonecraft reflected on humanity's past, present, and future in the hope of contributing to its improvement. She also thought deeply about human flourishing at the most personal level and knew only too well how the quality of the relationships we have with others undermines us or leads to mutual self-improvement.

However one sees her, what is certain is that her ability to inspire as well as to provoke remains undiminished. I believe she would be very pleased to know that.

BIBLIOGRAPHY

Primary Sources

Burke, Edmund. *A Philosophical Enquiry into the Origin of Our Ideas of the Sublime and Beautiful*, edited by James T. Boulton. London: Routledge and Kegan Paul, 1958.

———. *Pre-Revolutionary Writings*, edited by Ian Harris. Cambridge: Cambridge University Press, 1993.

———. *The Writings and Speeches of Edmund Burke, Volume 1: The Early Writings*, edited by T. O. McLoughlin and James T. Boulton. Oxford: Oxford University Press, 1997.

Coleridge, Samuel Taylor. *The Collected Work of Samuel Taylor Coleridge*, edited by Louis Patton, London: Routledge and Kegan Paul, 1970.

Lord Kames, Henry Home. *Sketches of the History of Man Considerably Enlarged by the Last Additions and Corrections of the Author*, edited and with an introduction by James A. Harris, 3 vols. Indianapolis: Liberty Fund, 2007. Vol. 1. Accessed April 4, 2017. http://oll.libertyfund.org/titles/2032#Home_1400 .01_103.

Smith, Adam. *The Theory of Moral Sentiments*, edited by D. D. Raphael and A. L. Macfie. Oxford: Oxford University Press; The Glasgow Edition of the Works and Correspondence of Adam Smith, 1976.

Tristan, Flora. *Flora Tristan: Utopian Feminist, Her Travel Diaries and Personal Crusade*, selected, translated, and with an introduction to her life by Doris and Paul Beik. Indianapolis: Indiana University Press, 1993.

Wollstonecraft, Mary. *Posthumous Works of the Author of* A Vindication of the Rights of Woman, *in Four Volumes*, edited by William Godwin. London: J. Johnson, 1798.

———. *The Works of Mary Wollstonecraft*, edited by Janet Todd and Marilyn Butler; assistant editor Emma Rees-Mogg, 7 vols. London: William Pickering, 1989, vol. 6.

———. *A Vindication of the Rights of Woman*, in *A Vindication of the Rights of Men, with A Vindication of the Rights of Woman, and Hints*, edited by Sylvana Tomaselli. Cambridge: Cambridge University Press, 1995.

———. *A Vindication of the Rights of Men*, in *A Vindication of the Rights of Men, with A Vindication of the Rights of Woman, and Hints*, edited by Sylvana Tomaselli. Cambridge: Cambridge University Press, 1995.

———. *The Collected Letters of Mary Wollstonecraft*, edited by Janet Todd. New York: Columbia University Press, 2003.

Secondary Sources

Andrews, Stuart. *The Rediscovery of America*. London: Palgrave Macmillan, 1998.

Bahar, Saba. *Mary Wollstonecraft's Social and Aesthetic Philosophy*. New York: Palgrave Macmillan, 2002.

Bergès, Sandrine. *The Routledge Guidebook to Wollstonecraft's* A Vindication of the Rights of Woman. Routledge: Abingdon, Oxon, 2013.

Bergès, Sandrine, Eileen Hunt Botting, and Alan Coffee. *The Wollstonecraftian Mind*. London: Routledge, 2019.

Botting, Eileen Hunt. "Wollstonecraft in Europe, 1792–1904: A Revisionist Reception History." *History of European Ideas* 39, no. 4 (2013): 503–527.

———. "Mary Wollstonecraft, Children's Human Rights, and Animal Ethics," in *The Social and Political Philosophy of Mary Wollstonecraft*, edited by Sandrine Bergès and Alan Coffee, 92–117. Oxford: Oxford University Press, 2016.

———. *Wollstonecraft, Mill, and Women's Human Rights*. New Haven, CT: Yale University Press, 2016.

———. *Mary Shelley and the Rights of the Child: Political Philosophy in* Frankenstein. Philadelphia: University of Pennsylvania Press, 2018.

———. "Nineteenth-Century Critical Reception," in *Mary Wollstonecraft in Context*, edited by Nancy E. Johnson and Paul Keen, 50–56. Cambridge: Cambridge University Press, 2020.

Bourke, Richard. "Edmund Burke and Enlightenment Sociability: Justice, Honour, and the Principles of Government," *History of Political Thought* 21, no. 4 (Winter 2000): 632–656.

———. *Empire and Revolution: The Political Life of Edmund Burke*. Princeton, NJ: Princeton University Press, 2015.

Brace, Laura. "Wollstonecraft and the Properties of (Anti-) Slavery," in *The Social and Political Philosophy of Mary Wollstonecraft*, edited by Sandrine Bergès and Alan Coffee, 117–135. Oxford: Oxford University Press, 2016.

Bromwich, David. *The Intellectual Life of Edmund Burke: From the Sublime and Beautiful to American Independence*. Cambridge, MA and London: The Belknap Press, 2014.

———. "Wollstonecraft as a Critic of Burke." *Political Theory* 23 (1995): 617–632.

Coffee, Alan. "Catherine Macaulay," in *The Wollstonecraftian Mind*, edited by Sandrine Bergès, Eileen Hunt Botting, and Alan Coffee. London: Routledge, 2019.

Conniff, J. "Edmund Burke and His Critics: The Case of Mary Wollstonecraft." *Journal of the History of Ideas* 60 (1999): 299–318.

Crafton, Lisa Plummer. "'Insipid Decency': Modesty and Female Sexuality in Wollstonecraft." *European Romantic Review* 11, no. 3 (2000): 277–299. DOI: 10.1080/10509580008570116.

———. *Transgressive Theatricality, Romanticism, and Mary Wollstonecraft*. Abingdon, Oxon: Routledge, 2016.

De Bruyn, Frans. "Edmund Burke the Political Quixote: Romance, Chivalry, and the Political Imagination." *Eighteenth-Century Fiction* 16, no. 4 (July 2004): 695–734.

———. "Edmund Burke," in *Mary Wollstonecraft in Context*, edited by Nancy E. Johnson and Paul Keen, 164–172. Cambridge: Cambridge University Press, 2020.

Devine, Harriet Jump. "'A Kind of Witchcraft': Mary Wollstonecraft and the Poetic Imagination." *Women's Writing* 4, no. 2 (1997): 235–245, https://doi .org/10.1080/09699089700200013.

Ferguson, Frances. "Theories of Education," in *Mary Wollstonecraft in Context*, edited by Nancy E. Johnson and Paul Keen, 246–254. Cambridge: Cambridge University Press, 2020.

Ferguson, Moira. *Colonialism and Gender Relations from Mary Wollstonecraft to Jamaica Kincaid: East Caribbean Connections*. New York: Columbia University Press, 1994.

———. "Mary Wollstonecraft and the Problematic of Slavery." *Feminist Review* 42, no. 1 (1992): 82–102. www.jstor.org/stable/1395131; reprinted in *Feminist Interpretations of Mary Wollstonecraft*, edited by Maria J. Falco, 125–149. University Park: Pennsylvania State University Press, 1994.

Ferguson, Susan. "The Radical Ideas of Mary Wollstonecraft." *Canadian Journal of Political Science / Revue Canadienne De Science Politique* 32, no. 3 (1999): 427–450.

Green, Karen, and Shannon Weekes. "Catharine Macaulay on the Will." *History of European Ideas* 39, no. 3 (2003): 409–425.

Gunther-Canada, Wendy. "The Politics of Sense and Sensibility: Catharine Macaulay and Mary Wollstonecraft on Edmund Burke's Reflections on the Revolution in France," in *Women Writers and the Early Modern British Political Tradition*, edited by Hilda Smith, 126–148. Cambridge: Cambridge University Press, 1998.

———. *Rebel Writer: Mary Wollstonecraft and Enlightenment Politics*. DeKalb: Northern Illinois University Press, 2001.

———. "Cultivating Virtue: Catharine Macaulay and Mary Wollstonecraft on Civic Education." *Women and Politics* 25, no. 3 (2003): 47–70.

Harris, Susan Cannon. "Outside the Box: The Female Spectator, 'The Fair Penitent,' and the Kelly Riots of 1747." *Theatre Journal* 57, no. 1 (2005): 33–55.

Hodson, Jane. *Language and Revolution in Burke, Wollstonecraft, Paine, and Godwin*. Abingdon, Oxon: Routledge, 2007.

Howard, Carol. "Wollstonecraft's Thoughts on Slavery and Corruption." *The Eighteenth Century* 45, no. 1 (2004): 61–86. www.jstor.org/stable/41467935.

Hudnut, William H. "Samuel Stanhope Smith: Enlightened Conservative." *Journal of the History of Ideas* 17, no. 4 (1956): 540–552. www.jstor.org/stable /2707787.

Janes, R. M. "On the Reception of Mary Wollstonecraft's A Vindication of the Rights of Women." *Journal of the History of Ideas* 39 (1978): 293–302.

Johnson, Claudia L. *Equivocal Beings: Politics, Gender, and Sentimentality in the 1790s. Wollstonecraft, Radcliffe, Burney, Austen.* Chicago: University of Chicago Press, 1995.

——, editor. *"The Cambridge Companion to Mary Wollstonecraft.* Cambridge: Cambridge University Press, 2002.

Johnson, Nancy E. "Early Critical Reception," in *Mary Wollstonecraft in Context,* edited by Nancy E. Johnson and Paul Keen, 41–49. Cambridge: Cambridge University Press, 2020.

Johnson, Nancy E., and Paul Keen. *Mary Wollstonecraft in Context.* Cambridge: Cambridge University Press, 2020.

Jones, Vivien. "Mary Wollstonecraft and the Literature of Advice and Instruction," in *The Cambridge Companion to Mary Wollstonecraft,* edited by Claudia L. Johnson, 119–141. Cambridge: Cambridge University Press, 2002.

Juengel, Scott. "Countenancing History: Mary Wollstonecraft, Samuel Stanhope Smith, and Enlightenment Racial Science." *English Literary History* 68, no. 4 (2001): 897–927. *Project MUSE.* DOI:10.1353/elh.2001.0033.

Kendrick, Nancy. "Wollstonecraft on Marriage as Virtue Friendship," in *The Social and Political Philosophy of Mary Wollstonecraft,* edited by Sandrine Bergès and Alan Coffee, 34–49. Oxford: Oxford University Press, 2016.

Kirkley, Laura. "Jean-Jacques Rousseau," in *Mary Wollstonecraft in Context,* edited by Nancy E. Johnson and Paul Keen, 155–163. Cambridge: Cambridge University Press, 2020.

Leddy, Neven. "Mary Wollstonecraft and Adam Smith on Gender, History, and the Civic Republican Tradition," in *On Civic Republicanism: Ancient Lessons for Global Politics,* edited by Neven Leddy and Geoffrey C. Kellow, 269–281. Toronto, Buffalo, and London: University of Toronto Press, 2016. JSTOR, www.jstor.org/stable/10.3138/j.ctt1kk65xt.17.

Maoulidi, Salma. "Mary Wollstonecraft: Challenges of Race and Class in Feminist Discourse." *Women's Studies Quarterly* 35, no. 3/4 (Fall–Winter 2007): 280–286.

Mayhew, Robert. "William Gilpin and the Latitudinarian Picturesque." *Eighteenth-Century Studies* 33, no. 3 (2000): 349–366. www.jstor.org/stable/30053947.

Moore, J., editor. *Mary Wollstonecraft.* International Library of Essays in the History of Social and Political Thought. Farnham, Surrey: Ashgate, 2012.

Murray, Julie. "1970s Critical Reception," in *Mary Wollstonecraft in Context,* edited by Nancy E. Johnson and Paul Keen, 57–63. Cambridge: Cambridge University Press, 2020.

O'Brien, Eliza. "Recent Critical Reception," in *Mary Wollstonecraft in Context,* edited by Nancy E. Johnson and Paul Keen, 64–72. Cambridge: Cambridge University Press, 2020.

O'Brien, Karen. *Women and Enlightenment in Eighteenth-Century Britain.* New York: Cambridge University Press, 2009.

O'Hagan, T. "Rousseau and Wollstonecraft on Sexual Equality," in *A Textual Introduction to Social and Political Theory,* edited by R. Bellamy and A. Ross, 123–154. Manchester: Manchester University Press, 1996.

O'Neill, Daniel. *The Burke-Wollstonecraft Debate: Savagery, Civilization, and Democracy*. University Park: Pennsylvania State University Press, 2007.

Pocock, J.G.A. "The Political Economy of Burke's Analysis of the French Revolution." *Historical Journal* 23, no. 2 (June 1982): 331–349.

———. "Introduction" to Edmund Burke, *Reflections on the Revolution in France*, edited by J.G.A. Pocock, vii–xlviii. Indianapolis: Hackett, 1987.

Pop, Andrei. *Antiquity, Theatre, and the Painting of Henry Fuseli*. Oxford: Oxford University Press, 2015.

Rawls, John. *The Laws of Peoples, with "e Idea of Public Reason Revisited."* Cambridge, MA: Harvard University Press, 1999.

Sapiro, Virginia. *A Vindication of Political Virtue: The Political Theory of Mary Wollstonecraft*. Chicago and London: University of Chicago Press, 1992.

Schulman, Alex. "Gothic Piles and Endless Forests: Wollstonecraft between Burke and Rousseau." *Eighteenth-Century Studies* 41, no. 1 (Fall 2007): 41–54.

Scott, Joan Wallach. "French Feminists and the Rights of 'Man': Olympe de Gouges's Declarations." *History Workshop* no. 28 (1989): 1–21. JSTOR, www.jstor.org/stable/4288921.

Sebastiani, Silvia. *The Scottish Enlightenment: Race, Gender and the Limits of Progress*. New York: Palgrave Macmillan, 2013.

Seeber, Barbara. "Mary Wollstonecraft: 'Systemiz[ing] Oppression'—Feminism, Nature and Animals," in *Engaging Nature: Environmentalism and the Political Theory Canon*, edited by Peter Cannavò, Joseph Lane, and John Barry, 173–188. Cambridge, MA: MIT Press, 2016.

Sen, Amartya. *The Idea of Justice*. London: Allen Lane, 2009.

Smither, Howard E. *A History of the Oratorio, Volume 2. The Oratoria in the Baroque Era: Protestant Germany and England*. Chapel Hill: University of North Carolina Press Books, 1977.

Spencer, Jane. "'The link which unites man with brutes': Enlightenment Feminism, Women and Animals." *Intellectual History Review* 22, no. 3 (2012): 427–444.

Sutton, Ian. "Roscoe circle" (act. 1760s–1830s). Published online by the Oxford Dictionary of National Biography, May 19, 2011. https://doi.org/10.1093/ref:odnb/101301.

Taylor, Barbara. *Eve and the New Jerusalem: Socialism and Feminism in the Nineteenth Century*. London: Virago Press, 1983.

———. "The Religious Foundations of Mary Wollstonecraft's Feminism," in *The Cambridge Companion to Mary Wollstonecraft*, edited by Claudia L. Johnson, 99–198. Cambridge: Cambridge University Press, 2002.

———. *Mary Wollstonecraft and the Feminist Imagination*. Cambridge: Cambridge University Press, 2003.

Taylor, Natalie Fuehrer. *The Rights of Woman as Chimera: The Political Philosophy of Mary Wollstonecraft*. 2004. Order No. 3125028. Available from ProQuest Dissertations & Theses A&I, 305185323. Retrieved from https://search.proquest.com/docview/305185323?accountid=9851.

Todd, Janet. *Mary Wollstonecraft: A Revolutionary Life*. New York: Columbia University Press, 2000, rev. 2014.

———. *Death and the Maidens: Fanny Wollstonecraft and the Shelley Circle*. London: Counterpoint, 2007.

Tomaselli, Sylvana. "The Most Public Sphere of All: The Family," in *Women and the Public Sphere: Writing and Representation, 1700–1830*, edited by Elizabeth Eger, Charlotte Grant, Cliona O. Gallchoir, and Penny Warburton, 239–257. Cambridge: Cambridge University Press, 2001.

———. "The Role of Woman in Enlightenment Conjectural Histories," in *Conceptualizing Women in Enlightenment Thought. Penser la femme au siècle des Lumières*, edited by Hans Erich Bödeker and Leiselotte Steinbrügge. Berlin: Verlag Arno Spitz GmbH, 2001.

———. "The Enlightenment Debate on Women" (reprint of 1985), in *The Enlightenment: A Sourcebook and Reader*, edited by Paul Hyland with Olga Gomez and Francesca Greensides. Abingdon and New York: Routledge, 2003.

———. "The Enlightenment Debate on Women" (reprint of 1985), in *The Enlightenment*, edited by Dena Goodman and Kathleen Wellman. Boston: Houghton Mifflin, 2004.

———. "Civilization, Patriotism and the Quest for Origins," in *Enlightenment and Feminism*, edited by Sarah Knott and Barbara Taylor. London: Palgrave, 2005 (Pb. 2007).

———. "Mary Wollstonecraft," *The Stanford Encyclopedia of Philosophy*, edited by Eward N. Zalta. Winter 2012 edition. http://plato.stanford.edu/archives/win2012/entries/wollstonecraft/.

———. "Mary Wollstonecraft: The Reunification of Domestic and Political Spheres," in *Geschlechterordnung und Staat. Legitimationsfiguren der politischen Philosophie (1600–1850)*, edited by Marion Heinz and Sabine Doyé. Deutsche Zeitschrift für Philosophie, Beiheft, 2012.

———. "Mary Wollstonecraft," in *Oxford Bibliographies in Philosophy*, edited by Duncan Pritchard. New York: Oxford University Press, 2016. http://www.oxfordbibliographies.com/view/document/obo-9780195396577/obo-9780195396577-0306.xml.

———. "Reflections on Inequality, Respect and Love in the Political Writings of Mary Wollstonecraft," in *The Social and Political Thought of Mary Wollstonecraft*, edited by Sandrine Bergès and Alan Coffee, 14–33. Oxford: Oxford University Press, 2016.

———. "Mary Wollstonecraft: Civil Society, Revolution, Economic Equality," in *Encyclopedia of Concise Concepts by Women Philosophers. Revolution; Economic equality; Civil society in Wollstonecraft*. Mary Paderborn University (UB) and the German National Library in Frankfurt/Leipzig (DNB), 2018. https://historyofwomenphilosophers.org/ecc/#hwps.

———. "'Have Ye Not Heard That We Cannot Serve Two Masters?' The Platonism of Mary Wollstonecraft," in *Revisioning Cambridge Platonism: Sources and Legacy*, edited by David Leech and Douglas Hedley. Heidelberg: Springer International, 2019.

———. *"French* philosophes," in *Mary Wollstonecraft in Context,* edited by Nancy E. Johnson and Paul Keen, 139–145. Cambridge: Cambridge University Press, 2020.

———. "Peace, Gender, and War," in *A Cultural History of Peace in the Enlightenment (1648–1815),* edited by Stella Ghervas and David Armitage. London: Bloomsbury, 2020.

———. "The Philosophes," in *Mary Wollstonecraft in Context*, edited by Nancy E. Johnson and Paul Keen. Cambridge: Cambridge University Press, 2020.

———. *"A Vindication of the Rights of Men,"* in *The Wollstonecraftian Mind*, edited by Sandrine Bergès, Eileen Hunt Botting, and Alan Coffee. London: Routledge, 2019.

Tysdahl, B. J. *William Godwin as Novelist.* London: Athlone Press, 1981.

Verhoeven, Will. "Gilbert Imlay and the Triangular Trade." *William and Mary Quarterly* 63, no. 4, third series (October 2006): 827–842.

———. *Gilbert Imlay: Citizen of the World.* London: Pickering and Chatto, 2008.

Wexler, Alice, and Emma Goldman. "Emma Goldman on Mary Wollstonecraft." *Feminist Studies* 7, no. 1 (1981): 114.

Wolfson, Susan J. "Mary Wollstonecraft and the Poets," in *The Cambridge Companion to Mary Wollstonecraft*, edited by Claudia L. Johnson, 160–188. Cambridge: Cambridge University Press, 2002.

Yousef, Nancy. "Wollstonecraft, Rousseau and the Revision of Romantic Subjectivity." *Studies in Romanticism* 38, no. 4 (1999): 537–557.

Note: Works by Wollstonecraft appear as individual index entries by title.

Burke, Edmund (*continued*)
  Wollstonecraft's commentary
    on, 1, 4, 8, 26–27, 40–41, 71, 81,
    86–88, 96–97, 113, 115–18, 123,
    139–53, 164–65, 184, 191, 204
Burney, Charles, *A General History
  of Music*, 30–34

Cambon, Maria Geertruida de, *De
  Kleine Grandison*, 6, 50
Carter, Elizabeth, 6
Catholicism, 30, 109, 149, 156
character: development of, through
  stages of life, 106–8; education's
  role in forming, 76–81, 103–5;
  effect of the arts on, 14, 20–21,
  28, 49; effect of the theater on,
  17–20; habit's role in forming,
  104; imagination's role in forming, 82–83, 87, 90; passions and,
  105–6; property's/inheritance's
  effect on, 160; will and, 103–4
charity, 77–79, 195–96
chastity, 193–94, 198
Chesterfield, Lord, *Letters to His
  Son*, 178–79
childrearing. *See* parenting
Christianity, 66, 109, 147, 176. *See
  also* religion
citizenship, 90, 169–71, 202
civilization: achievements and benefits of, 114, 121, 163; historical
  development of, 9, 37, 65, 80, 85,
  122–26, 130; human-animal relations in, 80; luxury as stage in,
  42; obstacles to human development in, 82, 89; poetry's role in,
  37, 40; political development of,
  130–34; religion as outgrowth of,
  111; Rousseau's views on, 118–19;
  uneven development in, 116–17;
  Wollstonecraft's views on, 114–22,
  174
class. *See* rank, social

Coffee, Alan, 128
Coleridge, Samuel Taylor, 35–36;
  "Kubla Khan," 36; *The Watch-
  man*, 35
commerce, 185–88
Cooper, William, 42
Corneille, Pierre, 16, 42–43
cosmopolitanism, 175
Cotter, Geo. Sackville, *Poems*, 43
Cowper, William, 35
Creationism, 109

Declaration of the Rights of Man
  (*Déclaration des Droits de
  L'Homme*), 125, 171
Declaration of the Rights of Woman
  and the Citizen (*Déclaration des
  Droits de la Femme et de la Citoyenne*), 174
dependence, 148–53, 197–98. *See
  also* slavery, enslavement, and
  domination
D'Erlach, Rodolphe-Louis, *Code du
  Bonheur*, 69
desire, 59–61, 177, 198–200
divorce, 203
domination. *See* slavery, enslavement, and domination
drink, 62
Dryden, John, 16, 35, 42–43; "The
  Flower and the Leaf," 42

education: age-appropriate, 108,
  179; and the arts, 50; body as
  subject of, 101–2; goal of, 110–11;
  habit's role in, 63, 82–83, 93;
  ideal of, 182–83; imagination's
  role in, 82–83; memory's role in,
  91–92; of men/boys, 179, 181–83,
  191–92; moral, 76–81, 103–5;
  nature as subject of, 47; reason's
  role in, 97–98; religion's role in,
  111; Rousseau's views on, 107–8,
  115; societal context of, 181;

habit, 63, 82–83, 93–94, 104
Halldenius, Lena, 128
Handel, Georg Frideric, 28–31;
    Judas Maccabaeus, 30, 38
happiness: fortitude necessary for,
    196; God as source of, 47, 109,
    161; human desire for, 74; in ideal
    world, 207, 208; labor associated
    with, 161; in personal life, 46, 49;
    public, 75, 124, 130–31, 158
Hazlitt, William, 35–36
Hegel, Georg Wilhelm Friedrich, 198
Henry IV, king of France, 190
Hints: on the arts, 23; on the beau-
    tiful and the sublime, 41; on
    imagination, 90; on the mind,
    30; on poetry, 37; as sequel to
    *A Vindication of the Rights of
    Woman*, 37, 110, 173; status of, in
    Wollstonecraft's oeuvre, 3
*An Historical and Moral View of
    the Origin and Progress of the
    French Revolution*: on the char-
    acter of the French, 161–62; on
    civilization's development, 114–15,
    122–26, 130, 205; on commerce,
    185; on England, 54; French Revo-
    lution as prompt for, 1, 143; on
    human nature, 75; on labor, 188;
    moral criticism in, 80; on politics,
    129–30; on the theater, 17, 42–43
historicity, of Wollstonecraft's
    thought, 9, 37, 58, 65, 102
Hitchcock, Robert, *The Macaroni, A
    Comedy*, 15, 15n7
Hobbes, Thomas, 113, 124
human nature, 73–81; animal vs., 73,
    94, 96–97, 118, 199; dignity of, 74;
    diversity of, 66–68, 70–71; fulfill-
    ment of, 130–31, 160–61, 171; God
    in relation to, 9, 30–31, 38–39,
    44, 49, 64, 78–79, 81, 99, 108–9,
    119, 207; goodness of, 131; nature
    in relation to, 9, 44, 49, 62–64;

perfectibility of, 75–76, 81, 98,
    119–21; reason as distinguishing
    feature of, 73, 94, 118–19; sexual-
    ity and, 59–62; social foundation
    of, 131–32; unity of humanity,
    65–69, 98; virtues of, 76–79;
    Wollstonecraft's conception of, 114
Hutton, Sarah, 83

ideals: of education, 182–83; of gen-
    der, 168–74, 193, 205–6; of hap-
    piness, 207, 208; of religion, 207;
    societal/civilizational, 166–74,
    184–85, 187–88, 197, 205–8
idleness, 160–62
imagination, 81–91; capacity for, 91;
    importance of, 81, 86–87; love
    dependent on, 61–62; moral
    development grounded in, 81–83,
    87, 90; negative effects of, 85–89;
    reason in relation to, 24, 36–38,
    41–42, 63, 82, 86, 90; role of, in
    art, 58–59
imitation: in art, 22, 26, 49–50,
    58–59; in behavior, 76, 104;
    in education, 92; of God by
    humans, 73; modernity and, 40;
    negative effects of, 22, 26, 59, 76;
    positive uses of, 26
Imlay, Fanny: father's abandonment
    of, 52, 72; illegitimacy of, 6; nam-
    ing of, 55; relationship with, 7, 55,
    167; relationship with Godwin
    and stepmother, 57; in Scandina-
    via, 4; suicide of, 56–57
Imlay, Gilbert: commercial activities
    of, 186; *The Emigrants*, 51–52;
    letters to, 15, 17, 46, 60–62, 77,
    86–87, 109, 167, 186; relation-
    ship with, 4, 51–52, 54, 56,
    60–62, 72; and slavery, 72, 186;
    *A Topographical Description of
    the Western Territory of North
    America*, 72

immortality, 98, 106, 108, 109, 119
Industry (slave carrier), 72
inheritance, 153–57, 159–60, 170.
   See also wealth
*Introductory to a Series of Letters
   on the Present Character of the
   French Nation*, 94

Jefferson, Thomas, 72
Johnson, Joseph, 1, 4, 21, 27, 45, 47,
   70, 144
Johnson, Samuel, 43, 51
justice, 194–96

Kames, Henry Home, Lord, *Sketches
   of the History of Man*, 66–67
Kant, Immanuel, 41; *Critique of
   Judgment*, 23
Kaplan, Cora, 59
Kingsborough, Lord and Lady, 4, 48,
   135–39, 161, 188

labor, 160–62, 185–88, 190
La Rochefoucauld, François de,
   201
*A Letter on the Character of the
   French Nation*, 85, 86, 175
*Letters Written during a Short Resi-
   dence in Sweden, Norway, and
   Denmark*: on civilization's development, 205; on commerce, 185;
   on the faculties, 84; motivations
   for writing, 1–2; on music, 30;
   publication of, 4, 5; Romantics
   influenced by, 36; on the theater,
   15, 19
Lewis, M. G., *The Monk: a Romance*,
   53
Liverpool Anti-Slavery Society, 72
Locke, John, 127
Louis XIV, king of France, 190
love and friendship, 53–62, 105,
   106, 141, 150, 197–202. *See also*
   marriage

lust, 60–61, 105, 197, 198
luxury, 8, 42, 58, 75, 102, 134, 181,
   188–91

Macaulay, Catherine, 6, 54, 192;
   Letter on Education, 103; *Obser-
   vations on the Reflections of the
   Right Hon. Edmund Burke on the
   Revolution in France*, 142
Macintosh, James, *Vindiciae Gallicae*, 143
MacKenzie, Catriona, 12
Mandeville, Bernard, 181
Marie Antoinette, Queen, 123, 146
marriage, 140–41, 154, 170, 198–203
Mary, A Fiction, 29, 137
Masham, Damaris, 5
Mazarin, Jules, Cardinal, 190
memory, 91–92
Mill, J. S., *The Subjection of Women*,
   117
Milton, John, 35, 180; *Paradise Lost*,
   42
mind and its faculties: association
   of ideas in, 92–93; balance of,
   82–83, 87–88, 99; body in relation to, 100–103; cultivation of,
   90; development of, 84; gendered views of, 95; operations of,
   93–95; soul equated with, 100,
   109; Wollstonecraft's conception
   of, 34. *See also* imagination; reason; sensory experience
modesty, 193
Molière, 16
Monthly Magazine, 38
Montolieu, Baroness de, *Caroline de
   Lichfield*, 51
moral criticism: on education's role
   in moral development, 76–81,
   103–5; goodness of human
   nature as foundation of, 74–76;
   in reviews, 10; of satire, 74; of
   social conditions, 112–14; of

A NOTE ON THE TYPE

{⚬⚬⚬}

THIS BOOK has been composed in Miller, a Scotch Roman typeface designed by Matthew Carter and first released by Font Bureau in 1997. It resembles Monticello, the typeface developed for The Papers of Thomas Jefferson in the 1940s by C. H. Griffith and P. J. Conkwright and reinterpreted in digital form by Carter in 2003.

Pleasant Jefferson ("P. J.") Conkwright (1905–1986) was Typographer at Princeton University Press from 1939 to 1970. He was an acclaimed book designer and AIGA Medalist.

The ornament used throughout this book was designed by Pierre Simon Fournier (1712–1768) and was a favorite of Conkwright's, used in his design of the *Princeton University Library Chronicle*.